THE
LINDSAYS OF AMERICA

A
Genealogical Narrative
and Family Record

Beginning with the Family of the Earliest Settler in the Mother State, Virginia, and Including in an Appendix All the Lindsays of America

Margaret Isabella Lindsay

"Every family is a History in itself and even a poem to those who know how to read its pages." —**A. Lamartine**

HERITAGE BOOKS
2008

HERITAGE BOOKS
AN IMPRINT OF HERITAGE BOOKS, INC.

Books, CDs, and more—Worldwide

For our listing of thousands of titles see our website
at
www.HeritageBooks.com

A Facsimile Reprint
Published 2008 by
HERITAGE BOOKS, INC.
Publishing Division
100 Railroad Ave. #104
Westminster, Maryland 21157

— Publisher's Notice —

In reprints such as this, it is often not possible to remove blemishes from the original. We feel the contents of this book warrant its reissue despite these blemishes and hope you will agree and read it with pleasure.

The genealogy chart between pages 22 and 23 is damaged, but because of its value, we have reproduced as much of it as possible.

International Standard Book Numbers
Paperbound: 978-0-7884-2198-3
Clothbound: 978-0-7884-7151-3

TO MY FATHER,

THE LATE

MAJOR GEORGE F. LINDSAY, OF THE U. S. MARINE CORPS,

AS A SLIGHT TOKEN

Of my profound respect and admiration for one who was in every way a true and noble gentleman, son, husband, father and officer! Who although I was denied the great boon and comfort of knowing him, losing him in my infancy as I did, yet whose character shines so beautifully forth, from all learned of him from my Mother and relatives, that the mind has often imagined it knew him; also for his deep interest in, and correcting early portions of the family genealogy, and

TO THE MEMORY OF MY DEAR MOTHER,

MARGARET FRASER LINDSAY,

Whose sympathy has encouraged me so frequently in this work,

THIS BOOK

IS AFFECTIONATELY DEDICATED

BY THEIR DAUGHTER.

PREFACE.

My Dear Kinsmen and Clansmen :

The following historical narrative and record of our family has long been a cherished wish of my heart from the moment that I began to read the stirring and interesting accounts in Scottish history and romance of our illustrious forefathers, but more especially after perusing those beautiful old books (in 3 volumes) entitled "The Lives of the Lindsays," by our noble and most talented transatlantic cousin, the late Lord Lindsay, Earl of Crawford and Balcarres, whom my father knew, and in the early stage of their acquaintance corresponded with, thus elucidating and establishing more thoroughly our descent from the House of Crawford and Edzell. Prior to this, my father had but the knowledge gained from a descendant of his grand uncle, Opie Lindsay of Virginia, of our early ancestry in this country, some of which was not satisfactory. This wish to give to the entire family a history of our ancestors, as well as to fulfill the intention my father had of making out a new record of the branch planted in Virginia, gave shape and meaning to my idea, until at length I made the first stroke of my pen in earnest of my labors. Many difficulties beset my path from time to time; the relatives who could have been interviewed to advantage were dead; letters were most tardy in bringing replies, and often *then*, further questions had to be returned, to be as patiently waited again for. When I hopefully wrote to some of our old court-houses in Virginia, in the vicinities our forefathers once resided in, looking forward to gain requisite data of births, marriages, deaths, wills, etc., I met with this response from the clerks of the courts: "The records of the early period I wished were long since lost by neglect, war, or destruction by fire." This was particularly so with the Fairfax court-house, as regards the early register of marriages. Fortune, however, favored me in the old Northumberland county court-house, that early portion of Virginia; here through the energies and kindness of its polite clerk, Mr. W. S. Crallè, I was enabled to gain a few important items, which he found in some of the old mutilated and time-worn records under his care.

My love, faith, and energy bore me along, year by year, for these last eight years, until at last my labor is over, and I can say, my work is done! As I progressed with my search after relatives and new fragments of history, one family of Lindsays after another sprang into notice, until I beheld, with surprise, that the clan on this side of the Atlantic was as large, if not larger, than that in old Scotland, England and Ireland. Verily, I said, the race flourished in these United States; and as the old branches wear out over there, here we have the twigs growing and strengthening year by year! The interest manifested in my subject was cordial and universal! Each bosom who answered me, seemed to be awakened with genuine pleasure and pride, and accorded me kind aid and words. It was this universal kindness and interest in my labors, together with several requests from different Lindsays, to mention their families in my book, that made me add the appendix herein.

I must not forget to mention that the gentle sympathy, and the assistance in discovering relatives, the ever ready ear and heart for me during all my work, until death took her from me three years and a few months since, that I received from my most devoted and noble mother, kept my love, faith, and energy in my task, in constant repair. To one and all of you, dear kinsmen and kinswomen, and the clan in general! I give sincere and heartfelt thanks for your aid and kindness, and trust you will deal gently in your criticisms on my book, only bearing in mind my great good will and heart to serve you and perpetuate our good and grand old name, so that after generations may have that knowledge of their forefathers which has so long been denied to many of you, and should it be that any Lindsay family in America has been neglected in my appendix, I pray their kind indulgence and forgiveness on the ground of not having or being able to gain information regarding them.

Those estimable volumes, "The Lives of the Lindsays," already mentioned, which several of you have inquired about, with a view to purchasing, I may here reply, are no longer obtainable, being out of print, as their publisher, Mr. Murray of London, wrote me. They first came out for the public in 1849, and were re-issued in 1859, the demand, I suppose, being so great for them. The author was doubly kind to my family in not only honoring my father with a set on their first publication in 1849, but in 1875 making my only brother, Walter Edzell Lindsay, the recipient of the later edition, and sent to him in the care of our clansman, the Reverend Dr. J. S. Lindsay of Virginia, who was then visiting Europe, and who had called upon Lord Lindsay by invitation.

We were a little disappointed to see that the alterations promised my father, had not been made in the re-issue (1859) of our pedigree given in volume 1, appendix, page 248, of the work.

CONTENTS.

CHAPTER X.

CHAPTER XI.

CHAPTER XII.

CHAPTER XIII.

CHAPTER XIV.

CHAPTER XV.

APPENDIX.

LIST OF ILLUSTRATIONS.

ARMS OF THE LINDSAYS'
OF
NORTHCUMBERLAND
AND
FAIRFAX COUNTIES,
VIRGINIA.

THE LINDSAYS OF VIRGINIA.

NORTHUMBERLAND — FAIRFAX COUNTIES.

CHAPTER I.

Remarks on genealogy — why families should keep it up — effect of good maternal influences — great men always indebted to their mother more or less for success in life — the proper pride for one's ancestry — Lindsay traits — Sir David Lindsay of The Mount Lord Lion King at Arms — his genius and character — love of King James the Fifth for him, his power, and the admiration for him in Scotland — his connection with the Lindsays in Virginia — wealth and rank of the Lindsays in Scotland.

Every family should have a record of its own whether they can trace back to a royal house, or only to that of a good and honest peasant, live under the protection of a monarchy or republic! The Holy Scriptures show us how genealogies were preserved and valued from all time. A knowledge of the virtues of our ancestors cannot fail to gratify us. To be prejudiced against genealogy exposes a want of kindly feeling and veneration,

Our progenitors, as Lord Lindsay truly remarks in The Lives of the Lindsays, "need not to have been heroes and heroines to interest us, to have been hallowed by a blaze of glory in high spheres, in war, or in the council chamber for us to love them."

It is rather in the domestic circle amidst those often unseen and private provinces, we note the truest and most telling virtues of heart and soul, the loving, devoted, and often sacrificing parent, child, brother or sister, whose heroisms are unnoted and unrewarded here, but whose virtues shedding around them in their lives the noblest lustre, takes root like the baby oak, and like that, keeps growing as a memory perpetually in the minds of posterity, and transmits to that posterity the good seeds of their moral beauty and worth, which if properly matured and *cultivated*, must bear again, in time, their characteristics, and make their descendants equally revered and loved; make those traits of virtue survive for generations, in greater or less degree.

Even the errors of our ancestors are our gain, for can we not draw lessons from the sorrowful consequences of their lives which must be beneficial to us in our life path?

For as we inherit the bad as well as the good parts of our fathers this knowledge of the frailties in the blood may be the "haven" upon which we can depend for a guard against a recurrence of them. If the gardener knows he can improve his apple orchard by grafting upon it a finer stock, so the mother, knowing of the crooked branches in her own and her husband's family, can by judicious care ingraft the seeds of a finer righteousness in the heart and mind of her child, the growing sapling, elevating and enlarging the virtues of the opening soul with moral precepts and teachings in that sweet and affectionate, almost unforeseen way, which only loving mothers know the secret of; which may fortify and enable it to resist, and more than probably triumph over those inherited weaknesses that might otherwise crush and blight its future.

This may be cited as one of the chief reasons *why* genealogical records should be more thought of and preserved in families.

I would have the "black sheep" of the fold, if there are any, brought forward into the light of day, and handed down in their real colors to posterity; not as families usually do, hide them or their memories away in secrecy and silence, until they are not only dead in body, but dead as to their deeds.

Whether those deeds be mild or violent ones; *hidden*, they work injuries to races yet unborn; *exposed*, they will stimulate to precautions which cannot fail to strengthen and purify both the minds and the bodies of after generations.

As those wise and talented men Bacon and Pope, respectively, said, "Knowledge is power" and "All our knowledge is *ourselves* to know."

There are other defects of character apart from actual moral delinquencies, which is also necessary for us to know about in the members of families.

Some men and women are blessed with strong will power and indefatigable energies. Such can go through life unaided, can steer themselves along unpiloted, but there are others of a more gentle, shrinking calibre who require the will and energies of the stronger ones to help them forward; to give their natures confidence and tone; in other words, to start them off, to *make* them come forward.

These are the separate natures which need the observant and intelligent mind of the mother to study and train, if she is permitted to.

Natures in one respect are like the Camelion, if such a simile can be allowed; they bear numberless lights and shades according to the objects with which they come in contact. Parents, watch and guard against these objects, being baneful; remember in a great respect you are responsible for the destiny of your children. The great Napoleon said, "The future destiny of the child is always the work of the mother."

And certainly history shows us there have been few great and distinguished men who have not been blessed either with an extraordinarily wise or a most excellently good mother, to whom they have been indebted for much of their success in life.

A reverence and pride for past kindred is totally distinct from that pride which would boast of a glorious line of ancestry. To all such unworthy ones I say in the lines of Chapman:

> "'Tis poor and not becoming perfect gentry,
> To build their glories at their fathers' cost,
> But at their own expense of blood or virtue
> To raise them living monuments."

The reverence and pride which is alone admissible and *true* is that which tends to *elevate* and stimulate our purposes to upright deeds and thoughts through life; so that, instead of leaning on our descent from an old and honorable race, we may "add by our own endeavors to the acquisitions of our ancestors."

Trusting my reader will pardon these few preliminary remarks, I will now introduce some things especially relating to our forefathers.

Running through every family there are more or less distinctive traits; those of the Lindsays are given in a pretty saying, a popular epithet, which has been assigned to them for ages — "Their lightsomeness or buoyant cheerfulness of character;" hence that old saying, "a Lindsay light and gay."

They have been proverbial for hospitality; they are excellent fighting men, eloquent in the extreme, and generally of handsome and distinguished appearance; of spirited temperament and powerful wills, and acquire fortunes easily, but in rare instances have the later Lindsays left wealth to posterity.

There have been men of the race in the days of the Stuarts who gave up life and property to the cause of royalty; some who clung to old traditions; others who worked for and upheld progression and liberty of thought and action with equal zeal.

One of the earliest poets and religious reformers in Scotland was one with whom our branch is perhaps particularly connected through marriage — Sir David Lindsay of The Mount, Lord Lion King at Arms to King James the Fifth. He was also early tutor to the young king. By his dramas and satirical descriptions he exerted a great influence against Papistry. It was one of our direct ancestors who married the great grand-niece of this famous Lindsay and assumed by the resignation of his father-in-law, a later Sir David Lindsay, his office of Lord Lion King at Arms and the titles and chieftainships of this branch, as you will see further on.

This honorable title of Lion King was borne by the chief of the heraldic corporation of Scotland; in those days of feudal and chivalric splendor, a most important office in the favor of the reigning king. Sir David Lindsay was appointed to this important office in 1530; he was looked upon as the chief judge of chivalry within the realm, and acted the part of official ambassador from his sovereign to foreign countries.

He visited the courts at Denmark, of Francis the First and Charles the Fifth, and proved himself on each occasion an able statesman in several of Scotland's commercial negotiations. After the expulsion of the Douglases when King James took the reins of government into his own hands, among the first things he did was to send him to Charles the Fifth at Brussels for the purpose of renewing the alliance which had existed for almost a century between Scotland and the Netherlands.

Nothing is positively known of his personal appearance, but we could not form a better idea of him than Sir Walter Scott's sketch of him in Marmion, canto 4, verse 7.

"He was a man of middle age;
In aspect manly, grave, and sage.
  As on king's errand come;
But in the glances of his eye
A penetrating keen and sly
  Expression found its home;
The flash of that satiric rage
Which, bursting on the early stage
Branded the vices of the age
  And broke the keys of Rome.
On milk-white palfrey forth he paced;
His cap of maintenance was graced
  With the proud heron-plume.
From his stud's shoulder, loin, and breast
  Silk housings swept the ground,
With Scotland's arms, device and crest,
  Embroidered round and round.
The double tressure might you see
  First by Achaius borne
The thistle, and the *fleur-de-lis*,
  And gallant unicorn.
So bright the king's armorial coat,
That scarce the dazzled eye could note,

In living colors, blazoned brave,
The Lion, which his title gave
A train, which well beseemed his state,
But all unarmed, around him wait.
Still is thy name in high account,
  And still thy verse has charms,
Sir David Lindesay of The Mount,
  Lord Lion King at Arms!"

Four Lions have belonged to the Lindsays of The Mount. In the Scottish rural homes of two hundred years ago and more, the works of Sir David Lindsay the Poet Lion King were seen side by side with the family Bible, these often constituting their sole library. It was out of such homes that many of Scotland's greatest inventors, poets, philosophers, navigators, and historians came. I have often had it related to me when in Scotland, that it used to be no uncommon thing in those ancient days when a discussion was on hand upon any thing in or out of the period, that some oracle of the party would say with sudden gravity or stern reproof, "Ay yer right for sae Sir Davet Lindsay tell 't us," or "na na its no sae in Sir Davet Lindsays books," thus illustrating the affection and respect with which his learning was held by his countrymen.

He was, says a writer on The Lives of the Scottish Poets, "a man of elegant taste and grand ideas, as great a philosopher as he was a poet, a detester of abuses and prejudices, and the secret projector of some of the most important improvements which soon after took place in the condition of his country." "He ever" (says another author) "remained a most intimate and confidential friend of James the Fifth, which honor he seems to have merited by the affection with which he served him, and by the honest and wise counsels which he never failed to offer him."

The Scottish Lindsays were loyal subjects and lordly chieftains, upholding rank and style at one period in Scotland, second only to the royal family. The feudal chieftains of the race intermarried through different generations, thrice with royal princesses. They held their courts and lived like princes.

"Their earldom, like those of Orkney, Douglas, March and others, formed a petty principality." Their estate was considerable and enabled them to fully sustain this grandeur. The Earls of Crawford at that time possessed more than twenty great baronies and lordships.

They have won distinction as soldiers, statesmen, cabinet-ministers, ambassadors, and clergymen, but their glories, alas! were too often dimmed by inferior posterity.

Fortune and lustre came to one generation, and sometimes ill fortune to the succeeding ones. Their alternations of fortune as given in the Lives of the Lindsays is at once striking and romantic.

CHAPTER II.

Walter and William de Lindsay our earliest ancestors in Scotland, 1116–33 — the latter from whom we descend — Baron Baldric de Limesay, their father, the Anglo-Norman, contemporary with the Conqueror William, the Norman — their connection — his vast territories in England — marriage of Lindsays to Royal Princesses — noble de Toëny ancestry of the Lindsays — latest discoveries, tracing the lineage back to Niord, King of Sweden, 40 B. C. — see chart of the de Toënys.

The first of our name and family who appeared in Scotland were two brothers, Walter and William de Lindsay, Anglo-Normans, sons of Baron Baldric de Limesay, according to the Norman spelling of the name, a Norman gentleman related to and contemporary with the Conqueror, who held the lands of Forfor, Henningby and others in Lincolnshire, England, under Hugh Lupus, Earl Palatine of Chester in 1086–7, at the time of the survey by William the Conqueror, entitled Doomsday Book; and who granted the tithes of Forfor and Oxcombe to the Abbey of St. Evroul near Evriaux in Normandy.

He had a brother, Randolph de Limesay, who flourished in 1086. His line dies out in heiresses, the elder of whom, Aleanora de Limesay, married her Scotch cousin, Sir David de Lindsay of Crawford, thus uniting the English and Scotch lines.

Walter de Lindsay, elder son of Baldric, figures as a magnate or great baron under David, the Prince of Strathclide or Cumbria. He is a witness to the celebrated "Inquisito," or inquest of Prince David into the possessions and tithes of the See of Glasgow within his territories in 1116.

There is no record of Walter's posterity; his brother William succeeds him in his possessions and favor as a magnate of Scotland, and a witness to the royal charters.

Of William's locality we have evidence; he resided in Roxburghshire, on the banks of the Leader, at his estate called "Ercildun," illustrious in song as the home in later times of Thomas the Rhymer, and near the Abbey of Dryburgh, to which he as well as his son Walter was a liberal benefactor; Ercildun is now Earlstone.

Their benefactions to the Church at Ercildun, besides some interesting representations of them upon seals, are preserved in the Treasury or Chapter House of Durham Cathedral, England. "The representations on the seals,— The Lives of the Lindsays say, exhibit "Walter and his son William, a lively type of the character of the young Norman noble." They are beardless and "are shown on horseback riding gently along, with falcon on wrist, unhelmetted, and with their shields hung carelessly behind them." William de Lindsay of Ercildun, and as he is also styled, of Luffness, the grandson of the first William, figures as a magnate of Scotland, and witness to the Charters of Malcom the Maiden and William the Lion from 1161 to 1200; between which extreme points of his career he appears in 1174 as one of the hostages fifteen, given in redemption of King William, after his capture by Henry the Second; and between 1189 and 1199 as High Judiciary of Lothian, which conferred paramount authority in all civil and criminal jurisdiction to the south of the two firths.

These justiciarships were the highest offices under the Crown, and were always held by barons whose power enabled them to enforce the regal authority in the execution of the laws.

He is the first of the Lindsays who is associated with the great mountain territory of Crawford, which formed the southern extremity of Lanarkshire; it is the highest district in the south of Scotland and this part was sometimes called the South Highlands. The Lindsays are said to have acquired this territory through the marriage of Sir David Lindsay, son of William, with a daughter of Sir John Crawford, about 1230, but there is no proof of this marriage, and William de Lindsay is known to have possessed it long before. The family held it till the close of the fifteenth century, that is, till the rebellion against James the Third in 1488, when David Lindsay,* Duke of Montrose, was deprived of it by the successful faction who gave it to Archibald Bell-the-cat, Earl of Angus, the great Douglas. Another story is that the Duke of Montrose exchanged it with Earl Archibald for lands in Forforshire. Later the name was altered by charter to Crawford-Douglas, but ancient usage prevailed over this charter, and the old name of Crawford-Lindsay was continued.

---

* This dukedom was given to David Lindsay, fifth Earl of Crawford, by James the Third as a reward for his great and faithful services to the Crown and to himself. He was created Duke of Montrose by charter, under the Great Seal, dated the 18th May, 1488, narrating his loyalty and the manifold acceptable services which, as it reads, "Our faithful and most dear cousin, David, Earl of Crawford, and Lord Lindsay, hath done unto us with unwearied good will — inasmuch as "he hath freely and often exposed himself, and his nobles and vassals for the defense of our person and Crown, and more especially of late, against those faithless lieges convened against the royal standard and majesty at Blackness" — by the tenor of this charter the king made him a duke, to be entitled and designated, in perpetual future times, Duke, hereditarily, of Montrose, conveying to him and his heirs for ever the castle and borough of Montrose with its customs and fisheries, etc., and the Lordship of Kincleven in Perthshire, the dowry of the king's late mother. This was the first instance of the rank of duke having been conferred upon a Scottish subject not of the royal family. This dukedom was enjoyed only during the life of David, Earl of Crawford, he had unfortunate family troubles, his sons disappointed him, being wild and ungovernable, and during the reign of James the Fourth his high positions for awhile were taken from him, that is his high offices around the Crown, but finally restored to him by his king who thus adhered to the charter granted by his father. His death took place in 1495 in his fifty-fifth year at Finhaven, and he was buried accordingly in the Gray Friars Church at Dundee. The dukedom sunk into dormancy after the duke's decease, his son, Earl John of Crawford, being deterred from assuming it for good reasons — his murder in a quarrel of his elder brother Alexander, Lord Lindsay. It was, however, claimed in 1859 by Lord James Lindsay, twenty-fourth Earl of Crawford, as the duke's heir and representative, but, although the line of descent and royal patent was so clear and convincing the House of Lords decided against him, an act of the British Peers many think most unjust.

Ere proceeding further I will give an outline sketch partly taken from The Lives of the Lindsays and other authorities of our Norman ancestors. From these works it appears that our forefathers are an offshoot of the noblest family of the Normans, and of a common male stock with Rollo and the Dukes of Normandy, and are descended from the royal houses of Denmark, Gothland and Sweden; as the chart given herein will show my reader, which traces our ancestry to Niord, King of Sweden, 40 B. C.

From Ivar Jarl, or Independent Prince of the Uplanders of Norway, I am indebted for pedigree to Lord Lindsay's Scotch history of the Clan; beyond that, as shown on the chart, I owe many thanks to a friend in the U. S. Navy, a gentleman of fond antiquarian tastes, and who has devoted much time and care to researches of this kind, and is, moreover, an Anglo-American gentleman of distinguished lineage, being descended, along with the Clebornes of Virginia, Alabama, etc., in the female line from the de Toënys through the noble families of de Stafford and de Clifford, of England. Lord Lindsay's pedigree of the de Toënys, our remote ancestors, begins with Ivar Jarl, or Independent Prince of the Uplanders of Norway, who was the representative of the Thorian race; the reputed descendant of Thor and of Thor's mythic ancestor Fornebter, King of the North, was the father of Eystein, surnamed Glumra, or the Eloquent; and Eystein was the father of Rognvald, surnamed the Wise and the Magnificent, and of Malahulc, the remote progenitor of the Lindsays.

"Rognvald submitted to Harald Harfagre, the first King of all Norway, and was by him appointed Jarl of More and Rumsdal on the western coast of Norway; he was father of Rollo, and great-great-great-great grandfather of

William the Conqueror, respectively of Normandy and England. Malahulc, our early forefather, accompanied Rollo in his expedition to Normandy, and became the ancestor of the great house of de Toëny, the hereditary standard-bearers of Normandy. Randolph de Toëny Malahulc's great grandson, who flourished under Richard the Second, had two sons, Roger surnamed the Spaniard, his successor, and Hugo."

"Roger rose in arms on the accession of William the Conqueror, refusing obedience to a bastard while other and more legitimate heirs of the royal blood existed; but he was defeated and slain. He was succeeded by his son Randolph, who accompanied the Conqueror to England in 1066, and became the ancestor of a long line of barons, the last of whom died in the reign of Edward the Second, while an equally illustrious race, the Lords of Stafford and Earls and Dukes of Buckingham, descended from Roger's younger son Robert."

"*Hugo*, the younger son of Randolph, and brother of Roger the Spaniard, settled on a manor not far from Rouen, and founded the family of de Limesay or de Lindsay, the names being identical and interchangeable alike in etymology and practice, in Normandy and Britain. He left two sons styled de Limsi, and de Lindesiaco, who, like Randolph de Toëny, accompanied the Conqueror to England in 1066, and continued the line of the Limesay succession, one of whom was Baldric de Limesay before mentioned, the father of the Northern branch of the family."

The original seat of the de Limesays, I should add, was at the manor of that name in the Pays de Caux near Pavilly, five leagues north-west of Rouen. They continued to flourish on the spot for many generations after the Conquest, and failed apparently, shortly after the middle of the thirteenth century, when the Sires de Frontebosc or Frombosc, a younger branch, succeeded to the property; their descendants in the female line, Comtes de Frontebosc and Marquesses de Limesay flourished till the French Revolution. Randolph de Limesay just mentioned, younger than his brother Baldric, who came over with the Conqueror, obtained about forty lordships in different counties of England, including Woverley in Warwickshire, that smallest but most famous of all England's shires, Birmingham was there, Kenilworth, Warwick Castle, Alcester, of the great needle industry, Dr. Arnold's Rugby was there, not to mention its greatest of all distinctions, it is the county of the softly-flowing Avon and of that Stratford wherein the great Shakespeare was born, also George Eliot the Authoress; seat of his posterity and from which they took their style as barons.

It was Aleanora de Limesay, his great granddaughter, one of the richest co-heiresses in England, who married her Scottish kinsman, Sir David de Lindsay, and carrying her estate to him vested the two lines in one, in 1199. The mother of Sir David was Princess Marjory, daughter of Henry, Prince of Scotland, a great grandson of King Malcolm Canmore, the Scotch king who married the fair and christian Princess Margaret, last, with her brother Edgar, of the Royal Saxon line of England, and who, with their mother, had taken refuge with the King of Scotland, on the conquest of England by the Normans.

Princess Marjory was the sister of King William the Lion of Scotland, and David, Duke of Huntingdon, the Sir Kenneth of Sir Walter Scott's novel — The Talisman. The name David, which has been such a favorite in the family for ages, is derived from him. Sir David de Lindsay of Crawford and Woverly, husband of Aleanora de Limesay, left three sons, Gerard, William, and Walter, also a daughter, Alice; the eldest son of whom succeeded first to the estates; his English possessions embraced the counties of Essex, Hertford, Oxford, Warwick, Leicester, Norfolk and Suffolk; his Scotch ones were also immense, comprising much of the lands in Lanarkshire, wherein his territory of Crawford was, besides several abbeys in other portions of Scotland. He left no issue and was succeeded in 1241 by his brother William, he in turn by his brother Walter in 1249, and he likewise by his sister Alice, who carried her estates to her husband, Sir Henry Pinkney of England, and whose grandson, Sir Robert, claimed the Scottish throne at the competition in 1292, through his grandmother, Alice de Lindsay.

This branch becomes extinct in 1301, and the chieftainships of the Lindsays is vested in a younger branch of the family, called the Lindsays of Lamberton, the founder of whom was Sir Walter de Lindsay, younger brother of the Sir David de Lindsay who married the heiress Aleanora de Limesay. For a time his house rose to greater power and grandeur than that of Crawford. For four generations the sons married heiresses, who brought them immense estates; the last male heir of this noted house, Sir William de Lindsay, married Ada de Baliol, eldest surviving sister of the unfortunate King John of Scotland, and ultimately eldest co-heir to her nephew Edward, pseudo King of Scotland.

This Sir William was killed in battle against Llewellyn, Prince of Wales, 1283, and the whole of his vast estates in England and Scotland, comprising in the former seventeen manors, besides towns and hamlets numberless, and over twenty-five Scottish sheriffdoms or counties, devolved on his daughter and heiress Christiana de Lindsay, wife of Ingelram de Guines, second son of Arnold third Count of Guignes and Namur, and Sire de Coucy in right of his mother Alice, the heiress of that house so illustrious in history and romance.

Christiana de Lindsay represented the ancient Scoto-Pictish dynasty of Scotland, the original Saxon line of England, including Edward the Confessor, Alfred the Great, Egbert and Cerdic, all centering ultimately in her direct descendant, Louis the Sixteenth of France, father of Marie-Therese-Charlotte de France, Duchess d'Angouleme. A detailed pedigree of this descent is given in the Appendix.

Then the ancient house of Crawford asserts its power and influence in Scotland, and we find a long line of knights, barons and earls, all upholding rank and honors under the separate Scottish and Anglo-Scottish sovereigns for generations. The first title of earl in Scotland was bestowed on David, Lord Lindsay, in 1398; the Earls of Crawford are consequently in precedence of all other Scotch earls, ranking as her premier earls.

The history of our de Toëny ancestors is said to be full of romantic incidents; their alliances were always with the families of the great feudatories or the sovereign houses in conformity with their distinguished origin. The romance of the middle ages attribute to them the chivalrous epithet of Knights of the Swan, as in the description by Matthew Paris, of Randolph de Toëny, son of Roger, the first settler in England. Doubtless later poets, like Tennyson and others, drew their hero knight from this ancient romance. The Lords de Toëny bore on their coat-of-arms lions and swans alternately; the earlier Lindsays likewise.

CHAPTER III.

Scottish ancestry continued — William de Lindsay of Luffness, 1236, succeeds as the representative of the Lindsays — House of Glenesk and Edzell — Walter younger of Edzell, our direct ancestor — his grandson David, the celebrated Bishop of Ross — his remarkable character — high honors — the only one of note to pray for the ill-fated Queen Mary on her execution — his son Sir Jerome or Hierome Lindsay of The Mount, Lord Lion King at Arms — his eldest son, David the Divine, founder of the Lindsay family in Northumberland county, Virginia — their title to the representation of the Lindsays of The Mount, and other honors.

The house of Crawford and Woverly, and also that of Lamberton becoming extinct in heirs male of the direct line, the honors and chieftainships devolved on William de Lindsay of Luffness, younger brother of Sir David and Sir Walter de Lindsay, spoken of in my last chapter. William was succeeded by his son, Sir David Lindsay of Luffness, 1233–49, who left two sons, Sir Alexander Lindsay of Crawford, and Sir William Lindsay the Chamberlain. Sir Alexander left a son Sir David Lindsay of Crawford, who flourished from 1314 to 1355; his wife was Mary Abernetheny, co-heiress of this old and powerful Scottish family; he left four sons, David was the elder, a gallant youth who fell in the battle of Nevills Cross at Durham.

Sir James Lindsay of Crawford, 1357, the second son, married his cousin, Egidia Stuart, sister of Robert the Second, and daughter of the High Steward, by the Princess Marjory, daughter of King Robert the Bruce; on account of their near relationship a dispensation was required from the Pope for their marriage, which was effected by King Philip of France.

Sir James had one son, Sir James Lindsay, afterward Lord of Crawford, and a daughter, Isabelle, wife of Sir James Maxwell of Pollock. Sir James Lindsay the second left co-heiresses in Euphemia and Margaret Lindsay, which makes this branch extinct in heirs-male. It is perpetuated by the third son of Sir David Lindsay of Crawford, Sir Alexander Lindsay of Glenesk, who married Catherine, daughter of Sir John de Stiveling or Sterling, and heiress of Glenesk and Edzell in Angus, and of other lands in Invernessshire.

Sir David's fourth son, Sir William Lindsay of The Byres, is the direct ancestor of the Byres-Crawford-Lindsay-Garnock branch, now represented by Sir John Trotter Bethune Lindsay, Lord of The Byres, and Earl of Lindsay, Kilconquah, Fife. The Earl of Lindsay established his claim as Earl of Lindsay in 1878.

The issue of Sir Alexander Lindsay of Glenesk, by his first wife, Catherine Sterling, were Sir David of Glenesk, the first Earl of Crawford, 1398 (who married the Princess Catherine Stuart,* fifth daughter of Robert the Second), and Sir Alexander Lindsay. He married secondly, Marjory Stuart, niece of Robert the Second, by whom he had Sir William Lindsay of Rossie, and Sir Walter, besides a daughter, Euphemia. Sir David Lindsay of Glenesk, first Earl of Crawford, had issue Alexander, second Earl of Crawford, and he in turn had issue David, third Earl of

---

* The Princess Catherine Stuart was the great granddaughter of Walter Stuart, the Lord High Steward of Scotland, who married the Princess Marjory Bruce, and founded the house of Stuart. The Princess Marjory Bruce descended from the marriage of Prince David Bruce, son and heir of the Great Bruce of Bannockburn, and Princess Joanna of England, daughter of Edward the Second, one of the Plantagenet kings.

Crawford (who married Marjory, daughter of Alexander Ogilvie of Auchterhouse, chief of that ancient race, and hereditary sheriff of Angus), and is the ancestor of a long line of earls and Lindsays, who finally die out in the direct line in an heiress, Margaret Lindsay of Spynie.

David, the third earl, had a second son, Walter Lindsay of Beaufort, who now perpetuates the male line, and is the progenitor of the houses of Edzell and Balcarres. Walter Lindsay's son was Sir David of Edzell, who died in 1528, and *his* son was Walter Lindsay younger of Edzell, who fell at the battle of Flodden, 1513, leaving a young widow and four sons; he is said "to have been one of the most gallant who fought under the king's banner, and one of the faithful band who, after the day was utterly lost, formed themselves into a ring and fought to the last in defense of their king, till he fell in the midst of them surrounded by a tower of their corpses."

He was not only his father's heir, but heir to his kinsman, David Lindsay, eighth Earl of Crawford, through Alexander, fourth Earl of Crawford, brother of Walter Lindsay of Beaufort, his eldest son David, therefore, succeeded as ninth earl; it is from his second son, Alexander of Edzell, we trace our ancestry. He was the father of the Rev. David Lindsay, the celebrated Minister of Leith, and Bishop of Ross, chaplain, and at various times envoy extraordinary and minister plenipotentiary for James the First of England and Sixth of Scotland.

He is said to have been the only noted minister who would pray for the ill-fated Mary Queen of Scots, at the moment when apprehending her instant execution. He was a man of uncommon ability and attainments, of varied travel, and besides his ministry held other high situations in the favor of the Crown. He accompanied the king on his matrimonial voyage to Denmark and united the royal couple. "He was skilled as a diplomat, and learned in the French and other tongues, and a most eloquent orator."

In 1600 he was appointed Bishop of Ross; he had always favored a moderate episcopacy, and was generally called on to argue in the disputations about it in the Church. It was this learned minister who baptized King Charles the First, and his elder brother, Prince Henry, who died in infancy; the latter of whom was baptized with royal magnificence in the Castle of Stirling, one of the favorite residences of the Scotch kings. The festivities and splendors of this christening were something truly gorgeous, not even in the nineteenth century could we have surpassed the arranging of the banquet and diversions created for the guests.

After many years' service at the English Court he was succeeded by his son-in-law, Archbishop Spotswood, the king's primate, and he returned to his ministry at Leith, where he died in 1613, at the advanced age of eighty-two or three. It is said he was amongst the earliest to join the Reformers; and was, according to his son-in-law, Archbishop Spotswood, "A man of a peaceful nature, wise and moderate, and universally beloved by all wise men." His remains are interred at Leith, a suburb of Edinburgh.

He left a son and a daughter; the son was Sir Jerome or Hierome Lindsay of Annatland, Jerome and Hierome being identical in those days, who married first, Margaret Colville, daughter of a Scottish Knight of Colville, by whom he had a son David (afterward the Reverend David Lindsay), baptized the 3d of January, 1603, the year of the union of the crowns of England and Scotland, and who was the founder of our family in America.

That which gave the bishop's son the most fame was his second marriage with his distant kinswoman, Agnes

Lindsay, daughter of Sir David Lindsay of The Mount, and the great-niece of the celebrated Sir David Lindsay the Poet, and Lion King at Arms, whom I mentioned in the early portion of this record. On this alliance with Agnes Lindsay, the heiress of The Mount, he became Sir Hierome Lindsay of The Mount, and was shortly after appointed Lord Lion King at Arms, making the fourth and last Lindsay who held this important and honorable office.

He left a son by Agnes Lindsay, called James Lindsay of The Mount, but the descendants of this son are extinct in 1714, according to the Lives of the Lindsays. Sir James Balfour then comes into possession of the estate, and his descendants hold it for sometime afterward, as this work further mentions. Who this gentleman was and how he became possessed of it I do not know; this very notable estate in Scotland, notable because it was the birthplace and home of one of Scotland's ablest men and earliest reformers, poets and historians, is in Fifeshire, across the Firth of Forth from Edinburgh where many of the Lindsays resided, and a few still reside.

It is here that the present head of the clan, Lord James Ludovic Lindsay, Earl of Crawford and Balcarres, has one of his country seats. The earl is likewise descended from Walter the younger of Edzell, who fell at Flodden. The author of the Lives of the Lindsays has kindly referred, in his book, to our branch of the family as being the present representatives of the Lindsays of The Mount, and furthermore that the direct heirs-male of this branch, were their descent *legally* substantiated, and all intermediate heirs extinguished, would be entitled to the chiefships of the Lindsays and successions to the family honors, on failure of the heirs-male of the body of James Lindsay, fifth Earl of Balcarres. See Vol. 2, § 5, page 281.

Deducing the descent from elder son to elder son, this honor would fall to my father's male issue, and failing the heirs-male of his body then to the branch of his family in Arkansas, of his uncle William Henry Lindsay, beginning with his *elder* son. Our representation of the Lindsays of The Mount must come through Sir Hierome's second son, James Lindsay, by Agnes Lindsay the heiress, whose issue is extinct in 1714, we being the heirs or next of kin by descent of this remote great-half-uncle.

Rachel, the daughter of David Lindsay, Bishop of Ross, and sister to Sir Hierome Lindsay, became the wife of Archbishop Spotswood, a most learned and accomplished divine and scholar, who wrote one of the finest histories of the Church of Scotland, which included a history of the times up to his era. She was the happy mother of Sir John Spotswood, who suffered greatly in the cause of Charles the First, and of Sir Robert Spotswood, President of the Court of Session and Secretary of State for Scotland, who sealed his loyalty to the same monarch on the scaffold, and of her daughter Ann, wife of Sir William St. Clair of Roslin, and grandmother of Governor Alexander Spotswood of Virginia, and thus through him, ancestress of nearly all the noted families of Virginia.

Walter, David and William are ancient Christian names amongst the Lindsays, and held on to with exceeding pride and tenacity by all of the blood and race; Alexander, John and James are also favorite names amongst us. The ladies have worn a more varied range, although Margaret, Ann, Elizabeth, Isabelle, Catherine and Mary, those old-fashioned names, seemed to have held their own with our grandmothers. Hierome, or Jerome as it is sometimes called in Scotland, came down from our forefather, Sir Hierome Lindsay of The Mount, Lord Lion King at Arms; it is frequently corrupted into Hiram. King James the Sixth shows his partiality for the Lindsays in the number which he retained about him, for we see him accompanied into England with Sir Hierome Lindsay's father, the venerable Bishop of Ross, also Sir John Lindsay younger of Kinfaunds, Sir James Lindsay, and Bernard Lindsay of Lochhill, Drum and Craigballe, County Tyrone, Ireland, descendants of Thomas Lindsay, the famous Snowden herald of Queen Mary's time.

Bernard Lindsay I believe to be the ancestor of those Lindsays in America whose forefathers emigrated from County Tyrone, Ireland. The Snowden herald had another son, Robert Lindsay of Tollyoge or Loughry of County Tyrone, who is also, in my opinion, an ancestor of some of the Scottish-Irish Lindsays settled in America. The Lindsays of Lochhill, Scotland, are a branch of the Lord Lindsays of the Byres.

It was the Poet King at Arms, Sir David Lindsay of The Mount, who proclaimed James sovereign of Great Britain, in all pomp and ceremony. The Lindsays were allied to James through his great-grandmother, Lady Elizabeth Lindsay, daughter of the fourth Earl of Crawford, and wife of John, first Lord Drummond, Darnley's grandfather.

Edzell Castle, the seat of these early Scotch ancestors, is now an extensive and picturesque ruin, and is situated not far from the river Esk in Forforshire, near the town of Brechen. Tradition reports that it was built by a family of the name of Stirling, from whom it descended by marriage to the Lindsays of Glenesk.

There are still to be seen by the Lindsay pilgrim or tourist the remains of its lofty apartments and the gardens or pleasance, whose crumbling walls show traces of the high state of artistic decoration to which they had once been subject as family shields or quarterings, "brackets for statues and sculptures in *alto-relievo*, representing the theological and cardinal virtues, the seven sciences, the planets, etc., in the allegorical style and manner of the followers of Niccola and Andria Pisano of the fourteenth century," a style of decoration unparalleled (Lord Lindsay believed) in those days in Scotland. It was the Lindsays who added these decorations to Edzell.

There were two fine towers; the larger, called Sterling's Tower, was older than the rest of the building, and is supposed to be one of those insulated keeps which were so necessary for safety and retreat in feudal times. Queen Mary honored Edzell by a stay of one night during her celebrated progress north, it was on the 25th of August, 1562. She held a council here, received ambassadors, and discussed affairs of state with her ministers and nobles. The room she slept in at Edzell afterward went by the name of the Queen's Chamber.

The old Norman-French way of spelling our name, as you will have seen, was de Limesay; the Scotch, Lindsay; the prefix de was held on to in Scotland for several generations, but finally dropped. The surname is supposed to be territorial, as hereditary territorial surnames were taken at that early date, 1050 and onwards, from the estates actually possessed either by those who bore the surnames, or by their ancestors.

There is a vast district in Lincolnshire, England, called "Lindsay;" the property of Baldric de Limesay, our Anglo-Norman forefather, lay within that district, but it is more generally believed that he derived his surname from some

Norman territory, the Lindsays being distinctly a Norman race, and bearing, ere their entry into England, a hereditary territorial surname, Lind or Lime, signifying a derivation from the linden or lime trees, and is probably, I think, the Teutonic part of the name, or taken from the fact of the immense number of linden trees upon their territory. There is a commune near Argentan in Normandy, France, called Sai or Say, which doubtless has something in connection with the derivation of the latter part of the name. The name also signifies Isle of Limes.

4

CHAPTER IV.

The Reverend David Lindsay, Episcopal clergyman of Wicomico parish, Northumberland county, in Virginia, our early forefather — he probably came to the colony during the reign of Charles the First, from 1645–55 — evidence of his vicinity in 1655 — account of the colonial ministry — early religious laws — death of the Reverend David in 1667 — inscription from his tombstone, possibly the oldest in America.

It is probable that our earliest forefather in this country, the Reverend David Lindsay, left the mother country during the reign of Charles the First, that is, between 1645–55. The earliest evidence I have found of his vicinity and occupation is the following, from an old book of court orders:

"Judgment is granted Mr. David Lindsay, (spelled Lyndsay) Minister, whereby he recovers 50 pounds Tobacco from Edward Coles."

Northumberland County Court
March 20, 1655.

From this evidence we can infer, I think, that he must have been located for some years in the colony. On the death of James, Charles the First's father, in 1625, the Reverend David was in his twenty-third year; he may then have been married or he may not, but, judging of the early marriages of his time, the former is extremely likely. We can give him a few years in Scotland, with the troubled and revolutionary period he lived in, and come to the conclusion he emigrated to Virginia about 1645, and thus entered upon his pastorate in the prime of life.

As appertaining to this pastorate I set down these other three items, also taken from old books of court orders of that time:

"21st of September 1657, Mr David Lindsay recovers of Thomas Lamkin 365 pounds of Tobacco.

October 1657, Mr David Lindsay, Minister, being behind 700 pounds of Tobacco of his last years salary in Wicomico parish, the Court orders that the said sum of 700 pounds Tobacco be levied out of the said parish (from every Titheable) by the Sheriff, &c. &c.

October 1662, Mr. David Lindsay was relieved of a fine imposed for performing marriage between two servants contrary to law. Northumberland County Court House.

The tumultuous times in Scotland and England during the reign of Charles the First, beginning with the religious wars, the Presbyterians in the former country and the Round-heads or Puritans in the latter country, the final execution of the king with many of his followers, including the banishment of others of note who had served him, among whom were not a few Lindsays, and the rising power of the Cromwellites, must have made great changes in many families and caused hundreds to seek peace, safety and comfort in expatriation, as history shows us they did.

The death in Scotland in 1642 of his father, Sir Jerome or Hierome Lindsay of The Mount, Lord Lion King at Arms, and this troubled state of his native country must have led our early forefather to seek a home in the new world. In 1642, as history says, "England fairly begins to get on fire with her great civil war. The dispute between arbitrary power and the rights of freeborn men grew so fierce and high that pike and bullet alone could settle it." Husbandry, industries, and all peace was at an end. To worship God in that form most suited to each man's conscience was denied. Our forefather not being a warrior, but a minister of the gospel, gladly turned his course westward, as that small band upon the *Mayflower* did about 1620, and sought to preach the gospel and to keep the gospel before the young colonists.

It may be interesting at this point to mention a few things concerning the ministers in the colony. The salary of a minister in the colonies, as fixed by law, was sixteen thousand pounds of tobacco per annum, that is eighty pounds current money; besides this, he is given, if he desires it, a dwelling-house and glebe, together with certain perquisites, as marriages, and funeral sermons. The fee for the first was twenty shillings, or two hundred pounds tobacco, for the second, forty shillings, or four hundred pounds tobacco.

Frequent acts were passed for the payment of ministers until the sessions of 1657–58, when church and state seem to have been radically divorced, and all matters relating to the church left to the control of the people. Prior to 1633 *all* dealing was paid for in tobacco. A curious style of currency? What a difference from those early days to these—then money as a mode of mutual interchange of barter was nothing; to-day, the breast of all America, young and old, throbs with a keen ambition to have and to make it.

In some parishes there were donations of flocks and negroes, which the minister returned when he died, or gave the value to the donators. By examination of the ancient records of St. Andrew's (Scotland's famous university) I believe that our early ancestor, the Reverend David Lindsay, was a student there. There is a signature thereon of a David Lindsay as being a student of St. Salvatore College of this University, January, 1618, and again, as having graduated M. A., July, 1621, which would make him at that time in his nineteenth year. Combined with the fact that his uncle-in-law, Archbishop Spotswood, was at the head of the university about this period, one can have but little doubt that the above record points to him, and that the influence of this talented uncle, historian of Scotland, as well as the king's primate, induced him finally to settle in Virginia, or at any rate, directed his attention to Virginia.

The London ministry, and, in particular, the Bishop of London, at one time instituted a movement to procure suitable clergymen to settle in the colony, as they were scarce. In 1620, history tells us there were but eleven parishes and five ministers in the whole colony, but this was, no doubt, some years previous to our forefather's arrival. The church in which the Reverend David Lindsay preached was the early Yeocomico or Wicomico church (spelled in both ways), situated near the Wicomico river, in Northumberland county, one of the earliest churches in the Virginian colony.

It was twice destroyed; first during the Revolution, and later again, through neglect, war, and age; but to show the reverence and love the people of this vicinity have for their ancient places of worship, peace once more reigning in our land, a subscription was raised not over five or six years since and a little wooden chapel near the site of the old Wicomico church built, and to-day people gather here to attend divine service.

Bishop Meade, in his history of "Old Churches and Old Families of Virginia," makes no mention whatever of our early forefather's services in Northumberland county; in fact there are several of the oldest families of this county and other counties omitted in this work, but doubtless the omissions were chiefly for lack of the proper source to gain the necessary information from.

For several years the old parish registry of Wicomico church was lost, but it finally turned up in another parish in Lancaster county, in Christ Church of that county, of which the Reverend Edmond Withers was pastor, who called the bishop's attention to it, and who copied some names from it for this book, but whether or not the Reverend David Lindsay was spoken of there as the early minister of Wicomico church, remains hidden to us, for I have made repeated inquiries and search for the ancient register, but can get no trace of it; certainly it was not restored, as it should have been, to the church to which it belonged, for naught is known about it by the present minister of this vicinity in Northumberland county.

Two names copied by Bishop Meade from the ancient register point conclusively to the Reverend David Lindsay's posterity. They were copied because the holders of the names were cited as vestrymen of St. Stephen's parish* of this (Wicomico) church. The first was John Opie, date 1714; the second, Lindsay Opie, 1781; both descendants, through his daughter, of the Reverend David Lindsay. As Northumberland county was not incorporated or formed until 1648, our early forefather was among its first inhabitants.

As can be easily understood, the ministers at this early period of the colony were the better learned and polished men belonging to it. Our early forefather's father, Sir Hierome Lindsay, was also possessed of besides "The Mount" of "Annatland," a seat in Scotland, where he resided ere his second union to his cousin, Agnes Lindsay of "The Mount." This former estate was by law, on the death of his father, the property of the Reverend David Lindsay, as the eldest son, but whether he came into possession of it or sold it ere coming to the colony, is a matter of doubt. Here probably he was born. "Duninno" is the name of another place occupied by Sir Jerome or Hierome Lindsay.

I believe both these estates were in Forforshire; Duninno, however, 'tis recorded, passed out of his hands when he possessed Annatland. He was evidently knighted by his king, for he is styled Sir Hierome or Jerome Lindsay of Annatland, before his marriage to his second wife, when he came into possession of The Mount.

---

* This parish was probably taken from the original Wicomico parish.

Therefore, it can be seen that the Reverend David Lindsay, by the Scottish law of knighthood, on the death of his father, became *Sir* David Lindsay, and all heirs-male of his body in the direct line forever afterward could be styled knights-baronet.

Northumberland must have been one of the best counties in colonial days, for James Waddell, the blind preacher of Virginia, remarked that "he found so much hospitality, intelligence, and polish, amongst the old Virginia gentry here, that he would cheerfully have passed his life among them." History asserts that about 1762, there was a brisk trade with Great Britain from the mouths of the rivers, and much generous piety amongst the merchants and planters of this region.

Westmoreland county, which was the native county of our illustrious Washington, adjoined Northumberland, in fact it was formed from the elder county, Northumberland, in consequence of which the latter is now one of the smallest counties in Virginia. This part of Virginia was called, in the past, the "Athens" of Virginia; for, in Westmoreland, some of the most renowned men of this country have been born, not only Washington, but some of the distinguished Lees, James Monroe, and others of note.

Colonial life is a subject very often written upon now by our best magazine writers, and forms most interesting matter to many, especially the genealogist and modern antiquarian. The habits, the manners and pastimes of our forefathers in early America were, of course, the prevailing habits, manners and pastimes of the mother country. The Cavaliers and the Puritans brought these things with them, as they did their love for freedom and liberty.

The minister of a parish was quite a small potentate. He not only preached the gospel on the Sabbath and other fixed days, married, christened, and read the burial service, but he heard the grievances of his different parishioners, and in some instances even administered the laws, which were those fixed by the London Company for Virginia. He might be given the position of what was then termed ecclesiastical commissioner, who was one appointed by the authority of the English Crown, through the Bishop of London. He kept an account of the clergy and all ministerial movements, as well as watched over the moral conduct of his flock. The old histories of Virginia give a curious account to us of the strict laws in force among the early colonists; it is here worthy of comment that although the desire for religious freedom and liberty was the elementary feeling that brought them to America, yet they were not slow in exacting and keeping up very stiff religious laws, and, to our modern eyes, unreasonable and unjust fines, sometimes the forfeiture of life.

For instance, here is an extract from Hawk's History of the Protestant Episcopal Church in Virginia:

> "Rule 6. Religious services by the inhabitants of Virginia during 1611. Sir Thos. Dale, Governor. "Every man and woman duly twice a day upon the first tolling of the bell shall upon working days repair unto the Church to hear divine service, upon pain of losing his or her days allowance for the first omission; for the second omission to be whipt; and for the third to be condemned to the galleys for six months; likewise no man or woman shall dare to violate or break the Sabbath by any gaming publique or private, abroad or at home, but duly sanctifie and observe the same both himself and his family, preparing themselves at home by private prayer, that they may be the better fitted for the publique according to the commandments of God and the orders of our Church; as also every man and woman shall repair in the morning to divine service and sermons preached upon the Sabbath day, and in the afternoon to divine service and catechising; upon pain of the first fault to lose their provision and allowance for the whole week following, for the second to lose said allowance and also to be whipt, and for the third to *suffer death.*"

God be praised that we live in this nineteenth century. Such strict and appalling laws seemed almost the quintessence to our eyes, of intolerant tyranny, yet they may have been necessary at that day, and for the control of rougher and hardier natures than existed as our country grew in intelligence and power. How the charming transparency of our climate must have delighted the colonist, after the denser, gloomier air of his native land; almost every object in nature must have been a source of delight, such abundant, picturesque and grand scenes as met his eye, must, indeed, have made him feel fully compensated for that tedious sea voyage.

There was no need of a scramble for any thing, the woods and the rivers and morasses yielded enough for all; for all, with strong and willing hands, to hunt for what they wished. As the red man gave way to his smarter brother with the pale face, and moved to other hunting grounds far away in the west, Virginia became, in truth, a garden of luxury and abundance to all who came from afar. But plenty encouraged indolence; there were no domestic manufactories beyond that which necessity required; every thing called comfort was imported from England. Tobacco planting was the only pursuit, and this, unfortunately, enfeebled the spirit of invention to a great extent.

Yet we know, when the occasion demanded it later on, this apparent indolence vanished as if by magic; when the hand of tyranny rose to destroy this peaceful method of living, and tried to intimate to this colony of self-exiled English, Scotch and Irish men, because they had exiled themselves they had no longer the rights of men, and must be treated as slaves, and were slaves, then the same spirit that rebelled against such action in the mother country rose with a redoubled fervor in this beautiful wild western home beyond the sea.

But all this was not in the life-time of our reverend forefather, he lived and passed away peacefully amongst the little settlement he had come to, in the capacity of their pastor and divine instructor, and was laid to rest by them on his plantation, "The Mount," and above his ashes was erected a tombstone, which, curious to relate, is to-day in existence.

In 1849 my father commissioned a relative to visit the old homestead and burying-place on it, and he took from the stone the following inscription, although it even then was difficult to decipher; it was surmounted by the engraved coat of arms of the family:

> "Here lyeth interred ye body of That Holy and Reverant Devine Mr David Lindsay, late Minister of Yeocomico, born in ye Kingdom of Scotland, ye first and lawful sonne of ye R^{t} Honerable Sir Hierome Lindsay. K^{nt} of ye Mount. Lord-Lyon-King at-Arms. who departed this life in ye 64th year of his age ye 3^{d} April. anno Dom 1667."

The most glowing eulogy that might have been written by man could not transmit to the Reverend David's posterity a better panegyric than those simple straightforward words engraved above his ashes. Holy and good, and an accomplished divine, he doubtless was, and we may accept this tribute to his memory, as from the *vox populi* of his day. It may be that his character closely resembled his noted grandfather, David Lindsay, Bishop of Ross; that he was also a man of peaceful nature, wise and moderate, and esteemed by all wise men, and that he did much to cast a refining influence around the rude homes of the colonists, sowing the simple words of the gospel in his vocation, and acting not only as a teacher and exponent of Christ, but as a teacher of all things good, and noble, and elevating in life.

Such an accomplished, learned, and wise grandsire, not to speak of his advantages of birth, education, and superior

THE EARLIEST BURYING PLACE OF THE LINDSAYS' OF NORTHCUMBERLAND, VA., SHOWING, TO THE LEFT, THE TOMB STONE OF THE REV. DAVID LINDSAY.

associates in Scotland, *must* have made him no ordinary man; and could we draw away the veil hiding the past from us, and look upon the people of his vicinity and parish, with himself moving in their midst, I venture to take upon me to say that I have not overestimated him in my suppositions. Some authorities of the past tell us that the oldest *existing* tombstone and inscription in this country was on the banks of the Neabsco creek, in Fairfax county, Virginia, the date upon it going back to 1608, but present authorities of the locality assert that the date, although much obliterated by age, can only be traced to 1678. If this is truly the correct date, then the tombstone of the Reverend David Lindsay can carry off the honors of antiquity.

The Lindsay burying ground, a picture of which I have given my readers, is on the original homestead of the family, on Cherry Point Neck, Yiocomico or Wicomico river, Northumberland county, now owned by Mr. William Harding of Northumberland. I am sorry to say that the burying ground is sadly out of repair, overgrown with weeds and brushwood, and an altogether wild and desolate looking little spot, the tombstone of our first forefather sunken in its masonry and fast beginning to tumble into mother earth. It seems a pity that its honorable antiquity is not tended with more care and veneration, but the long absence of those of the blood and name in the old locality has doubtless much to speak for this.

CHAPTER V.

The family of the Reverend David Lindsay — his wife Susanna Lindsay — had evidently malicious friends in the colony — she is living in 1665, two years before her husband's death — dies presumably between this and the execution of his will in 1667 — items of court concerning her — copy of the Reverend David's will — his daughter Helen Lindsay, his heiress, sole legatee, etc., also, supposition of his son Robert's death before 1667 — the Opies of Northumberland early connections of the Lindsays, through Helen, daughter of the Reverend David.

The knowledge handed down to us regarding the family of our early forefather is, that he had a son Robert, who was our second forefather in Virginia, and this record seemed a thoroughly accepted one with all our elder relatives, who, it must be supposed, knew more about our genealogy than we do. It is true, they misapplied the name of our first ancestor, calling him Robert instead of David, but my father corrected this error during his researches into the family pedigree, and through a comparison of notes in his correspondence with the late Lord Lindsay, Earl of Crawford and Balcarres; said comparison of notes enabling us to deduce our descent from Sir Hierome Lindsay and Margaret Colville, his first wife, parents of the Reverend David Lindsay.

Tradition gives us nothing respecting our early foremother, the wife of the Reverend David, all endeavors to find out any thing of her amongst the elder relatives has been in vain. That she was living in Northumberland in January, 1665, two years prior to her husband's death, I ascertained through this old court item.

I.

"Robert Lindsay made oath concerning a statement of one Richard Thompson who circulated a malicious and scandalous report about the wife of Mr. David Lindsay, *for which he was indicted and convicted* by Court."

Northumberland Court House Records, January, 1665.

II.

"In May 1659 Susanna Lindsay is sued by one William Bound and he was non-suited."

Northumberland Records.

What this malicious and scandalous statement made by Richard Thompson in reference to the wife of our early forefather was, the intervening years and silence of ages hide from us; imagination could conjure up many suppositions, and so weave some unhappy chapters in his book of life. Perhaps her nature and intentions were misunderstood, or perchance she was a very beautiful woman, and evil and cruel men lay pitfalls in her way, and did much to annoy and traduce her, seeing she scorned them.

We must remember the crude young country and the age she lived in, and doubtless the rough characters of the colonists at that early period. Whatever the malice was, the offender and slanderer was meted out punishment by the court of that day as the reader sees, and *we*, her descendants, must accept *this* as evidence of her being more sinned against than sinning.

Her Christian name was Susanna, according to the old court records. The second item of court of date prior to 1665, of May, 1659, speaks of a Susanna Lindsay being sued by one William Bound, and who is nonsuited. If this points to her, then we must believe that she was not living with her husband at that time as the suit is only in her name; again she comes off victorious in her suit, and William Bound, like Richard Thompson, has to retire ignominiously.

The Robert Lindsay referred to in the old court item, No. I, was doubtless her son Robert. Like her he must have died between 1665 and 1667, as he is not mentioned in his father's will. At his deposition in court, in 1665, for his mother, he was twenty-four years of age; his death may have been the result of some accident. Tradition gives us little or nothing respecting him, except that he was a planter and inhabitant of Northumberland county, married and left a son called Opie.

The disturbed state of the country in those early times, and up to the Revolution, and all through that rebellion, and our late civil war, has made it impossible to obtain any satisfactory or continued data from the Virginia court-houses. The ancient papers and registers kept therein of the marriages, births, deaths, and general doings of the different parishes in colonial times, having in nearly every instance been lost or destroyed in some way or other, as I said in my preface.

Even the church registers were not exempt from disturbance; there are no church registers of very early date, I believe, existing in Virginia to-day. It is really quite a marvelous thing, therefore, that I was able, with the aid of the gentlemanly clerk of the Northumberland county court-house, Mr. W. S. Crallè, to stumble across what evidence I have in regard to our earliest American ancestors; the one or two ancient records remaining in the court-house were musty, frail and mutilated, and without index, so that the task of examining them was not an easy one.

Northumberland was among the early portions of Virginia settled by the colonists. Westmoreland, Northumberland, Lancaster and Richmond, all early counties, are joined together and are bounded on the east by the Potomac river and Chesapeake bay, and on the west by the Rappahannock river, and are intersected by small rivers, as the Wicomico in the second.

The first evidence I had that our early ancestor, the Reverend Sir David Lindsay, left a will, was the following court item:

> "A probate of will was granted on petition of Mistress Helen Lindsay *daughter* to Mr. David Lindsay in April 1667."
> Records of Northumberland County Court House 1667.

I was naturally anxious to obtain, if possible, a copy of such an ancient document, but my hopes seemed destined to disappointment, for examination of the ancient fragments of record revealed nothing more for me, until after several months went by, and a short time since a letter came from Mr. Crallè telling me another search had made him successful, the will was found! It is needless to say how pleased and gratified I felt. The following is a copy of it, also the legal attestation by the clerk of the court as to its discovery.

You will note that our early forefather mentions therein no wife and no son, which leads me to suppose that both were dead when he executed it; the said execution was made on the day before his demise. See date of death upon his tombstone in preceding chapter. If his wife were not dead he could not deprive her of dower, and *something* must have been bequeathed to his son by the law of inheritance, in those days the son usually coming in *first* for his father's real and personal estate, or he may have provided for him during his life-time.

The will of the Reverend David Lyndsay (copied exact):

"In the name of God amen. I, David Lyndsay, Minister of God now in Virginia, being now deseased in body, but of perfect memory doe now make my last will and testam^{t}. Imp^{s} I bequeath my soule to the almighty, my Savior and redeemer, by whose passion I have assured hope to —— Eternally wth him in happiness.

Item. I give and bequeath my body to the earth to be buried by my Exect^{x} in decent and Xtian buriall. Item. I bequeath all my goods, lands, chattels, debts, servt^{s}, moveables, or whot else is mine unto my loving daughter Helen Lyndsay whom I constitute, appoint, and ordain my lawfull execut^x to this my last will and Testam^t to be fulfilled. and I do hereby give and bequeath my whole estate to my loving daughter Helen Lyndsay, to her, her heirs, exec^r & adm^r, and I do grant and acknowledge this to be my last will and Testament by my subscription and seale in the 2^d day of Aprill in the year of the reigne of o^r Soveraigne Lord Charles, King of England Scotland France and Ireland, and in the year of o^r Lord 1667.

DAVID LYNDSAY.

Signed sealed & a^d in the
presence of James Claugton (or Clayton)
The mark of Clem Arlidge.
GEORGE DEASON.

The — of Aprill 1667 this was proved to be the last will and testament of Mr David Lyndsay dec^d by the oaths of James Claughton and Clem Arlidge & is recorded.

Letter certifying to the finding of the above will by the clerk of the Northumberland Court House.

State of Virginia
Northumberland County, to wit,

I Wm S. Crallè, Clerk of the County Court of said county, do certify that the writing on the opposite side of this paper (meaning his letter) is a copy of the Will of David Lyndsay as found in an old mutilated record book in Clerks Office, of said county, copied as accurately as I could considering the style and legibility of the writing in said book, with the omission of one word which immediately precedes the word "eternally" as found at the beginning of 6th line, which omitted word I was unable to make out. Given under my hand this 4th day of April 1888.

Wm S. CRALLÈ. Clerk of the
County Court of Northumberland Va

Cotemporary with the Lindsay family there lived, in Northumberland, the family of Opies, who came from England, being, likely by their name, of Cornish origin, and as the descendants of this family have the Lindsay blood in their veins, and are hence connected with us, I cannot more fittingly end this chapter than by a short record of them.

Thomas Opie, the founder and first of the name in Virginia, married Helen, the daughter of the Reverend David Lindsay, and their son, Captain Thomas Opie, Jr., lies buried beneath the same tombstone as the Reverend David, for the following inscription records it:

"Here also lyeth the body of Captain Thomas Opie Jr of Bristol, *grandson* of Mr David Lindsay, who departed this life 16, November 1702."

Captain Thomas Opie had a son, John Opie, who died in 1722, leaving a wife, Ann, and sons, Lindsay Opie, Thomas Opie, and a daughter, Susanna; Lindsay Opie lived, married and died in Northumberland county, in 1746, leaving a wife, Sarah, and sons, John, Thomas, George A. and a daughter, Ann. Either one of these sons was the father of Lindsay Opie, who was a wealthy planter in Northumberland during 1775. He was father to Hierome Lindsay Opie, born 1758, in Northumberland county, and who died in Baltimore 4th October, 1839, aged 82; also father to Juliet Opie, Mrs. Hopkins; Margaret, Mrs. Parker, widow of General Thomas Parker of Virginia, who left a daughter, Susan, who married General Stephen Mason of Virginia; and of Jane, who married a Mr. Clarke of Kentucky, and left a son, Hierome Lindsay Opie Clarke, and of a son by a second marriage, Major Leroy Opie, paymaster United States army, who was killed in Virginia by robbers, in the discharge of his duty, while traveling.

Hierome Lindsay Opie, who died in Baltimore in 1839, resided a number of years in his native county and served as a member in the Legislature. His first wife was a daughter of Judge White of Virginia, by whom he had four children who died young; his second was Miss Muse, their children were Hierome Lindsay Opie, who married Miss Lauck of Martinsburgh, W. Va., and had the following three children by her: 1, Hierome L. Opie, 2, Thomas, and 3,

Mary, Mrs. Meade of Virginia, niece-in-law to the late Bishop Meade. The elder son is a lawyer in Covington, Ky., and is married; he had an elder son named Hierome Lindsay Opie. Thomas is a well-known surgeon of Baltimore, Dean of the College of Physicians and Surgeons there. The daughters were Margaret, Mrs. Riddle of Delaware, and Mary, Mrs. Norris of Virginia, who left a son William Opie Norris; and Virginia, Mrs. R. H. Butcher of Success, Warren county, Va., whose daughter is Mrs. General R. Ayres, U. S. A. Hierome Lindsay Opie, Sr., died in Baltimore in 1862, his wife in 1883. This latter family of Opies was known and highly thought of by my father, who indeed regarded them as his cousins as they did him. At all times there appears to have been a strong pride and attachment between the two families. Down to this generation the reader will notice the perpetuation of the favorite name of Hierome Lindsay in the Opie family, and of Opie in the Lindsay family.

The state of the Virginia colony at this early period of which I write was well calculated to call upon any native mechanical genius which was within the settlers; nearly every family contained its own tailors and shoemakers, every family tanned their own leather, almost every house had a loom and every woman was a weaver; necessity may well be said, in those times, "to have been the mother of invention." There was, very likely, in every parish some one whose natural ingenuity enabled him, not only to help himself, but his neighbors, far above expectations.

With the few tools they brought with them to Virginia, these early forefathers of ours performed wonders. Their plows, harrows with wooden teeth, their sleds, their copperware and pewterware for domestic use were usually made by the colonists. The first water-mills were then called tub-mills; it consisted of a perpendicular shaft, to the lower end of which a horizontal wheel of about four or five feet in diameter is attached; the upper end passed through the bed-stone and carried the runner after the manner of a trundle head. These mills were inexpensive and were serviceable. Instead of bolting cloths sifters were in general use; they were made of deer skins, in a state of parchment stretched over a hoop and perforated with a hot wire.

CHAPTER VI.

Opie Lindsay, grandson of the Reverend David, the last Lindsay of Northumberland — copy of the inventory of his movable estate — Robert the second, his son, his settlement in Fairfax county, and becoming the founder of the Lindsay family of this county — date of arrival supposed to be about 1743 — copy of his will — importance of women in legal matters signing their family name with their husbands, etc. — Robert Lindsay's family — calling his plantation in Fairfax "The Mount" — times, condition of affairs in Virginia.

Opie Lindsay, like his father, Robert Lindsay, did not follow the sacred calling of the ministry. It is highly probable that the difficult educational (especially ecclesiastical) advantages of his day were meagre, making such a profession to his eyes impracticable, or the life of the planter was more to his liking; he lived and died a planter of Northumberland, married and had a son Robert, thus making the second of the name and of whom I speak later on. I was not successful in obtaining a copy of his will from the old records of the county, but the following copy of the inventory of his movable estate will, no doubt, prove interesting as revealing to our nineteenth century eyes and minds knowledge of the possessions and house furnishings of an early colonist, and I presume one who was then called comfortably off. The reader must calculate the appraisers' values will not *overrate* things by any means.

Inventory of the movable estate of Opie Lindsay, Esq., deceased, of Northumberland, Virginia, September 20, 1727.

"Pursuant to an order of Court September the 20th 1727, ordered by the worshipfull Court of Northumberland that we whose names are hereunder mentioned have according to the said order appraised the Estate of Opie Lindsay Dec^d Viz :"

	L.	*S.*	*d.*
To one cow and calf	1	12	00
Two do 2L 10 (2 Bulls	4	00	00
One heifer	0	15	00
Tenn head of hogs	2	10	00
Two Eues	0	10	00
Two Shoats	0	02	00
one young Mare	2	00	00
46^lb of New puter at 16^d p^t	3	01	04
8½ of old puter at 10^d p^t	0	07	01
one pott 30^l at 3^d p^t: (pot hook	0	07	06
one pott (pot hooks 37^l at 3^d p^l	0	09	03
18½^l of old Iron at 1^d p^l	0	01	06
1 Brass Candlestick 1 skimmer & some lumber	0	04	00
1 Linnen wheel & 1 p^r Tow Cards	0	08	00
Two Cider Casks 3 (frying pan and pestle	0	09	00
1 Chest 3 (& 1 Sifter	0	04	00
some lumber	0	12	00
1 plow & 1 Gigg	0	08	00
1 Cider Cask, washing Tub & Two old Barrells	0	07	00
1 Saddle 2^s & Two Chests 10^s	0	12	00
Two boxes 2^s & 1 Table	1	02	00
1 Silk rugg 1 blanket 1 p^r sheets 1 bed 1 boulster 1 pillow 1 Trundle bed sted. and 1 hide	4	00	00
1 bed boulster 1 sheet 1 blanket 1 Rugg 1 bedsted & 1 hide	2	05	00
8½ of Cotton at 16 p^l	0	11	04
To Wareing apparrel	0	12	00
1 Gunn 2^s6 & 6½ of wool at 6 pr pound	0	05	09
1 auger 1 shoemaker pincers and Nippers & some lumber	0	08	00
1 Lot of Wedges	0	07	00
3 Hides & 1 Tanfatt	0	03	00
2½ Doz of Coat Buttons	0	01	00
1 Cap	0	01	00

	L.	S.	d.
To 27½l of Nails	0	13	04
1 Mare and Two Colts..................	3	05	00

Appraised pr

GRIFFIN FANTLEROY,
MATT KENNER,
JAMES STRAUGHAN.

JOHN SMITH.

October the 18th 1727.

This Inventory of the Estate of Opie Lindsey Dec[d] was exhibited into Northumberland County Court by John Smith administrator of the said dec[d] and on his motion is admitted to Record.

Teste
R[d] LEE. Clk Curt.

Of the precise date of the removal of Robert Lindsay, son of Opie Lindsay, from Northumberland to Fairfax county, nothing is extant, but from a bond executed by him in 1743 to one William Taylor, for sale of a certain tract of land in Cherry Point, Northumberland county, which bond states that the tract of land mentioned in same, was left by one Thomas Austin to him for life, and that he was then a resident of Fairfax county, we may infer that he came to Fairfax prior to 1743.

I obtained the above copy of recorded bond from the Northumberland court-house. The county of Fairfax was formed in 1742, hence only a year previous to the execution of this bond by our ancestor, Robert Lindsay; it was taken from Prince William county; the land of this county, "and indeed, as Howe's history says of the whole of the tide-water of Virginia, is flat and sandy," but other parts inland are exceedingly fertile and beautiful, and some hilly.

I know of no cause why Robert Lindsay abandoned Northumberland for Fairfax. Possibly he saw greater chances to improve himself by securing richer and better soil for his planting pursuit. All or a great portion of the lower lands of the Potomac, and all along the Chesapeake, had begun to wear out through the excessive tobacco planting for years, as history tells us, and in all probability for this reason, if for no other, our forefather thought it wise to change his locality. It is a great regret to me that I have been unable to collect so little knowledge from amongst our oldest relatives about this Robert Lindsay, the founder of the family in Fairfax county, and his wife, I have gleaned naught beyond her Christian name, and this was from his will.

The absence from nearly all wills (whether of this or past generations) of the full name of the wife precludes the possibility in this way of posterity learning who were their foremothers, and as mothers have such an influence upon the human race, this is unfortunate. A woman who is well born, in my opinion, should always sign her family name to that of her husband's; a man in mentioning his wife, in his will, should add her family name after his, as "my wife Jane Williams *nee* Brown," for then it serves as a family record. One can never tell of what invaluable service this might prove to establish monetary claims to later generations.

But to return to Robert Lindsay; although regretting my inability to gather much respecting him, yet from this scrap of information here and there I learned that he was a thorough Virginia gentleman of the old school, of noble countenance and bearing, of extremely strict religious principles, being a faithful member of the Church of England, and was proud of his good name and descent, and his coat-of-arms patented.

He owned a large plantation in Fairfax county, several slaves, and was looked upon as one of the wealthy gentry of his neighborhood. The name given to his home was "The Mount," in honor, no doubt, of the one in Northumberland, which had received its title from the original homestead in Scotland.

The early part of the eighteenth century, in Virginia, is somewhat barren of incident beyond the local changes, the replacing of the colonial governors and under officers, and members of the House of Burgesses, but with the breaking out of the French and Indian war times change, the peace heretofore lying over the land is surcharged with the echo of war, the rattle of musketry, the din of battle, the parting of husbands and wives, mothers and sons, to go forth to fight for their country and homes, and amidst this the wrongs inflicted upon the colonies by the mother country, fans a smouldering resentment into angry heat, and the great war for Independence begins with that first skirmish upon Bunker Hill.

Through all this Robert Lindsay the second lived; I have no knowledge of *his* being a fighter for the cause, but doubtless he aided in some way. There was flour needed for bread, and tobacco for the camp, *all* dare not abandon the fields and looms. There must be the sower and reaper as well as the soldier, one cannot do without the other; and there must be the Legislature.

In view of these stirring times the youth of the country suffered considerably from a lack of proper schooling; educational facilities were stunted, schools broken up, and, therefore, the only instruction that could be given to the children was that imparted under the parental roof, often the only education received by many of our ancestors.

Sometimes a pupil so advanced by his parents was taken under the tutorship of the parish minister, who received him into his family as a proof of regard and friendship for some especial ones of his church. Several of Virginia's noted sons were thus given a classical finish to their studies. The celebrated Chief Justice Marshall, Francis Lightfoot Lee, and some others not upon my memory at this moment, are an illustration.

The planters' homes were generally built of clapboard wood, not over two stories, and double, with the entrance in the center; some were of freestone and a few of brick. I have heard that our great-great grandfather's, Robert Lindsay, was of the latter; there were not many rooms, but these were large and furnished in keeping with the style of that day. The quarters for the slaves were outside, consisting of small log cabins, and depended in number on the quantity of the slaves on the estate. If the planter had but a few he could always hire more from his neighbor when he required extra hands for his harvesting. The ladies of the family, besides superintending the domestic concerns of the house, employed a great part of their time in spinning, and usually, in this way, supplied the entire family, including their servants, with clothing.

It was not unfrequently woven on the estate, some families having looms of their own. According to the old custom some housewives were also good in the arts of dyeing the cloth into neutral tints. An aged relative, after listening to my mother and me in a vocal duett one day, during a visit to us, made the remark, pointing to the piano, "when I was young my piano was the spinning wheel, and right pretty music it seemed to make along with those of mère's and my sister's wheels. We counted it an accomplishment to be a quick, good spinner."

The most aristocratic ladies occupied their leisure then in carding the flax. In Virginia and Maryland, during those days, the youth called their parents père and mère; it can doubtless be accounted for by the introduction of the idioms of the French court into the English court, and hence brought from the mother country by the early settlers to the colony.

Some years before the death of this great-great grandfather the war of Independence had ended by the declaration of that independence in 1776; and finally the inauguration of General Washington as first president of the United

States. He lived up to seventy, if not eighty years, and died in the year 1784, at "The Mount," the home he had settled years before. The following is a copy of his will, taken from the records of the Fairfax court-house and kindly sent to me by a distant kinsman residing near there.

"The Will of Robert Lindsay Esq., of "The Mount".

"In the name of God, amen. I, Robert Lindsay of the county of Fairfax and the parish of Fairfax being very sick and weak of body but of perfect mind and memory thanks be given unto Almighty God for the same, and calling to mind the mortality of my body and knowing that it is appointed for all men once to die, do make and ordain this my last Will and Testament. That is to say, principally and first of all, I give and recommend my Soul into the hands of Almighty God that gave it, my body to the earth to be decently buried at the direction of my Executors hereafter named, nothing doubting but at the General Resurrection I shall receive the same and arise to Glory! thro' Christ our Lord to whom be honor and praise forever more, Amen. And as touching such worldly estate wherewith it hath pleased God to bless and bestow on me in this life, I give, devise and dispose of in manner and form following Viz– Item. I give and bequeath unto my son William Lindsay ten pounds current money as it runs, and for him therewith to be content. Item, I lend to the use of my beloved wife Susanna Lindsay during her natural life, the Plantation whereon I now live, with the nigroes.

Viz Elisono, Lucy, Selmiah and Harry, likewise all my household goods, and moveables, excepting such things as shall be hereafter named and bequeathed. Item, I give and bequeath unto my dear and well beloved son Opie Lindsay all my Lands excepting such parts as shall be hereafter named, to be freely by him and his Heirs, possessed, but if in case he should die without any heirs that then the said Land should descend to Thomas Lindsay and his heirs. Item I give and bequeath to my dear and well beloved son Thomas Lindsay one hundred and fifty acres of land whereon he now lives, beginning at the line of Pearson at the mouth of a small branch bedding in my field towards Col Wrens thence running with the most convenient line to Colonis line formerly fully to conclude one hundred and fifty acres of land to him and his heirs lawfully begotten, but if in case he should die without heirs for his wife Martha Lindsay to peacefully posess and quietly to occupy during her life and at her death for the land to descend to Opie Lindsay or his heirs.

Item, I also give unto my son Thomas Lindsay at my wifes death a nigro girl named Selmiah with all her increase forever excepting as before excepted and then the one half of the said nigro and her increase unto my daughter Mary Ann Boggess and her heirs and the other half to descend to my son Opie Lindsay and his heirs, also I give unto my son Thomas Lindsay an equal part of all my household goods and moveables as in heirship before mentioned at the death of his Mother.

Item, I give and bequeath unto my son Opie Lindsay one best bed and furniture, and two cows and yearlings, and at his Mothers death to have the Plantation whereon I now live, also nigro Harry and an equal part of all my household goods and moveables to him and his forever and at any time hereafter as soon as this my will be in force for him to have one eue and eue lamb and one whether also my great coat. Item. I give and bequeath unto my dear and well beloved daughter Mary Ann Boggess the land at the Falls Church that I bought from Mr John Hust to her and her heirs forever, on condition that she, her heirs, or assignes do at the reasonable request hereafter when properly required do make or cause to be made unto my son Opie Lindsay his heirs or assignes a good and sufficient Lease for ninety nine years, and the said Lease to specify certain three acres of Land if so much and to be receivable forever at the annual rent and usuries as in price to the amount of six pounds current money of Virginia to be paid by the holder of the Lease to the bequeathed Mary Ann Boggess or to her heirs or assignes.

I also bequeath unto my daughter Mary Ann Boggess one eue and eue lamb and one wheather and at my wifes death for my daughter to have a nigro fellow named Elsono and his wife Lucy and one named Ned which is *in* her possession and an equal part of all my household goods and moveables to her and her heirs forever also I give her two thousand pounds of coap Tobacco to be paid out of my estate by my executors hereafter named, and lastly I do anominate and appoint my dear and well beloved sons Opie Lindsay and Thomas Lindsay to be my whole and sole executors of this my last Will and Testament, truly, utterly, disannuling and revoking all and every other former testaments, wills, and legacies, bequests and executors heretofore by me made, willed, and bequeathed, ratifying and conforming this and no other to be my last Will and Testament.

In witness whereof I have set my hand and affixed my seal this eleventh day of September (1784) one thousand seventh hundred and eighty four

Interlined before sealing and sealed thus —— (her) and his wife Lucy.

ROB^rt^ LINDSAY.
(*Robert*)

Signed and sealed and acknowledged in the presence of

his
ALEXANDER (A. B.) BEACH
mark
JOHN SAWER
His
LUKE FIELD
mark
JAS WREN

At a Court Cont^d^ and held for the county of Fairfax 16 November 1784 this Will was presented in Court by Thomas Lindsay one of the Executors herein named who made oath thereto and the same being proved by the oath of John Sowyer and James Wren is admitted to Record and the said Executors having performed what the Laws require a certificate is granted them for obtaining a probate thereto. Ex' in due form.

Test, P. WAGENER.
Clk. of the Court.

I have now brought the Lindsay reader down to the eighth in generation from our gallant young Scotch ancestor, Walter, younger of Edzell, who fell at Flodden. The early transatlantic Lindsays could not boast of such worldly position and renown as their Scotch ancestors, but all must bear in mind that this was a new country; there was not much going on during the early colonial days in which any one talent could show itself above another.

Our first American forefather as you have seen belonged to the sacred calling of the ministry, and for the next four generations his descendants follow the business vocation of every one of the gentry in Virginia and other parts of the colonies, that of cultivating tobacco, the chief production of the country. We trust they were honest, upright, Christian men and women, and although they left no glory to posterity they left no stain, which, after all, is the better proof of true aristocracy.

> "When our souls shall leave this dwelling the glory of one fair and virtuous action is above all the scrutcheons on our tomb or silken banners over us."
>
> J. SHIRLEY. 1666.

And surely we *must* feel that there was one or more virtuous actions in the lives of these past ancestors which the veil of long flown years hides from us. It was a virtuous, aye, a heroic action to exile oneself and family to a crude, wild and virgin land, there to suffer privations and lack of those comforts of the body which the mother country afforded them ; yet none grew disheartened, it seemed, or turned back, but with stout hearts and steadfast spirits they put brain and muscle to work and formed settlements, created homes, raised churches, enacted laws, and so began the foundations of a country which to-day rises so proudly to confront, with her great progress, wealth, prosperity and unity, the mother countries of Europe.

All honor and glory then to *all* America's early forefathers.

CHAPTER VII.

Opie Lindsay of "The Mount," Robert Lindsay's second son — considers himself the head of the family — great ceremonies at "The Mount" during the funerals of relatives — their interment in the family burying ground — curious way in which Opie Lindsay writes his love letters — his three marriages — wedding clothes and cake of each marriage always preserved — Robert and Opie, his first two sons, and their families, the former the founder of the Lindsays in North Carolina; the latter of the Lindsays of Crab Orchard, Kentucky.

The will of Robert Lindsay of Fairfax county has shown us that he left at his death three sons and but one daughter; the sons were, first, William, secondly, Opie, thirdly, Thomas, and a daughter Mary Ann. A descendant of the daughter has some indistinct record of a son John, and is the only one I find who has. If he existed, he must have died long before his father; I have gained no knowledge of him whatever. William, his eldest son, seems to have branched out early in life for himself, and as his fortunes and descendants require considerable space, I will leave *his* history and theirs to another chapter.

Opie Lindsay, his second son, was a great favorite of his father; he is said to have resembled him in a marked degree, both in appearance and character. He has been described to me by a relative, as a gentleman of strong characteristics, unusually handsome physique, tall, broad, and muscular, and possessing finely-cut, aristocratic features. His will power was great, his habits methodical, and his observance of all religious ceremonies extremely strict; he was evidently a most faithful and dutiful son of the church of his fathers. He was also clannish and proud of his old Scottish name and descent, and, 'tis said, made a journey once to Scotland to visit the old homestead in the land of his ancestors. It is to his and my father's deep interest in the family that we owe a preservation of the knowledge which has descended to this generation, of its ancestry.

Many people, aye, even the members of good families not unfrequently, sneer at the love of genealogy implanted in some bosoms, but if it were not for just such warm and enthusiastic, not to speak of reverential spirits, scaling the mountains of the past, step by step, and tracing out the lives of those who existed therein and recording them carefully, what would be known of any family? History is the greatest teacher the world has; should there cease to be historians how would man discover his progression? History is a record of the world's family, as family history is a record of *one* of the world's families.

Opie Lindsay served for a while, in youth, in the Revolutionary war as bearer of dispatches from one position of the army to another, and had some narrow escapes of detection from the British, which it is said he was fond of relating. On the death of his father, and latterly his mother, and coming into possession of "The Mount," his parents' plantation, he settled down to the Virginia life of a planter, and the war over, and peace being established, began to grow in prosperity. He looked upon himself as the head of the family despite his having an elder brother, but it was doubtless on account of his inheriting the paternal homestead.

Whenever a death took place in the family the remains were often conveyed to "The Mount" for interment in the burying ground of the family, which was, after the old colonial fashion, on the plantation. Friends and relatives far and near were expected to attend, the old house was thrown open, the table was set and piled up with good things, the four ends of the table-cloth being tied with huge strips of black cloth, and mourning rings or souvenirs of some kind prepared for the nearest of kin of the deceased; and during the reading of the burial service Opie Lindsay placed with his own hands on the casket of the departed relative, an ancient plate containing some salt that also looked stale and musty with many years.

I do not discover his object in this custom, but can only associate it with an idea that it was as a last compliment to the memory of the deceased, meaning they had been "as the salt of the earth." A tree generally marked the position of the grave of the departed in the family burying ground. In writing his love letters (and no doubt they were numerous, for he was married three times) the word "love" was invariably left standing by itself. I am told he was a naturally eloquent and graceful talker and letter writer. He was a great reader of the events of his time, as at his death, quantities of the first Virginia newspapers were found. He also gathered about him a good little library of books.

These newspapers, an aged relative told me, were queer and oddly-printed little journals; in size no larger than an ordinary theatre program. She remembers having seen one when, as a child, she was visiting "The Mount" with her mother; "The Mount" then being in possession of his youngest son and daughter. At his death, which occurred at a ripe old age, the wedding clothes and some wedding cake of each of his wives were found in a good state of preservation.

By his first wife, who was Miss Margaret Lamkin, of the distinguished Lamkin and Chatam families of Virginia, he had four children, all sons, whose names were as follows: Robert, Opie, Thomas, and William. Robert was the founder of a branch of Lindsays now residing in North Carolina. He settled a home there on the river Dan, in Rockingham county, and with the paternal pride and affection named it "The Mount," after the one in Fairfax county, Virginia. His wife was Miss Elizabeth Wren, by whom he had five children. William Lindsay, the elder son, married and died, leaving two sons, George Robert Lindsay and William Carter Lindsay, both of whom are married and have families.

Robert, the second son, was a physician, and died unmarried.

John, the third son, still survives; he is a gentleman considerably advanced in years. Succeeding to the family homestead, with patient and careful industry he kept it up as a fine and flourishing farm, and thereon raised his family, six in all. He stood true to the Union cause during our Civil war, and afterward served twice as a representative in the North Carolina Legislature. His wife was Miss Nancy Law of North Carolina. His children are William R. Lindsay, Tamalane B. Lindsay, Eugene K. (who died a soldier in our late war), Virginia (Mrs. Marshal A. Black of Madison, North Carolina), Indiana (Mrs. James Davis of Red Shoals, North Carolina), and Fanny (Mrs. Daniel W. Busick of Madison, North Carolina).

The eldest son, William R. Lindsay, resides on his father's farm, "The Mount," he married Miss Nannie Meador and has by her two children, Amelia W. and John Motley Lindsay. William R. Lindsay graduated at Wake Forest College, North Carolina, and I am told served two terms in the State Legislature as a representative from Rockingham county, and declined the honor of a third nomination. His brother, Tamalane B. Lindsay, has a farm at Douglas, ten miles distant from "The Mount," which he calls "Deep Springs." His wife was Miss Rhoda R. Scott, a niece of ex-Governor David Ried of North Carolina, also United States senator for one term. They have one child, a daughter, Annie Scott, born to them in 1881.

8

Mr. John Lindsay makes his home principally with his youngest son Tamalane B. Lindsay. His daughter's, Mrs. Black's, children are Josephine, Theodosia, Nannie, Viola, Clifton and Marshal; the first is married to a Mr. N. F. Ried of Virginia, by whom she has two children. Mrs. Davis' children are Lindsay and Margaret.

Mrs. Busick's children are Essie, Charles, Tulia, Oscar and Daisey. Emily Lindsay, the elder sister of William, Robert and John Lindsay, married a Mr. Bledsoe and left a numerous family.

Mary Lindsay, their younger sister, married a Mr. Dolin and has by him a large family, who reside at Madison, North Carolina.

Opie Lindsay, the second son of the elder Opie Lindsay, and brother of Robert Lindsay, who settled in North Carolina, emigrated about 1790, along with his brother Thomas Lindsay, to Kentucky. He brought his wife with him (who was a Miss Bates of Virginia) and settled a home three miles from Crab Orchard, Kentucky. His children by this marriage were Julia, Mrs. Burgess of Fluvanna county, Virginia, who had the following family, viz.: Pleasant M., Alfred S., Daniel M., Octavia C. and Henry C., all residents of Virginia.

Samuel Lindsay, who married, first, his cousin, Rebecca Lindsay, by whom he had no issue; secondly, Lucinda Yowell, by whom he had six children, none of them living, however, beyond childhood. Samuel Lindsay died in Boone county, Kentucky, November 28, 1879, after having acquired a nice little fortune, it is said.

Sarah, who died unmarried. Alfred, who married Miss Dyer of Baltimore, Maryland; the children surviving of this union are William D. Lindsay of New York, married to Miss Ida Hunter of Washington, D. C., and the father of five children, named Ida W., Grace E., Hunter, George W., Maud E.

Alfred Lindsay of New York married to Miss Emma L. Snyder of Baltimore, and father of four children, Olive, Alfred, William I. and Ella A.

Melville Lindsay of Washington, D. C., manager of the Goodyear Rubber Works, on Ninth street, who married Miss Eloise Briscoe of Delaware, and is the father of William B., Melville, Clarence A. and Janvier.

Montgomery Lindsay, who married Miss Bertha Hopler of New Jersey. Estelle Lindsay and Ella Lindsay, unmarried, and residents of East Orange, New Jersey.

Mr. and Mrs. Alfred Lindsay, Sr., the parents of this recorded family, were a truly good and exemplary couple — and their home was a beautiful illustration of christianity, peace and love, which shed its beneficent influences around their children. Mr. Lindsay, I am told, was a tall, delicately-formed and most-refined-looking gentleman, with dark-brown hair and eyes. They lived in Washington, D. C., for some years.

Opie Lindsay of Kentucky married, secondly, Miss Nancy Roder, by whom he had six children: Elizabeth Scott (Mrs. Dr. De Lancy Egbert), who left no issue; Opie Lindsay, who married Polly Delancy, and has eight children; Martha Lee, who married Morris J. Harris, a native of Zelon, Poland, but raised in Posen, Prussia, who emigrated to America in 1840, to Crab Orchard in 1842, and identifying himself with Crab Orchard, grew rapidly in favor and prosperity. He early acquired a knowledge of the English tongue, was a man of strong principles and a most devoted husband, father and friend, and died universally loved and respected, November 6, 1883. Their children were six in number; two girls and three boys are living; one of the former is Mrs. H. L. Steger of Crab Orchard, Kentucky, who has two young daughters, Leah and Eva.

Nancy L. Lindsay, unmarried. Eveline W. (Mrs. A. Smith).

Ruben Carben Lindsay, who married Miss Belle Sparks, and had a child, which died in infancy. They are also deceased.

CHAPTER VIII.

Further record of the family of Opie Lindsay of "The Mount"— Thomas his third son — his emigration to Grant county, Kentucky — one of the fathers of that State — his family — William, Fanny, John Opie and Hierome, other children of Opie Lindsay of "The Mount."

Thomas Lindsay, the third son of Opie Lindsay of "The Mount," as previously stated, emigrated to Kentucky about 1790, and settled, I believe, in Grant county. His wife, who was a Miss Rebecca Brannen of Pennsylvania, accompanied him to Kentucky. He was, evidently, a gentleman of high aims and progressive spirit, for he desired to have his family well educated, and gave them every opportunity in his power for being so.

The fact of his leaving his home in Virginia to push his fortunes on new ground and amongst strangers, evinces his love of progression even in those early days in which he lived and moved. It may be interesting to his descendants, as well as to his elder brother's, Opie Lindsay's, descendants, to make a little historical notice of Kentucky about the period of their settling there.

It was not admitted to the Union as a State until 1792. The father of Kentucky, as is pretty generally known, was Colonel Daniel Boone of North Carolina, who, along with his brother and a companion named Stuart, and some few others, made rambling tours here for the purpose of hunting the buffalo, and thus discovered the beauties and advantages of this region. In September, 1773, Daniel Boone, with his family, relatives, and many friends whom he had induced to follow him, made the first settlement in Kentucky. It was not far from Clinch river, and was called Boonesborough. This settlement was effected with great peril, for the Indians were extremely hostile; they had several battles with them, and many of the settlers were killed, amongst them Boone's son. The savages once carried off his daughter, but she was afterward recovered.

The part where Boone settled was then a portion of Virginia. For some time he devoted his energies to building forts, and laying roads, and surveying the country; and the fame of his enterprise, and the fineness of the climate, and the abundance of game and rich soil, spread abroad, and numbers of families from the adjoining States followed him to this new country, not afraid to share similar privations, and fears of attacks from the Indians. The settlement must have been rapid, for in nineteen years after the first settlement by Boone it is incorporated as a State of the Union.

Thomas Lindsay's descendants can thus see that their forefather was doubtless subjected to many adventures and privations in his new home, and that he neither lost courage or pride in it, for he raised his family here and died, at last, honored and respected by all around him. His grandchildren may proudly look back upon him as one of the early fathers of the justly celebrated State of Kentucky. His children's names were Dorcas, David, Elizabeth, Rebecca, Thomas R., and Opie John, who all married.

Dorcas' husband or family, if she had any, I have not been furnished any knowledge of.* David's wife was a Miss Melvina Oglesby, by whom he had six children. Elizabeth was

* Could she have been connected in any way with the following? There is a tradition in Frankfort, Kentucky, how true I do not know, that Santa Anna, the celebrated Mexican general, was born in Kentucky, or was of Kentucky parentage, and of the blood of Lindsay, his mother or his grandmother having been a Kentucky Lindsay, a circumstance he was fond of relating when on a visit to this State, after having become distinguished.

a Mrs. Jos. Kirkpatrick and died shortly after her marriage. Rebecca became (as previously recorded) the wife of her cousin, Samuel Lindsay. Thomas R. had two wives; his second wife was Marietta Hutsell, by whom he had three children, Anna, William and Ella.

Opie John, the "Benjamin" of the family, seems to have been the "bright star." He studied medicine with great zeal, and graduated with distinction at the Transylvania University of Lexington, Kentucky. He was the first Mason in his county, occupying high rank in the order, and an old line Whig, and, under the new Constitution, was the first elected representative from Grant county to the Kentucky Legislature, where he showed marked ability. He was a remarkably fine-looking man, courtly in manner, extremely clannish, and celebrated for his hospitalities, and drew around him all the distinguished men of his State.

Dr. Lindsay's wife was Miss Emily Clarkson of Bourbon county, Kentucky, and said to have been a noted "belle" of that county, which has long had a reputation for its handsome women. Her mother's family, the Trabues, of Huguenot descent and probably from Virginia, were one of great pride and wealth in the State; she was a granddaughter of M. Duprey of France, head of an old French family of wealth and distinction. The issue of this marriage were three children, Alice, who became Mrs. W. L. Collins of Kentucky; Julius, still single and a resident of Grant county, Kentucky, and Davidella, who is the wife of Thomas M. Worcester, a prosperous merchant of Cincinnati, Ohio, a lady of much benevolent energies in her church, I have heard, and a general favorite in society. Neither ladies have children.

William Lindsay, the fourth son of Opie Lindsay of "The Mount," remained in Virginia, and marrying his cousin, Maria Lindsay, a daughter of his uncle, William Lindsay, settled on a plantation near his uncle and father-in-law in another part of Fairfax county, where he resided until his death in 1844, aged 48. He was a most amiable gentleman, with a pleasant face, gentle, kindly blue eyes, fair complexion and auburn hair, and dearly beloved by his children.

Having given a record of the children of Opie Lindsay by his first wife, Margaret Lamkin, I must proceed to his issue by the second and third wives. The second was a Miss Jett, who did not long survive her marriage; she left a child, which died in infancy.

The third was a Miss Howerton of Montgomery county, Virginia, a lady of excellent family and considerable personal attractions, by whom he had three children, Fanny, John Opie, and Hierome.

Fanny never married; she was, I am told, a most estimable lady, of noble-looking face and figure, of sincere religious belief and devoutly pious, and died at a fair old age at the residence of her cousin, Margaret Lindsay, Mrs. Swink of Fairfax county, Virginia.

John Opie also remained single. He was noted amongst his relatives for extreme kindness of disposition, his love for, and pride in, the clan Lindsay, and careful preservation of all his father's papers relating to the family, and as the antiquarian *upon* the family history. His face was genial and pleasant, his figure manly and dignified. During part of his life, up to within his father's death, he took the management of "The Mount," and for a few years afterward lived there with his sister and brother, when the old homestead had to be sold to pay one of his half-brothers his portion of the estate, as one of the heirs.

It was a great pity, for had this not occurred the old homestead of our joint forefather, Robert Lindsay, who founded it, would doubtless have been existing, and in the possession of some of the name or blood, to-day, and a place for all to visit with a great amount of reverential pride and interest. This spirit of disbanding and breaking up old home places is distinctly American, and for the preservation of home ties and affections, generally detrimental ; yet, on the other hand, it shows the *progressive* and *independent* dispositions of Americans, and had its good results, for by this spirit in the youth of a country it creates enterprise, settles and builds up new States, and finds fresher channels for fortunes, and encourages energy.

Hierome, or as he was generally called, Hiram Lindsay, the youngest of Opie Lindsay's children, was a planter, married and left several children, but for some reason or other, none of his relatives seemed to have much interest in his family. It was said his wife belonged to a very plain family. One of his daughters who was a bright, promising girl, my father, I am told, offered to educate, but at fifteen she ran off and married a young man of very humble origin and no energies; so the story goes.

John Opie Lindsay died at his bachelor home in Alexandria, at a fair old age.

"The Mount," or a portion of it, is now owned by a family of German descent, called Klock.

CHAPTER IX.

William Lindsay of Laurel Hill, in Fairfax county, the elder son of Robert Lindsay of "The Mount"—his wife Ann Calvert, a great granddaughter of Lord Baltimore—her remarkable beauty of person and character—her long widowhood—raising ten children—account of Susanna, her eldest.

The reader will have noticed in Robert Lindsay's will that he makes his smallest bequest to his elder son in these words:

Item. "I give and bequeath unto my son William Lindsay ten pounds current money as it runs and for him therewith to be content."

Although there is no tradition to the effect that he was not on good terms with his father, still those words must make his descendants suspect he was evidently not in as high favor with him as were his brothers, Opie and Thomas. I am told he was a remarkably handsome man, daring and adventurous. He began to battle with the world at an early age, and showed wonderful aptitude for making, though not retaining, money. He was generous, almost to a fault, and kept open-house to friends and strangers alike, in the usual warm-hearted Virginia way. He was an excellent host, full of repartee, spirit, and good humor, and the stranger left his board always his good friend.

In appearance, as I have been told by an aged relative, he was tall and muscular, and inclined to portliness, his face was decidedly of an aristocratic type, his complexion clear, his cheeks bronzed, hair dark-brown, and he had extremely penetrating gray-blue eyes, that could sparkle with fun or blaze in anger, with equal force and animation. He served in the war of the Revolution in one of Virginia's militia regiments, and received a severe wound at the battle of Guilford Court-House, under General Green, which battle took place in May, 1781.

His first home was settled in Colchester, Prince William county, Virginia, where he did business, principally that of selling for the planters; in modern term was a commission merchant, and was what was called in his day a wealthy man. His children were born in Colchester, with the exception of the youngest ones. In the time that he resided in Colchester, it was *the* shipping port of the Potomac, and held the important position in this respect that Alexandria did afterward. It was situated on the Occoquan river, which ran into the Potomac, and was on the lands of my great-great grandfather, through my Grayson kin, Doctor Peter Wagener, one of the wealthiest land-holders of the vicinity. (See acts of the Virginia Legislature of the colony, 1753, wherein the town is mentioned as being on the land of the said Doctor Peter Wagener, "that it would be very convenient for trade, and that commissioners shall be appointed to lay out said town and call it Colchester;" which act was carried out and settled upon by the Legislature.)

There is a tradition in the family that William Lindsay made two or three fortunes, and lost two or three. His latter home was in Fairfax county, not far from the Occoquan river and his former place of residence, and perhaps some ten or twelve miles from "The Mount," the paternal homestead. The plantation consisted of about a thousand acres, and on one of the elevated portions of this he erected his house, which was called "Laurel Hill." The homes of nearly all the Lindsays who could conveniently arrange it, were built on some hilly location. It was probably a feeling with them, also a belief, that the original home in Scotland was built (owing to its name) on elevated ground.

As far as I have been able to ascertain from some of our aged relatives, William Lindsay married about the year 1766 to 1767. His wife was Miss Ann Calvert of Culpepper county, Virginia, whose father came from the eastern shore of Maryland; a great granddaughter of Cecil Calvert, Lord Baltimore, the founder and proprietor of Maryland. The Calverts were of royal descent from the Norman King William the Conqueror of England, the Saxon King Edward the Elder, and the Capuchin King Henry the First. (See Mr. Browning's book "Americans of Royal Descent.") And if blood is indicative of queenly appearance and bearing Mrs. William Lindsay bore undoubted evidence of her lineage.

She was but a little over fifteen at the time of her marriage and already famous for her loveliness of person and character. For the benefit of her female descendants I will add what I have gathered in regard to her style. She was about the medium height, symmetrical and graceful in form, her countenance of delicate and noble contour, complexion of dazzling fairness, the cheeks generally tinged with a soft rich pink, her dark-brown eyes full of brilliant lustre and heavily fringed with the darkest lashes, mouth mobile and expressive, head proudly set on lovely shoulders and crowned by dark-brown hair, small, well-shaped hands and feet, and her smile was the last, but not the least, of her unusual inventory of charms. She was somewhat cold and reserved in her demeanor to strangers and acquaintances, but to those she loved and cared for, most gentle, frank and winning. She retained her beauty to a remarkable age (I would that her secret of its preservation had been handed down to us, if secret it was), as 'tis said, seeming to grow lovelier with her years.

She survived her husband many years, dying at length at the age of seventy or more, at the home of her son-in-law,

Mr. Renald Grimes, at Patapsco, Prince William county, Virginia, in the year 1822, and was buried at Laurel Hill. My father, when a boy, was her especial pet among the grandchildren, and she frequently, he told my mother, patted him approvingly on the head, as she remarked, in accents of pride, "my child, if you had your rights, you ought to be a lord." These words of his old grandmother, he said, haunted his youthful imagination until he began to wonder why they were said, and it was greatly owing to them that he began to investigate the family history later on with such zeal. He was born under her roof, and it is told me christened on her knee by her priest, for she was of the Roman Catholic faith of her family. Her priest came twice or thrice a month to Laurel Hill from Alexandria to say mass for her, as she was unable to go so far to church.

William Lindsay was not permitted to enjoy his new home very many years; he died here in the prime of manhood, of that painful disease, gout, about the year 1792–3, during the very early childhood of his youngest children, Thomas and Catherine, and was the first adult laid away in the family burying ground on the plantation. His widow and children continued for a number of years at Laurel Hill; it saw many a sad and many a festive occasion; children were married from this home, grandchildren were born here, and the remains of dear relatives were carried thence to their last resting place, in the rear of "grandmère's garden," as the saying was.

The grandmère was not only a lovely looking old lady but an exceedingly neat, careful and excellent housewife, and her system and regime a pattern to all her children and grandchildren. None could excel her at the spinning wheel, even in her advanced years, and no family had finer linen, homespun as it was called, than hers. Her usual attire, I am told, was a homespun gown on week days, with a French mull kerchief arranged prettily about her neck, and snowy white mull Normandy cap. On the Sabbath, and festive occasions, she donned a rich, dark turk satin that might stand by itself for quality, and the white mull kerchief gave way to a daintier lace kerchief, with finer cap to match.

She ruled by love and yet firmness; her slaves and all the attendants about the plantation revered and loved her. None were kinder where sickness and distress was, and gave readier assistance and sympathy, whether at neighbors or among the negro cabins; for the plantation hands, as was the usual custom, had each (that is the heads of families) a cabin to herself or himself. Even the faithful maid-servant of the grandmère, unless in case of sickness or for children, resided, at night, in her husband's or father's cabin, coming to the mistress' house in the morning.

The old lady was a fond gardener, and tenderly and proudly (ere she grew very old) brought up and watched her rose trees, the numerous varieties of which she was famous for, and to this day some of those rose trees bloom and bear fragrant roses as of yore. She had also a bed of notable cactus. Her rich and elegant silverware for table use, which was used daily, was a source of much admiration and pride to the younger portion of her family. The best set of candlesticks, an aged relative has told me, were so heavy and so tall that it took a strong man to lift them. She had her teapot and served this then expensive beverage to all her family, on certain occasions only. Chiccory and coffee were greatly used in that day, and also milk, with strong liquors for the men. The old homestead is a sample (for it is still standing and occupied, although by strangers) of the homes of the well-to-do planters of a hundred years ago.

The accompanying picture in this chapter is a copy of a hurried sketch I made of it on the occasion of my first visit to it a few years since. It is built of well-seasoned North

LAUREL HILL.

Carolina pine, which has withstood the wear and tear of the elements, not to mention "old time," most bravely. On either side are the old type colonial chimneys, which afforded, inside the rooms, those prodigious fireplaces of which we read in history and romance as affording such scope for the "yule log" to blaze and crackle so cheerily from for those gathered around it on winter or holiday nights, or the fugitive from justice, or the child at play. The ground on which the house stands is moderately high and reached by a serpentine carriageway of gradual ascent, and the surroundings are picturesque. You look from the dormer windows in front, as far as the eye will reach, over a gently undulating valley of green sward and woods, which terminates, at last, in a shining silvery streak, varying in size and serpentine in shape, which you would imagine a creek if you did not know was a glimpse of the lordly Potomac, once called, ere Lord Fairfax re-named it, Cohongoruton, which was the ancient name given to it by the Indians.

To-day the busy rattle and rumble and shrill voice of the steam horse is heard and seen piercing its rapid way through the near foreground, and numberless little villages peep forth now here or there, showing that man will come where the scene is promising and beautiful. The famous old Telegraph road, used throughout the Revolution for the mail and armies, and in direct communication with Mount Vernon, passed the dividing line of Laurel Hill. Sometimes, 'tis said, regiments halted here and the hospitalities of the old homestead were called into action, and always with credit to it. If there could have been any historical-loving soul of ready pen in the family at that period (and possibly there may have been, which knowledge is lost to us), what a number of interesting items I now might be relating to you from ancient journals of these stirring war-times of our grandfathers.

From the recollection of an aged relative, the oldest surviving granddaughter of William Lindsay and his wife, I am indebted for the following dates of the births of their children, the family Bible having been lost in the Grimes family.

An infant, died young	born	1767
Susanna	"	1769
George Walter (my grandfather)	"	1771
William Henry	"	1773
Ann or Nancy	"	1775
Hierome or Hiram	"	1778
John	"	1780
An infant, died young	"	1783
Sarah	"	1785
Maria	"	1787
Thomas	"	1789
Catherine, called Kitty	"	1791

Ten of the above grew to manhood and womanhood. I. Susanna, usually called by the young relatives Aunt Sue, their eldest daughter, was a most amiable and kind-hearted woman, with pleasing face and figure, the latter of which grew portly with her years. In youth her hair was of a fine chestnut hue, and her blue eyes mild and full of kindly light; she had one of those soft, winning dispositions that endeared her to every one. She married twice. Her first husband was William Triplett of Fairfax county, and a member of one of the best county families, but to whom she had no children. He served his country in the war of 1812 and, I think, was killed therein. Her second husband was a Mr. Johnston, by whom she had a son named Hierome Lindsay Johnston, who at nineteen left his home with friends to hunt, as was supposed, but was never seen by his widowed mother or relatives again, nor was there any clue ever found as to his whereabouts or death.

This was a sad blow to her who was a second time a widow, but time, the real healer of all earthly sorrows, at last softened the pain, and her affectionate heart found, by degrees, a refuge and source of comfort in a nephew of her first husband, whom she had adopted as a boy, and who proved the staff and shield of her declining years, Leolin Jamison, in whose house, in Alexandria, Virginia, she passed peacefully away ere reaching seventy.

CHAPTER X.

Colonel George Walter Lindsay, elder son of William Lindsay of Laurel Hill — his sad death in his early prime, 1810, in Washington, D. C.— his wife, Judith Grayson — her fine character and appearance — distinguished family and connections — their five children, Major George Frederick, John, Anne, Mary E. and Benjamin Grayson Orr — who they married — *their* children.

II. The second surviving child and elder son, born to William and Ann Calvert Lindsay of Laurel Hill, as you will have noticed, was George Walter Lindsay, born while his parents resided in Colchester, Prince William county, 1771. I have always heard that he was of most engaging appearance and manner, inheriting much of his father's bright, sunny disposition, and withal dignity of bearing; he had a fair complexion, ruddy with health, chestnut colored hair, handsome gray-brown or hazel eyes, keen and full of intelligence and humor, a graceful, elegant figure, and springy foot-step, and was a general favorite amongst relatives and friends.

He was enterprising and industrious, and most desirous of winning a high position for himself in life, and all he undertook was with this aim, but his career was cut short in his early prime by an untimely death. The unsettled state of the country as he grew to manhood, the constant hostilities about this time with the mother country interrupted greatly the advancement in business, or in professions, of hundreds of Virginia's youth. Their arm was constantly called upon to aid in the deliverance of their country from oppression and wrong, and all had to obey who could. Like father like son, even the tender lads rendered what assistance they were able in the colonial wars.

George Walter Lindsay was early appointed a lieutenant of one of the militia regiments raised for the war, in his native place, and served in several engagements with the British in Virginia and Maryland. He rose to the grade of colonel, having finally a detachment under his charge, and retired at the close of the war with this rank. About 1801 he married Judith Grayson of Prince William county, Virginia, daughter of the Reverend Spence Grayson of "Bell Air," in that county, an Episcopal clergyman of noted eloquence and highly cultivated tastes, a graduate of Oxford in England, and niece of the distinguished Colonel William Grayson, military aide to General Washington, afterward Senator Grayson, the first appointed senator (1784) from the mother State to our Federal Congress, whose colleague was Richard Henry Lee, and who was also one of the framers and ratifiers of our Constitution.

For the benefit of his collateral descendants, I make a copy of the following from How's History of Virginia, page 442:

"In June, 1788, he was a member of the Virginia convention which was called for the purpose of considering the present Constitution of the United States. In this assembly, rendered illustrious by men of the first talents, he was very conspicuous. His genius united with the eloquence of Henry, in opposing the adoption of the Constitution. While he acknowledged the evils of the old government, he was afraid that the proposed government would destroy the liberty of the States. His principal objections to it were, that it took from the States the sole right of direct taxation, which was the highest state of sovereignty; that the limits between the National and State authorities were not sufficiently defined; that they might clash, in which case the general government would prevail; that there was no provision against raising such a navy as was more than sufficient to protect our trade, and this would excite the jealousy of European powers, and lead to war; and that there was no adequate checks against the abuse of power, especially by the president, who was responsible only to his counselors and partners in crime, the members of the Senate."

It further says of Senator Grayson:

"His great abilities were united with unimpeached integrity."

In Miss Grayson's veins flows some of the best blood of Virginia; her mother was a Miss Mary Elizabeth Wagener, a daughter of Doctor Peter Wagener, at that time one of the most prominently rich men, along with his son-in-law, the Reverend Spence Grayson, in Prince William county, Virginia; he was a very distinguished county gentleman and physician, a vestry-man of Powhick Church, where General Washington worshipped, a descendant of good old Holland Dutch stock, and son of the Reverend Peter Wagener, D. D., Rector of Sisted, in the county of Essex, in England, in which town and county Doctor Wagener was born the 5th of April, 1717.

His wife, whom he met and married in Virginia, was the beautiful Catherine Robinson, only daughter of the Honorable John Robinson, one of his majesty's counsel in Virginia, afterward speaker of the House of Burgesses, who was the one to receive General Washington at the close of the war and deliver to him his notable speech; and whose cousin, the Tory officer, Colonel Robinson, at the close of the war went to England to assume the family title, Earl of Ripon, etc., and its accompanying estates. Through the Wageners, she was connected with the Beverleys, the MacCartys, the Balls (Washington's mother's family), and other distinguished Virginia families; through her father, the Reverend Spence Grayson, she claimed descent from Captain Joseph Monroe, the father of President James Monroe, her grandmother being Susanna Monroe, the sister of Captain Joseph Monroe of the noble Clan Monroe of Scotland. Her sister, Susanna Monroe Grayson, was the wife of Lund Washington, Esq., a second cousin of General Washington. She was born at the handsome old Grayson estate, "Bell Air," in December, 1780, and died at her home in the city of New Orleans, Louisiana, September 18, 1851, of congestive chills, in her sixty-ninth year, the last surviving member of her parents' numerous family, they having raised to manhood and womanhood fourteen out of fifteen children.

She was noted, as were all her sisters, for unusual personal attraction; she was a clear, rosy brunette, tall, plump, and queenly in figure, highly accomplished, played well upon the guitar, and sang sweetly, and was as winning and noble in character as in looks; one and all of her relatives were devoted to her. It has often been related to me that on the occasion of their marriage, a handsomer or more distinguished-looking young couple never stood before a clergyman to be united in the bonds of matrimony. She married twice after the death of her first husband. Her second husband was the Honorable Mr. Lemon, a representative in Congress from Mississippi, who died two years after their union, of yellow fever at Natchez, Mississippi, leaving her considerable wealth.

Her third husband was the Reverend Mr. Richardson. She left no children by either of these gentlemen—a son was born to her by Mr. Lemon, but he died in infancy.

Colonel George Walter Lindsay settled a home latterly in Washington city, on Capitol Hill, and was residing there with his family at the time of the accident which caused his death. It was the custom of his day for the head of each family to go every morning to market, the market being then, as now, on Pennsylvania avenue; he was riding there one morning on a spirited horse, which was so wild and restive as to attract universal attention from passers-by. A friend accosted him once and told him it was safer to get off than to ride it; the Lindsay spirit shone out well in his reply, "Never! until I conquer the beast." He was a splendid horseman, as were nearly all the Virginians, and doubtless would have succeeded in his wish, but the girths of the saddle broke, he was thrown and dragged a considerable distance, and death ensued a few hours after being carried home to his wife and children; this took place in the year 1810, in the thirty-eighth year of his age.

I am told his remains were interred in the Congressional cemetery at Washington. Mrs. Lindsay, latterly Richardson, was buried in the Grayson vault at Yazoo city, Mississippi. Many of her relatives resided in Mississippi and Louisiana. Colonel George Walter Lindsay had by her three sons and two daughters, viz.:

George Frederick (my father)	born	1802
John	"	1804
Anne	"	1805
Mary Elizabeth	"	1807
Benjamin Grayson Orr	"	1809

The two eldest were born at Laurel Hill. George Frederick, who was my father, was not more than seven or eight years of age when his father died, and he told my mother he had, therefore, little or no recollection of him; all his knowledge of him was through relatives. He was appointed to the West Point Military Academy when but fourteen years of age, and was, 'tis said, the youngest cadet ever appointed to this academy. He passed through the Point most creditably, graduating in four years, saw service first as an ensign in the field, and was afterward commissioned by President Monroe as second lieutenant of the Second Regiment of Infantry, 1st of July, 1820. He went through both land and sea service; he served in the Florida and some of our Indian wars, and resigned latterly from the army to enter the Marine Corps, wherein he rose rapidly; he finally accepted, from choice, a position on the staff, as major and quartermaster of the corps, in which capacity he was serving at the time of his death, at his residence, 1301

K street, Franklin square, Washington, D. C., the 27th of September, 1857.

To enumerate my father's fine qualities might seem like vain glory from his child, who did not know him, having lost him in her infancy, but her ear ever rejoiced in listening about him from her mother and relatives; suffice to say that he was a good son, and hence a good and affectionate husband and father, and ever a ready and sympathetic friend, too kind and generous by far perhaps, as his generosity, in many cases of his army and navy friends, was not repaid. His widow and orphans discovered this on the settlement by the former of his estate. I can be excused, perhaps, for also adding the journalistic tribute and words of a friend on hearing of his demise: "He was a true man; in our view, one of nature's noblemen; he has served his country faithfully and well, may his rest be one of peace." As my mother told me, he had a commanding and military bearing joined to a distinguished-looking and handsome figure; his height was five feet nine or ten inches, his weight about one hundred and seventy-five pounds, his chest broad, his hands and feet small and shapely, and his step unusually firm and springy; his skin was very clear and fair, but his face, as he advanced in years, became slightly bronzed. As a general thing he wore no beard or mustache; his hair was a dark-brown, his forehead high, his eyes of a dark-gray-blue and penetrating and stern, until he smiled, when the whole aspect of his countenance changed from excessive dignity to almost childlike simplicity, his laugh was joyous and musical, and he had a keen sense and appreciation of all that was beautiful and refined, whether in people or objects.

He was married twice; his first wife was not much over sixteen, and he not twenty-one, at the time of their union; she had her early home in Plattsburg, New York, where he first met her; she was Mary J., the daughter of the gallant

Colonel Malancthon Smith of the United States Army, and sister of Captain, afterward Rear-Admiral Malancthon Smith of the United States Navy, now retired. After a happy marriage of many years she passed away, in 1850, at the handsome country home of her husband, Manor Hill, in Westchester county, now a part of New York city. Her illness was long and painful, but she bore it with christian-like and noble patience; I have always heard she was a lady of much refined beauty of person and mind, and warmly loved by all her relatives and friends.

The children of this marriage were William Grayson, Beverley Grayson, George Frederick and Mary Osborne. William Grayson met with an untimely death at the tender age of ten or eleven years, at Pensacola, Florida, where his father was then stationed—he fell from a tree, broke his arm and died of lockjaw; he was a remarkably quick and precocious child, with the blonde beauty of a girl. Beverley Grayson was the only one of this union to survive his father; he had a classical education, had traveled abroad, was of a distinguished, refined person, with regular features, and reserved, rather shy manners; he studied for awhile at medicine, but the civil war breaking out disconcerted his plans; he finally enlisted in the Eighty-seventh New York Volunteers, under General McClellan, was taken prisoner at the battle of the Chickahominy, carried to Libby Prison, where he sickened and died, as reported by a returned comrade and fellow prisoner.

George Frederick received, at the close of his education, an appointment as second lieutenant in the Marine Corps, and served in the Mexican war; he died of dropsy of the heart, in February, 1855, on board ship, en route home from California on sick list; was found dead in his cabin. He was a tall, sprightly and handsome blonde, only twenty-three years of age at his death. Mary Osborne, like her elder brother, met with an untimely death, due to an accident; she was a child of five or six years, and on an errand to the kitchen for her father, where, in the absence of the servant, she attempted to get hot water from the kettle on the fire, her clothing caught fire, and ere assistance was rendered she was burned too severely to recover; she was buried in the city of Philadelphia, where her father was then stationed.

About 1852 my father married, in Boston, my mother, Miss Margaret Fraser of Scotland, then on a visit with her father and sister to America. Her father was John Fraser of Scotland, editor and proprietor for many years of "The True Scotsman" of Edinburgh; an ardent reformer, philanthropist, and for a while politician; a gentleman of wide intelligence and action in his native country, and honored with the friendship of some of the most distinguished men of his time, at home and abroad. My mother had a fair, dainty coloring of face, large blue eyes, of the pure tint of the summer sky, her forehead was moderately high, the countenance a classical oval, with refined, delicately cut features, hair dark brown, her figure slender and five feet three inches in height, and her feet and hands small. Her friends delighted in her fluent and intelligent conversation, and her beautiful singing, which was that of the true artist; her voice was a rich and sweet soprano, of great breadth, flexibility and cultivation; she sang always with her whole soul in her music, whether it was in rendering one of her beautiful Scotch ballads or brilliant Italian cavatinas. She had a brief but happy married life, and survived my father about thirty years; living in all that time solely for her children, educating and caring tenderly for them. She took them to Europe several times, and gave them all the advantages that lay in her power. She died, after an illness of four months, of the same disease as my father (dropsy) at her residence, 1301 K street, Franklin Square, Washington, D. C., on

February 2, 1886. Her gentleness, patience, and hope during illness were sublime; her end sweet and peaceful as befitting the close of a truly pure, unselfish, and noble life. "Her faults were few, her virtues many." She bore my father three children, Walter Edzell, Margaret Isabella (the writer of this Record), and Anne Barnard. The first was born at his father's country-seat, Manor Hill, previously mentioned, and when but a young infant, accompanied our parents to Scotland, where he was somewhat romantically christened. See the following account of the christening, from a Scotch paper of that year, 1853:

"BAPTISM EXTRAORDINARY. — An interesting, novel, and romantic christening took place a few days ago on the 140th anniversary of the Battle of Flodden, on the battle-ground where King James IV fell, September 10, 1513, surrounded by his nobles and chivalry of Scotland. Captain G. F. Lindsay of the United States Marine Corps, who recently left the United States as bearer of despatches to the American legations at London and Paris, being in Scotland on a visit to his wife's relatives and his own kinsmen, conceived the notion of having his infant son christened on that reputedly glorious, though fatal field to Scotland. For this purpose a party was made up, and the Rev. Patrick Brewster (brother to the great Sir David Brewster), of the Abbey Church, Paisley, a friend of his wife's family, the Frasers of Newfield House, near Johnstone, was invited to officiate at the ceremony, and who kindly consenting to do so, the party proceeded by railway from Edinburgh to Berwick, where they took carriages and drove fifteen miles to the battle-field, and on the margin of Camphill Burn, a beautiful little stream running through the field into the river Till, the infant boy was baptized from the water of that limpid stream, under the name of Walter Edzell, in memory of the gallant young Walter of Edzell, who fought under the king's banner, and was one of the faithful band who, after the day was utterly lost, formed themselves into a ring, and fought to the last in defense of their king, till he fell in the midst of them. Captain Lindsay had many ancestral kinsmen killed in that bloody battle. Among them was Earl John Lindsay, of Crawford, the chief of the clan, and Walter, the younger of Edzell, his direct ancestor, who left four sons, David, afterward the ninth Earl of Crawford, Alexander, John, and Robert, the two last of whom were killed at the battle of Pinkie, in 1547." Many interesting details are given in the Lives of the Lindsays, vol. i, pp. 186–192, and vol. ii, p. 281.

I was born at my father's city house, 57 Walker street, New York city, within sound and sight of Broadway. My sister Anne Barnard (named after Lady Anne Barnard, *nee* Lindsay, who wrote the beautiful poem "Auld Robin Gray") was born at her parents' Washington home, 1301 K street, N. W., and died in New York in 1860, aged three years. Walter Edzell Lindsay married June 12, 1882, Miss Florence G. Turner of Washington, D. C., a daughter of Dr. T. J. Turner, a medical director in the Navy, and has one child, a daughter, Florence Edzell, born 18th October, 1887, at the old family homestead on K street, in Washington.

John Lindsay, second son of Colonel George Walter, and Judith Grayson Lindsay, was born at Laurel Hill, in Virginia, in 1804, and died in Washington in his twentieth year, unmarried. He was, I have heard, a remarkably handsome young man, and noted for his unusual height; at sixteen years of age he measured six feet six and a half inches in his stocking feet. Mr. Gales, editor of "The National Intelligencer" of Washington, in alluding to his death, said, "He represented one of the finest specimens in the *genus homo* of the banks of our Potomac."

Anne Lindsay, their third child, was cut off at a tender age by a sad fate, similar to that of my half-sister, Mary Osborne Lindsay; she was playing in an empty room at her grandmother's home, Laurel Hill, and finally, as a source of fun, amused herself lighting papers and throwing them behind her, when her clothes suddenly ignited, and although she ran screaming to some of the family, ere assistance arrived she was too seriously burnt to survive many days. She was (my father often told my mother) a child of an unusually sweet and merry disposition, and gave promise of growing into a lovely woman.

Mary Elizabeth Lindsay was a sprightly and striking looking brunette, and married at seventeen or eighteen a physician of Alexandria, Virginia, named Roberts, and died soon after the birth of a daughter, which was adopted by its grandmother Lindsay, then Mrs. Lemon, who at about the same time had a son to her husband which, however, lived but a few months, and hence the little motherless granddaughter took the place of the lost one in the care and affection bestowed upon it by the grandmother ever afterward; she nourished it as her own, and taught it to call her mother. She took her to Mississippi with her, and on the death of her husband, Mr. Lemon, she settled in New Orleans, where Mary Elizabeth Roberts received her education, and, about 1837, was married to a promising young lawyer there, Charles E. Mount, by whom she left three children, Thomas E., Pauline, and Charles E. Mrs. Mount passed away in New Orleans after a long illness, in October, 1873, her husband in 1881. Thomas E. Mount is a widower with two or three children, and resides in Vicksburgh, Mississippi (data of 1874). Pauline is married to Mr. Myford McDougall, the son of a Scotch gentleman, and a descendant of the ancient House of Lorn; he is a planter in Louisiana, their home is called "Palestine," and is in Tangipaho Parish (Peace Grove P. O.), Louisiana. She has the following children living: Robert Lindsay McDougall, Kate McDougall, Frank McDougall, Hester McDougall, and a son Lindsay McDougall, all nearly grown, except the last named.

Benjamin Grayson Orr Lindsay, the last born of Colonel George Walter, and Judith Grayson Lindsay, accompanied his mother to Mississippi and resided with her until his death. He was a lawyer by profession, and practiced law for a while with his talented cousin, also a lawyer, Spence Monroe Grayson, Esq., of New Orleans, Louisiana. In appearance he was said to resemble his brother George Frederick quite strikingly; in disposition he was generous and warm hearted; of considerable ability, but lacking in concentration and steadiness of purpose. He passed away about 1837–8, after a short illness of congestive fever, in the thirty-first year of his age, unmarried, and was buried from his mother's residence in New Orleans.

CHAPTER XI.

William Henry Lindsay, the third born, and second son of William and Ann Calvert Lindsay of Laurel Hill — his death at Barnaby, in Prince William county, in 1823; his enterprising widow, Catherine Sanford Lindsay — their children, the emigration of herself and family to eastern Arkansas in early times, his grandchildren, etc.

III. William Henry Lindsay, the third child, and second son of William and Ann Calvert Lindsay of Laurel Hill, born, as already recorded, in 1773, was a well-to do planter in Prince William county. He died in his prime, July 8, 1823, of bilious congestion, at his fine estate called "Barnaby." He was, I am told, a splendid type of the Virginia gentleman of his day, six feet in height, weighed two hundred and fifty pounds, and was fond of the sports then indulged in by the gentlemen, and a most generous entertainer. His intimate friend was the celebrated John Randolph of Roanoke. He was married in 1804 to Miss Catherine Washington Sanford, daughter and heiress of Joseph Sanford, Esq., of "Barnaby," in Prince William county, by his second wife, Margaret Ann De Barry, who descended from an old and honored family of Barrymore, Ireland.

Mrs. Catherine Sanford Lindsay, widow of William Henry Lindsay, seems to have been a lady of remarkable energies and enterprise, courage and benevolence. Not long after her husband's death, she disposed of her Virginia lands, gathered her worldly goods together, and with her young family emigrated to eastern Arkansas. The journey in those days, as can be imagined, was not effected from such a distance without great endurance, trouble and expense. Arkansas was then only a Territory, and principally inhabited by Indians, said to be the remnants of the most powerful tribes in America.

The first settlement made by the whites was at the Indian village of Arkansas, on the river of that name, in the year 1685. The first inhabitants, and emigrants who joined them for many years, were French; the progress of the colony was not rapid. Little Rock, the early seat of its government, was laid out only in 1820, and in 1836 Arkansas was admitted to the Union as a separate, independent State.

Mrs. Lindsay's route to Arkansas was in all probability through Kentucky, until she reached the Mississippi river, thence down that river to Memphis, Tennessee, from which point she, no doubt, crossed into Arkansas by the easiest means, settling near Pine Bluff, in Jefferson county, which is in the eastern part of the State. The Arkansas river, which runs through it, and its outlets afford abundant irrigation to, and thus render this country quite fertile. Nearly eight hundred miles across the continent! Think of that, for a weak woman and a young family to accomplish for a new home! Her travels, without doubt, at that time, were fraught not only with many hardships, but stirring adventure, which might form an interesting volume if the incidents could have been preserved.

Twenty years she lived in her new home, a fine plantation, seeing her children grow up around her. There was no woman in eastern Arkansas, I have heard, better known and respected than she was. Her actions were noble and energetic, her deeds of charity numerous, and her hospitalities unbounded. Industry and inheritance had blessed her with wealth, which she used with a liberal hand, and when at last she passed from earth, December 5, 1848, in the sixty-fourth year of her age, she was mourned for with sincere and genuine grief by all who knew her.

In personal appearance she was of noble and handsome form and face, warm and genial in manner, intelligent and fluent in conversation, and of surpassing energy in all matters she took in hand. Such an ancestress one may justly be proud of, and let it be hoped that many of her descendants take pattern from her life, and that her excellent qualities have been transmitted to her posterity. She was truly one of the mothers of the great Bear State. The following are the eight children of William Henry and Catherine Sanford Lindsay, who were all born in Virginia.

I. Margaret Ann, born November, 1805. Died at two years of age.

II. Edward Washington, born May 27, 1807. Died June, 1861, in his prime; he married in Arkansas, late in life, his cousin Catherine Triplett, the widow Stonnell, and the daughter of his aunt, Mrs. Sarah Triplett *nee* Lindsay, of Fairfax county, Virginia, and had two children, Mr. George Lindsay, who married Belle McGuyher of Arkansas, and Kate Lindsay, now Mrs. De Boyd Smith; both are residents of the old homestead in Jefferson county, Arkansas.

III. William Henry, born August 27, 1810, died at the age of fifty-seven, in November, 1867. His wife was Miss Catherine Cockrum, by whom he had five children as follows: Catherine, Samuel, John, Julia, and Fisk; only two are living, Mr. Samuel Lindsay and Mr. Fisk Lindsay. The former bore a distinguished part as a captain in our recent Civil war on the Confederate side, losing an arm in battle; he served in one of the Arkansas State regiments. He is, I am told, a gentleman of pleasing face and manner, and extremely kind-hearted. His second wife was a Miss Moore, by whom he has two children living, Ora and Joseph. He owns a farm in the State, and is said to be comfortably off. Mr. Fisk Lindsay is married, and has some children, whose names have not been furnished me.

IV. John Randolph (named after his father's distinguished friend) was born March 20, 1813, and died in his forty-eighth year, of consumption, December, 1861. He married, in 1837, Sarah A. Puller, by whom he had ten children, only three are living, Edward, Kate and Charles, and are residents, I believe, of Arkansas.

V. Margaret Ann, born March 6, 1816. Died June, 1861, in her prime. Her husband, Mr. Israel Embrey, belonged to an old and wealthy family of Arkansas. She bore him twelve children, five of whom are living, Jordan, Mary Caroline, William, Flowers, and Edward Embrey. She was married to Mr. Embrey in 1835.

VI. Catherine, born October 21, 1818. Died in childhood, 1825.

VII. Mary Offut, born May 23, 1821. Died March, 1860, in her prime. She was married, in 1836, to the Reverend Fontaine Brown, a presiding Elder of the Methodist Church in Arkansas. He was an ardent and strong advocate of the Confederacy, and suffered largely on this account, having been imprisoned by the Union authorities, and not liberated till the close of the war, and died shortly afterward from the privations and hardships endured therein. Five children survive of this union, Catherine, James, Walter, Fontaine, and Adelaide Brown.

VIII. Frances Sanford, born May 19, 1823, and still living. On May 22, 1840, Miss Frances S. Lindsay married Judge and Colonel Joseph W. Bocage of Pine Bluff, Arkansas, one of the most enterprising and leading spirits of Pine Bluff, and a lineal descendant of a distinguished French family called "Du Bocage" in France. He possesses some interesting relics of his family. His mother was a native of Martinique, W. I., daughter of Governor Pierre Lavoisier, and niece of the celebrated French chemist, Antoine Louvent Lavoisier, who was guillotined the 8th of May, 1794.

He was born the 8th of May, 1819, on the Island of St. Lucia, W. I., but coming to this country from the West Indies, at an early age, with his recently widowed mother, meeting with shipwreck and rescue on the way, from the effects of which his mother died soon afterward, he was given to by that mother, on her deathbed, and raised by a distinguished lady-relative (on his father's side) of North Carolina. This lady, in due time, entered him at Donaldson College, in her State. On the death of this relative, having found that although heir to a large estate in the West Indies, through the Wilberforce and Channing act (by which England emancipated her slaves in those countries), it was of no use, he made a bold start out into the world to try his fortune, and having youth, talent, and energies, after many privations and struggles, step by step, rose to his present honorable position. When he finally landed in Arkansas, his lot fell in principally with the French and Indian settlers of Chicot county, where his mother-tongue stood him in good need.

By degrees he identified himself with Pine Bluff, in Jefferson county, and grew as it grew. He served during the recent war, on the Confederate side, as colonel of the Second Arkansas Infantry, a regiment he had assisted to raise. He also served twice as State Attorney of the Arkansas Legislature, and occupied other high civil positions in the gift of the people. He is at present a member of the firm of "Johnson & Bocage," real estate agents, in Pine Bluff. Both Judge and Mrs. Bocage have been described to me as a distinguished-looking couple, of somewhat past middle age, and as intelligent, highly-esteemed, well-to-do citizens of that city. They have the following family living:

I. Mary Etto Walters, married to Captain J. W. Smith, a son of Governor Nathaniel Smith, and mother of four children. II. Edward Washington, who married Miss Julia

Brown of Georgia. III. Frances Irene. IV. Flora Toinette. V. Charles William. VI. Annie Reyburn. The younger son, Mr. Charles William Bocage, seems from all accounts to have inherited a great portion of his father's enterprise, genius, and energy of character. He is a civil engineer by profession. At nineteen years of age (which is but five years since) he had completed two divisions on the Texas and St. Louis railroad, and a division in Illinois, on the Toledo, Texas, and Rio Grande railroad. He is probably the youngest civil engineer in our country, ever intrusted at that age with a division of his own.

On the 5th of June, 1883, the youngest daughter, Miss Annie R. Bocage, at sixteen years of age, graduated with the highest honors, carrying off the gold medal offered to the most proficient in the senior class at the Columbia Female Institute (by Christ Church), at Nashville, Tennessee.

I am told Mrs. Bocage is truly a Lindsay in looks, having "the strong, positive features of her father predominating in her countenance, with the delicate outlines of the lower portion of her mother's face."

CHAPTER XII.

Ann or Nancy Lindsay, the second daughter, and Hierome, John and Thomas, the other sons of William and Ann Calvert Lindsay of Laurel Hill — John's bravery and death while capturing a pirate vessel on the high sea during the Revolution — marriage of Thomas, and the early loss of his wife — his unhappiness, and flying to sea to escape from it if possible — is never heard of again — his vessel supposed to have been shipwrecked.

IV. Ann or Nancy Lindsay, as she was called, born as recorded in 1775, was said to have been a delicate-looking and beautiful young girl, of the purest blonde type, and most gentle and amiable in disposition; she married at seventeen years of age, about 1792, a Virginia gentleman named Woodrough, and died the following year, leaving no issue.

V. Hierome Lindsay, the fifth child and third son, born in 1778, inherited considerable genius, talent and ingenuity, and love of music. He was moderately tall, of graceful, slender figure, handsome in face and refined in manners. He was a soldier in the Revolution, going as a substitute 'tis said, for his brother William Henry, who, being married, was unable to leave his family. At the close of the war he settled down as an assistant planter in one of his sister's homes in Fairfax county. He was fond of constructing articles of furniture and ornaments, and playing on the flute, which he was a good performer upon. He died at his sister's home, of quick consumption, in the thirty-fifth year of his age, unmarried, and was universally regretted by all who knew him.

VI. John Lindsay, sixth child and fourth son, born 1780, was looked upon as the hero of the family. He entered and showed a strong predilection for the army at an early age. He was of early-matured manhood, and of great personal bravery and attractions. He was tall, slender and agile, with unusual energy and strength of body. He had dark, piercing gray-blue eyes that seemed to grasp things with wonderful intelligence and rapidity. His voice was strong, clear and commanding, and his movements of nervous quickness. When eighteen years of age he looked all of twenty-eight. His elders, recognizing his talents and abilities, were always attached to and proud of him, and listened to him as they would their equal. Many predicted for him a distinguished future, but fate, destiny, or whatever you may call it, seemed against him.

The men of this family all died ere their prime, with the exception of one, William Henry, as you no doubt noticed. After serving with zeal and bravery in the Revolutionary army, and also in the navy, he became a lieutenant on board a privateersman called "The London Packet," which was chiefly fitted out by Baltimore merchants to protect their trade with France during the second war with Great Britain. There was at this time a great deal of annoyance from pirates on the sea and along our coasts, and one vessel in particular had become outrageously insolent and destructive, and in consequence a terror to the sailor. This vessel the captain of the privateersman determined to meet and destroy, and for days he chased her, until the pirate, strong in her recent victories, stopped and showed fight somewhere on our Atlantic not many miles from land. The contest was fierce and deadly; at the outset of the engagement the brave captain of the privateersman was fatally wounded, and Lieutenant John Lindsay, although the junior officer, there being another on board his superior, seeing some wavering of the privateersmen, flew to the captain's recent post, and while the balls and shot whistled around him and through his hat even, issued commands in his commanding young voice. It was reported that he not only commanded with unwonted nerve and intelligence, but fought back some of the pirates, who tried to board the ship, like a lion. At last victory was to the privateersman; the pirate vessel was riddled and slowly sinking, and Lieutenant John Lindsay was getting the surviving prisoners on to his ship; he was standing, calm and brave, watching his men do their duty, and the dark, dirty pirates in chains coming across the gang-way, when whiz! a shot felled him down like a nine-pin to the deck, and his young life slowly but surely ebbed away ere nightfall. The shot had been fired by one of the pirates. He was but nineteen years of age at his death. The vessel's company, in recognition of his bravery, had a handsome, large gold locket made, and a painting in ivory executed on it, showing the two ships in battle; below, a tombstone with a lady and two small children as mourners, which signified his widowed mother and youngest brother and sister.

This souvenir, along with his hat riddled with shot, they presented with an eulogistic letter to Mrs. Ann Calvert Lindsay of Laurel Hill, in honor and memory of her noble son. The locket was a gift from her to my father in his youth; the Grimes family held it as a loan from my father for several years, and then it was most kindly rendered back to my brother and myself a few years since by our cousin, Mrs. Helen White *nee* Grimes of Little Rock, Arkansas.

IX. Passing over the other daughters of the family until a new chapter, I conclude this portion with Thomas Lindsay, born 1789, the ninth child, and fifth and youngest son of William and Ann Calvert Lindsay of Laurel Hill. He was of manly proportions, tall and muscular, and fine-looking, like his brothers; the only son with brown eyes like his mother, to whom he was devoted at all times; he was her "baby boy," and therefore the longest in the home circle. He married young, a very sweet and pretty young girl, a Roman Catholic, named Matilda Wells, who belonged to an honored old family of the eastern shore.

His love for and devotion to her was almost worship, so that on her death, a year or so following their union, he became inconsolable; before this he had preferred the quiet life of a planter and business man; he was engaged in business for a short time in Occoquan, Prince William county, a few miles from Laurel Hill; now he longed to leave home and enter upon more stirring scenes, and the times were ripe for them. He entered the services of the army, but finally became a junior officer of a privateersman called "The Wildcat." This vessel did considerable service to protect our coasts from pirates and the British, and was then wrecked, or sunk at sea by the enemy, a few years later, with all hands on board; a portion of the wreck bearing her name was picked up at sea. Thus Thomas Lindsay passed out of existence in the twenty-sixth or seventh year of his age, and without issue.

Of all these five promising sons of a noble and devoted mother, it is sad to see they were nearly all swept away from the arena of life at such an early age, and by deaths so distressing; only one of the five died in his bed, and out of the five but two left issue to become progenitors of future Lindsays.

Chapter XIII.

Sarah, Maria and Catherine Lindsay, the younger daughters of William and Ann Calvert Lindsay of Laurel Hill — who their husbands were — their children and grandchildren — a few remarks about women — what countries favor their educational advancement the most.

Mention has been made of Susanna and Ann or Nancy Lindsay, the elder daughters of the family, and now I have the remaining daughters to bring before your notice. Like their brothers, they lived in the most stirring era of our country, they heard and saw more of the soldier and sailor than of the peaceful citizen. Their ears were constantly taking in the incident of battle, defeats or victories; their hearts were often rent by parting with father, lover, husband, or son, and there was that awful hour when the news came, saying "he is dead," that parting was forever! Those were the days that tried men's and women's capacities, intellectually, physically, morally; that developed and gave them patience, courage, strength of purpose, and patriotism! Much had to be sacrificed for a grand purpose!

They were only shortly removed from the pioneer settlers of the country who had hewn the way and earned their land for *them* if the primitive law of man, "that to the stronger shall the spoils go," is to be the test. Had they not, these settlers, battled with the Aborigines; had they not gone through many privations and hardships; yet their Saxon pluck and will seemed ever quenchless, and the women suffered in unison with them. It is to the sacrifices, devotion, endurance, prudence, thrift, and sagacity of women that many a country, not to mention a family, owes its success; and the more enlightened and cultivated its women are, so it continues to rise in power.

Great Britain! Switzerland! and our own glorious United States give the freest encouragement to that end, as statistics show us. Germany, although she has given some intellectual female brains to the world, is yet stubbornly against her advancement. France is struggling for her; as yet it is only at Paris that she can carry through a complete course at the universities if she desires to. In the Netherlands there are no *enactments* to prevent her attending university lectures, or taking degrees, and the public schools are well kept up and attended in the different cities. Belgium is gloomy and feroce, and will not listen to any thing in her educational favor, but the question is agitated from time to time in her council chambers.

Spain, Portugal, Russia, Denmark, Sweden, Norway, Austria and Spanish South America are far behind in their desire to give university advantages to women. Better the hymnal and missal in her hand than books on philosophy, logic, and the sciences generally. But pardon this little flight; to return to the younger daughters of William and Ann Calvert Lindsay:

Sarah Lindsay, born in 1785, the third daughter and seventh child who grew up, and usually called Sally by her relatives, was a lady of endearing qualities; she cannot be too highly estimated for womanly intelligence and virtue, both as daughter, wife, mother and friend. In her youth she was tall, slender, and rounded, with well-cut and expressive features, dark-blue eyes, and pretty brown hair, and a clear, healthful complexion. In middle life she grew into the portly matron. She possessed a wonderfully clear, far-seeing, and active brain, and was a clever plantress; these duties devolving upon her during her widowhood. She was a loving and industrious daughter, and left Laurel Hill sorrowfully, when at an early age she was united to Mr. George Triplett of "*Round Hill,*" in her own county, a brother of William Triplett, who was her sister Susanna's first husband.

Mr. Triplett was the elder member of an old and wealthy Fairfax family, and the beautiful old plantation of Round Hill welcomed its new mistress with its gayest aspect and cordiality; but the fond husband was torn at last from the side of his wife, although he came back from the army from time to time to visit his home. He became a captain and then a major in our army during the second war with England, and rose to considerable distinction, and at length fell, another victim to the cause of liberty. I have been told that he was a gentleman of most estimable character, and agreeable in face and form, with all the Virginia urbanity and warmth of manner.

After bringing up a large family and attending to the many cares of her estate, a dreadful calamity befell the widowed mother—the beautiful old home, where her bridal days had been spent and her children born, was destroyed before her eyes by fire, the inmates barely escaping; many family relics, and nearly all the household furniture was lost. The shock to her nervous system was too great, and her health gave way; she died a year or so later in the fifty-fifth year of her age. The following are the names of her sons and daughters, and their children:

I. George William Triplett, a remarkably fine specimen of manhood, tall, well-developed, and energetic and quick of movement, of noble character, and who, 'tis said, bore the greatest likeness to his mother. He married Miss Jane R. Dale, a descendant of the old Dale family of Ireland, and niece to the celebrated orator and statesman John C. Calhoun. The issue of their union were Richard C., Sarah J., Ella M., George W., and William Powell; all survive except Ella M., who died a few years since, of consumption. The sons and the daughter reside at the old paternal homestead in Fairfax, "Round Hill."

II. Charles Hector; who emigrated years since and settled in Pine Bluff, Arkansas. He has been spoken of as a noble-looking, white-haired old gentleman; his wife was a Miss Hester A. Dunlap, and died some years since. Mr. C. H. Triplett rose to prominence as a farmer of Jefferson county; he died October, 1887, aged seventy-eight.

His three children are Sarah Lindsay, now Mrs. John L. Buck of Pine Bluff; Marion, who married a cousin, William Lindsay, and Charles H., married to Estelle Holland, and resident of Pine Bluff.

III. John Thomas; no record furnished me of him.

IV. William Walter, who married Mary De Bell of Fauquier county, and left two sons, William and Charles F., who are farmers of Fairfax county.

V. Francis Frederick (still living); Mr. Francis F. Triplett is a fine-looking gentleman, of middle age, and bears his years well, considering he has had struggles since the war with adversity and the manifold cares of a large family, and losing his partner in life during his children's young life. He is a farmer at his home called "Flagg Hill," in Fairfax county. He married Mary A. Wheat, by whom he has the following children: [1]George, [2]Walter Jones (who married Mary Cross), [3]Francis Asbury, [4]Effie Wheat (who married John L. Monroe), [5]Mary Florence, [6]Katherine Lindsay, [7]Frederick Osion, [8]Harriet Edith, [9]Irving Everett, [10]William Wallace.

VI. Catherine, a very handsome woman, noted for her gay spirits and daring horsemanship in youth. She married, first, Edward Stonnel of Fairfax, and had by him one son, Triplett Stonnell, who died young. Her second husband was her cousin, Edward Washington Lindsay of Arkansas. (See record of William Henry Lindsay.) She died in her early prime, of consumption, while visiting her relatives in Virginia.

VII. Marion, who died in her girlhood.

Maria Lindsay, the fourth daughter of William and Ann Calvert Lindsay of Laurel Hill, born 1787, like her sister, was gifted with fine features and well-proportioned figure; her face was strong and finely chiseled, her eyes very dark-brown, her skin a clear, fresh brunette, and her hair a dark chestnut; she was tall, and in later years, full and plump, as befitting her age. Her talents were shown in her spinning and dyeing, her deftness in home surgery, for it was no uncommon thing for her to set a broken limb when no surgeon was near; and also to attend to all the sickness and ailments of her slaves and cattle. She kept a hospitable house, and her table was rich with luxuries concocted by her hands, or under her superintendence. She was an earnest member of the Methodist Episcopal Church. She married, young, her full cousin, William Lindsay, younger son by the first marriage of her uncle, Opie Lindsay of "The Mount," Fairfax, and a few years after her marriage, settled on her portion of the paternal estate, where their home was erected, and which they called "Marble Hill." This home, like her sister's, Mrs. Sarah Triplett, some years later, met with destruction by fire, and the different children being scattered by marriage, and her husband dead, she was induced to go to Georgia, by her son there, and went in 1847, accompanied by a younger son and two daughters. Here she died, two years later, in her fiftieth year, her heart having fretted under the change of home and circumstances. Her children were: I. Ann Maria, born 1810, at Laurel Hill, who married, late in life, a widower of Fairfax, named Dawson, by whom she had one child, a son, John Dawson, who is married to Myrtle Cockerell, a cousin of Senator F. Cockerell of Missouri, and by whom he has five children, Lindsay

Dawson, Anne M. Dawson, William Dawson, Maggie Lee Dawson, and Charles W. Dawson. They reside at Marble Hill, in Fairfax, which is farmed by young Mr. Dawson. Mrs. Ann M. Dawson is a lady past seventy, and still bright of speech and memory, and to whom I am much indebted for a great deal of family history. She is the oldest living member of her mother's family, and a resident on the once flourishing Lindsay estate in her neighborhood. She owns about three hundred acres, all left now of the Laurel Hill property.

II. Margaret and Catherine (twins), born in 1812, also at Laurel Hill. They were fine-looking brunettes in youth, and attracted the beaux of the neighborhood to a large extent. It is related of them that, owing to their strong resemblance to each other, some funny incidents occurred. One is, that Catherine, who was shy and bashful, had an admirer whom she would not admit as such, and that Margaret, full of girlish mischief, made out she was Catherine one evening to see if any thing the swain might say would commit him. It was in the dusk, the ruse was effectual, the youth grew tender, etc., and the next day she had her sister stand confessed.

Margaret married a merchant of Alexandria, named Leolin S. Nicholson, who died there in 1838, aged twenty-seven. The issue of the marriage were two daughters and a son; Mary Frances, Margaret Ann, and William. The first married a German gentleman named Nunar, and died in July, 1867, childless. The second became Mrs. John W. Ellis; her husband was born and reared in Richmond, Virginia; she, and her husband, and mother removed from Alexandria, Virginia, to Macon, Georgia, where Mr. Ellis entered into business; nine children blessed their union, three of whom are grown and married, and have families. The eldest, W. W. Ellis, married Miss Mary P. Collier; issue, one child. The eldest daughter, Frances V., married Mr. T. E. Clements of Albany, Georgia; issue, four children. Ella S. married Mr. W. H. Freeman of Florida, where they reside; issue, three children.

The remaining six are Emma L., George Frederick, Joseph O., Harriet J., John C., and Mary N. William Nicholson died young. Catherine Lindsay died unmarried.

III. Sarah Louisa, born at Laurel Hill, 1815, died a widow, at Haigler, Nebraska, July 21, 1887, aged seventy-two. She married in Alexandria, Virginia, an Englishman, from Nottingham, England, named Atkinson. They emigrated after a while to Wisconsin, where he became a farmer and miller; issue, Alexander, Louisa (Mrs. Fay of Iowa), John, Lindsay, and Laura (Mrs. Black, who died in 1888). Alexander Atkinson is a merchant in Omaha, Nebraska. Lindsay Atkinson is a land agent and land settler in Haigler, Nebraska, and a young man of much enterprise and perseverance, and one of the pioneers of Haigler, a quickly-growing town of the West.

IV. Hierome Melancthon, or "Hiram" as his relatives called him, was born in 1817, at "Barnaby," his uncle William Henry Lindsay's residence, in Prince William county, Virginia. His middle name was bestowed upon him by my father when a young man, while on a visit to his aunt, Mrs. Maria Lindsay, and was in honor of his first wife's father, Colonel Melancthon Smith, U. S. A. Hiram M. Lindsay started into the world at an early date to seek his fortunes, and after several experiences, he landed in Macon, Georgia, where he soon rose into prominence as a business man, and amassed considerable money.. He entered the Confederate army and became a colonel ere the close of the Rebellion. The war was disastrous to him as to others, and he was nearly ruined; he had to start life afresh, but declining years and ill-health were against him, and I am told that he has not been able to retrieve his losses. He is now a resident of Birmingham, Alabama. Mr. Lindsay in early manhood was a fine specimen of youth, good looks and stately bearing; he married in Georgia, in 1846–7, Miss Mary A. Flint, by whom he had a large family. The eldest, Alice Victoria V., married twice; her first husband was a Mr. Hull, a New Yorker; her second is Mr. Lorenzo Baker, a native of Pennsylvania, by whom she has one child, Edith Douglas; Mr. and Mrs. Baker reside in New York, at 306 West Thirty-first street.

The second daughter was Talulla H.; the third, Florence Ethel, who married a Mr. Benner, and by whom she has a son, Henry T.; her husband died a few years ago; she is sadly afflicted by insanity at intervals, and is an inmate of the State Insane Asylum of Georgia.

The fourth child, William M., is an enterprising and rising young merchant in Birmingham, Alabama. He married, when very young, a Miss Hetty Phillipps of Georgia, by whom he has three children, Mabel, Maud and Clarence. Fifth, Mary Ann (dead). Sixth, Thomas F. (dead). Seventh, Mattie V. (dead). Eighth, Anna Eloise, now Mrs. Henry Myer of Kingston, New York. Ninth, Minnie Lee (dead). Tenth, Robert Lee A., residing in Birmingham, with his father. Eleventh, Samuel Stonewall, a resident of Birmingham.

V. William, born in Colchester, Virginia, died in childhood.

VI. Mary Elizabeth, born at "Mount Pleasant," in Fairfax, Virginia, in 1822, the farm then owned by her father; she married a gentleman in Georgia, by the name of Davenport; he died September 30, 1879. Her children are all grown, and are, Charles Edward, Catherine Louisa, Calvert Lawson, Margaret Lindsay, Emily Maria, and Josephine. The elder daughter is married to Joseph Bruker of Savannah, Georgia. Calvert L. is married to a Miss Mamie Calahan of Georgia. Mrs. Mary Elizabeth Davenport is a resident of Augusta, Georgia; address, 436 Taylor street.

VII. Charles William, born at Laurel Hill in 1827; he removed in 1847 to Georgia, with his widowed mother and two sisters, Margaret and Mary. He latterly became a planter of Hardy, Mississippi. He married a widow, by whom he had one child, a daughter, called Fanny Maria, who is married to a well-to-do planter of Coffeeville, Mississippi, named R. T. Wimberly. Mr. Lindsay is now a widower, and not in any special business; he still lives in Mississippi.

Catherine, or Kitty, as she was called, the last and youngest daughter and child of William and Ann Calvert Lindsay of Laurel Hill, was born in Virginia in 1791; she possessed an unusually sweet and amiable disposition and character, and also personal attractions; was a brown-haired blonde, with dark-brown eyes, and a sweet, yet dignified expression of countenance; her figure was rounded and graceful, and of medium height. A relative has told me who knew her, that she made one of the most beautiful *old* ladies it had ever been his good fortune to see. She evidently inherited this gift "of growing old gracefully and beautifully," from her lovely mother, Mrs. Lindsay of Laurel Hill. She was married at sixteen years of age, to a wealthy and handsome young West Indian, called Reynald Grimes, and the subject of their courtship being somewhat romantic, it bears relating, I think.

Young Grimes was born and raised on the magnificent plantation of his father, on the island of Barbadoes, and ere he was a few years old, was affianced to the only daughter and heiress of his father's neighbor and bosom friend, planter Woodrough; the friends having, as young bachelors, cherished the idea, if they ever married, of having a family alliance of this kind. The young people grew up with the understanding that they were to marry. Ere this, young Grimes, desirous of traveling a little, was allowed by his father to take a sea voyage to the United States. "He came, he saw, he conquered," the heart of fair Kitty Lindsay of Laurel Hill, but although he loved the young girl, he dare not, in honor, address her, knowing of that other fair girl he had left behind him in his island home; he now found that he did not love *her* as he loved the pretty Kitty. He returned home at length, and lay bare his feelings to Miss Woodrough, who, like a true and noble woman, released him from his engagement; his father died a short while afterward, and his mother also being dead, the young man hastily sold his large estate and emigrated to, and bought a new one in Virginia, where he soon brought his bride, Kitty. The only request Miss Woodrough had made when she released him from the engagement was, that he was to correspond occasionally with her, and to name his first daughter after her, which he promised.

The union proved a most happy one, and a large family was born to them. Adversity traveled to them, however, and after several blissful years, nearly all their great wealth was swept from them. Mr. Grimes was not as successful in his Virginia plantation as his father had been in the West Indies; he did not seem to understand the Virginia methods, it was said; his losses affected his spirits and health, and in 1831, he died suddenly of a stroke of apoplexy, at his supper table, in the very prime of his manhood. The last word on his lips was the name of his wife. The family had done what Miss Woodrough had asked, but the correspondence was neglected by degrees, and finally ceased entirely; years afterward Miss Woodrough died an old spinster, leaving an immense fortune; the Grimes were not remembered; it is probable she felt their silence as lack of interest. The following are the children of Catherine or Kitty Lindsay Grimes, and Reynald Grimes:

I. Mary Isabella Woodrough, who married, at seventeen, Captain Robinson, of the noted old Robinson family of Virginia, by whom she had two daughters, now married; she died in 1875, suddenly, without warning, of heart disease.

II. John, who also fell dead suddenly, in the streets of Washington, of the same disease, leaving five children.

III. Ann, who became Mrs. John Carlisle of Lauderdale, Virginia; she also died suddenly of apoplexy, leaving a husband and seven children.

IV. Susan, who married O. B. Gibson of Washington, D. C., and died shortly after his death, of quick consumption, 1873.

V. Helen, who married, in 1864, Dr. A. P. White, a native of North Carolina, but for some years, and until his death, a well-to-do resident of Arkansas. He died of heart disease in 1877, leaving his widow a fine plantation and a town-house in Little Rock. She had no children of her own, but has adopted a relative's daughter, whom she takes as much interest in as if her own.

VI. William, unmarried, resides with his sister, Mrs. White of Little Rock.

VII. Charles, died October, 1883.

VIII. Reynald, died in 1841, aged twenty-six years.

IX. Sarah, single, resides with her sister, Mrs. White of Little Rock.

The death of Mrs. Catherine (Kitty) Lindsay Grimes took place in Washington, D. C., in 1867, in her seventy-sixth year; her remains were interred in the Grimes lot, at the Congressional Cemetery.

CHAPTER XIV.

Thomas Lindsay of "Mount Pleasant," in Fairfax, the youngest son of Robert Lindsay of "The Mount" — his gentle and affectionate wife Martha Scott-Fox — their nine children — who they married, and their children.

Thomas Lindsay of Mount Pleasant, born as recorded, November 13, 1750, the youngest son of Robert and Susanna Lindsay of "The Mount," was also a gentleman of the old school, courteous and dignified in manner, of fine and pleasing features, tall of stature, not stout, of quick yet stately step, punctilious in religious affairs, a vestryman of his church, and one of the highest respected citizens of Fairfax county. He inherited his homestead from his father, upon which he lived comfortably the life of the southern planter. The plantation was a few miles from historic old Falls Church, and adjoining "The Mount," and tradition says, one of the prettiest in the neighborhood. It is now owned by a Mr. William Shreeve. He married a young widow of Pennsylvania, Mrs. Martha Fox, *nee* Scott, whom all her children revered and loved devotedly, her character was so gentle and winning. She was a firm, yet affectionate mother, an excellent house-wife, and gracious hostess, and truly religious. Her acts of charity were many; a tale of distress ever found her a sympathetic listener and helper. Tradition does not treat of her personal appearance, but her descendants need not repine; because she was not a noted beauty, her deeds will live longer after her; beauty too often dies when buried in the tomb. Thomas Lindsay passed from earth at a ripe old age, September 14, 1830, his disease being paralysis, which he had for several years; his devoted partner followed him the following year, and curious to relate, in the same month, September 21, 1831. Mrs. Lindsay was born November 6, 1757, and also passed away at a very old age. They may be called a veritable "Darby and Joan." Nine children were born of the union of this excellent couple.

I. Robert, born May 26, 1779; killed by lightning, along with some companions, while boating on the Potomac, 17th of July, 1805.

II. Samuel, born November 20, 1781. He married a Miss McDougal of Virginia, by whom he left two accomplished and charming daughters, Martha A. and Mary Eliza; the former married a physician of Alexandria, named W. P. Gunnell, and, some years later, removed with him and her family to Austin, Texas, where he left her a widow. Her children are grown, and are, Jenny Lindsay Gunnell, who is married to Mr. ———, Ada Byron Gunnell, married to Mr. ———, Marion Campbell Gunnell, Mouter Gunnell, the only son, a young physician, and Laura Richards Gunnell. All, I believe, are now residents of Waco, Texas. The latter daughter, Miss Mary Eliza Lindsay, spends her winters between Baltimore and Washington, and her summers in Virginia, where she frequently delights her numerous cousins and friends by her lively and pleasing manners, and agreeable, witty conversation. She truly bears out the saying, "One of the Lindsays light and gay." Samuel Lindsay, their father, was one of the wealthiest merchants of *old* Alexandria, but the Civil war scattered the greater part of the estate left by him to his widow and daughters.

III. David, born May 25, 1784, married a Miss Lucy Parker of Clark county, Virginia, a relative of the noted Judge Parker of Winchester, Virginia. He emigrated many years ago, in example of some of his relatives, to Kentucky, and became, in time, a well-to-do farmer of Mason county, and died at a good old age, leaving a young family, two sons and one daughter. The elder son, Richard Alexander, is a wealthy farmer of the same county, and possesses, I am told, one of the largest and best cultivated farms in this locality. He has been described to me as a most genial and pleasant gentleman of sixty-five; he has four sons and two daughters. His eldest son, Josiah, by his first wife, who was a Miss Jane E. Parker, and his cousin, is married (wife was Mary Ellen Botts), and has four children; by his second wife, Malinda Alice Ball (now deceased), he has William Parker, David, Richard Madison, Lucy Dudley, and Eliza Lee, the youngest being now seven years old. Maysville is the name of the town he resides in, but North Fork is his post-office. The second son, William T., died in Kentucky, in 1879, leaving two sons and a daughter. The elder son, H. P. Lindsay, is proprietor of the Commercial Hotel, Xenia, Ohio. Richard Lindsay, the second son, is married, and resides on his farm in Maysville. Lucy, the daughter, married a farmer of the same place. Lizzie, daughter of David, became, first, the wife of a clergyman of New York, named Craig, by whom she had two sons, Lindsay and Fairfax Craig; secondly, the wife of a wealthy gentleman from Paduka, Kentucky, at which place she died many years ago.

IV. Nancy, born August 5, 1776, married a gentleman named Braddock Richmond, a member of Congress from Rhode Island, and died in Washington, D. C., 10th of December, 1810, leaving a son, Thomas Lindsay Richmond, who studied for the pulpit but died ere his ordination.

V. Susanna, born 23d of February, 1789; died ——; married a gentleman named Moore, of Fairfax county, a descendant of the famous Sir —— Moore of Colonial history, by whom she had three sons and a daughter. The younger son was Francis Moore, who was a young gentleman much endeared to his relatives for his lovely and genial disposition and natural brightness of mind. Death deprived them of him in 1852, in his young manhood. Robert Moore was the elder son, of whom I have no record. Thomas Moore was the second. The daughter I have also no record of.

Mr. Thomas Moore is now the best established lawyer of Fairfax Court-House, where he has made his home for many years, the firm name being "Thomas Moore & Son." He married quite an intelligent and highly-refined lady, Miss Morris of New York, a great grand-daughter of Lewis Morris, one of the signers of the Declaration of Independence, and a full cousin of Mrs. ex-Secretary Hamilton Fish, who bore such a conspicuous part in social life during President Grant's term of office. The issue of their marriage are: I. Robert Walton Moore, now his father's partner, and at present a member of the Virginia Legislature. He is a most intelligent and agreeable young gentleman, and his honors sit gracefully upon him. Mr. Moore is a graduate of the University of Virginia. II. Susanna Lindsay, who married, a year or two since, a Mr. Donohue of Fairfax county, and died recently, leaving him two children. III. Jane Morris. IV. Bessie Rutherford (dead). V. Helen Stuyvesant. VI. Edith May. VII. Lucy Kean (dead). VIII. Margaret Lindsay.

VI. Elizabeth, born 15th of March, 1792, married on the morning of the 5th of August, 1824, in the thirty-third year of her age, at her father's home, Mount Pleasant, by a Baptist minister named Johnston, to Henry Fairfax, Esq., of Prospect Hill, near Dumfries, Prince William county, and Freestone of the same county; a gentleman of wealth and good family, a descendant, like old Lord Fairfax of Virginia, of Henry Fairfax, fourth Baron Fairfax of Cameron, who died in 1688, who was the oldest son of the Hon. Rev. Henry Fairfax of Bolton-Percy in Yorkshire, England.*

---

*See the Fairfax chart.

The issue of this marriage between Elizabeth Lindsay and Henry Fairfax were two children: I. John Walter Fairfax, born at Prospect Hill, Prince William county, 30th of June, 1828. He inherited a fine estate from his parents, was a gallant officer of the Confederate service, rising to the rank of colonel. I have heard that his elegant homes "Freestone" in Prince William county, and formerly "Belle Grove" in Loudon county, used to afford the finest entertainment in the hunting season, to President Grant and his friends. He married Mary Jane Rodgers, daughter of Colonel Hamilton Rodgers of Loudon county, Virginia, on the 27th of September, 1848. The following is a record of their family:

I. Henry, a civil engineer by profession, and a gentleman of considerable means; residence "Oakhill (formerly the seat of President James Monroe)," Loudon county, Virginia. II. Hamilton R., residence New York city; he was married June 1, 1887, to Eleanor Cecilia, daughter of Mrs. William P. Van Rensselaer of Manursing Island, New York, a young lady of fine old Knickerbocker stock, and an heiress; issue, a daughter born 1888. III. John W., residence New York city. IV. Elizabeth Lindsay, wife of Lieutenant Charles Ayres of the U. S. Army, son of the late General R. Ayres of the army; she has two children. V. Lindsay, residence in New York city.

These last three sons are united in business in New York under the firm name "Fairfax Brothers," and are most intelligent, prospering, and fine-looking young gentlemen.

II. Martha Lindsay, daughter of Henry and Elizabeth Lindsay Fairfax, like her brother John Walter, inherited a fortune from her parents; she figured as quite an heiress and belle in the palmy society days of Alexandria, and was surrounded by many of the brightest beaux of Virginia, of her time. Her hand and heart were won at last by a handsome and clever young lawyer, Thomas Bolling Robertson, Esq., a descendant of good old Scotch stock, and, moreover, of the famous Indian Princess, Pocahontas. After a happy union of many years, Mr. Robertson was called from earth, in the seventieth year of his age, March , 1887, at his residence, "Galemont," Broad Run, Fauquier county, Virginia, where his widow, daughter, and two of his sons chiefly reside. Mrs. Robertson, or "Cousin Mat," as her relatives are fond of calling her, has one of the warmest and kindest hearts which ever beat beneath human breast. In conclusion, I can pay her no truer or higher compliment, when I say that she has inherited all the pious and womanly virtues of her grandmother, Mrs. Martha Lindsay, whose namesake she is. One of her largest virtues, according to the great Napoleon, is her raising seven handsome and well-educated sons, the youngest of whom, it pleased the Supreme Being to deprive her heart and hearth of, a few months previous to her husband; a fine-looking and exceedingly smart young lad, named Murray. The following is a record of her family:

I. Mary Barnard. II. Thomas Lindsay, who married, in the fall of 1887, Miss C. Boyer of Virginia, and is a physician in Fincastle, Botetourt county, Virginia; issue, a son born 1888. III. Bolling, residence at Galemont, Fauquier county, Virginia. IV. Walter, who married Miss Carrie Wyville of Washington, D. C., about three years ago, and is in business in Chicago. V. Mercer, residence Dallas, Texas. VI. Henry Fairfax, who is in business in Broad Run, Fauquier county, Virginia. VII. Powhatan, who married Miss M. L. Chapman of La Plata, Maryland, 8th of February, 1888, and is in business in Baltimore.

VII. Josiah, born 17th of November, 1794. Died 22d of February, 1813, aged nineteen; single.

VIII. Margaret, born 26th of November, 1797. Died ——. She married a gentleman in Fairfax county, named Swink, by whom she left two or three daughters; one is Mrs. Hunter of Fairfax county, Virginia; another is Mrs. Henry Alvord, wife of the distinguished and able principal of the Maryland Agricultural College near Washington, D. C., a Northern gentleman, and a descendant of the fine old Alvord and Welles family of Massachusetts, and the eldest is Mrs. Landstreet, wife of the Rev. Mr. Landstreet of Virginia, a retired Methodist minister. It is said that Mrs. Margaret Swink was a gentle and affectionate lady, and much esteemed by all who knew her.

IX. Thomas Walter, born 22d of July, 1800. Died 18th of August, 1802.

CHAPTER XV.

Mary Ann Lindsay, only daughter of Robert and Susanna Lindsay of "The Mount"; her excellent qualities as daughter, wife, and mother ; her marriage to Mr. Boggess ; subsequent family—her descendants—her death in Alexandria in 1822—burial at her brother Opie's home, "The Mount," etc., etc.

I have now to mention the remaining child of our earliest Fairfax forefather, Robert Lindsay of "The Mount," who seems to have been his only daughter, and the youngest but one, of his children, coming to the household before her brother, Thomas Lindsay, having been born, according to her family Bible, the 9th of October, 1747. She was an affectionate and dutiful daughter, dignified, and gentle in manner, of tall and well-rounded, yet slender figure in youth, but toward middle life, portly and large. She had regular and handsome features, and in the words of an aged descendant, who has some recollection of her, was an unusually good and noble woman in every way. She was a fine housewife, a strict church woman, and was admired and loved by a large circle of her relatives and friends. Her marriage took place from "The Mount," her father's home, at an early age, to a planter in her native county, Mr. Henry Boggess, a respected citizen of the vicinity, who was born, according to her Bible, May 7, 1736. His ancestors, I am told, were either from Spain, Portugal, or Italy, and the original spelling of his name, Boggio, or perhaps (as I think), Boggessa. There are families in Italy of these names. The strong Italian or Spanish types of faces among many of his family and clan, point to their probable origin. She and her husband made their home near her father's, a home which he bequeathed to her at his death ; here her children were all born and raised; she brought them up religiously, and after the best pattern of her time, giving them what educational advantages she could, and teaching them all those maternal lessons that she benefited by from her mother. The result was, honest, handsome and healthy-looking, well-regulated men and women.

She died at an old age, at the house of a relative in Alexandria, in April 27–28, 1822, and was interred, with all due solemnity and honor, in the family burying ground, at "The Mount," where her brother, Opie Lindsay, then resided. As daughter, wife, and mother, she had acted well her part, and her descendants can look back to her character with pride and affection. Ten children were born to herself and husband.

I. Robert Boggess, born November 8, 1765; he married Miss Nancy Dickey of Virginia, by whom he had eleven children, names not known.

II. Vincent Boggess, born April 28, 1768, married Miss Margaret Scott; six children.

III. Lindsay Boggess, born September 20, 1770, married Miss Milly Janes, August 12, 1792. Died February 7, 1848, aged eighty-eight. He had nine children, the first four of whom were born in Fairfax county. In 1801 he moved from Fairfax with his family and settled west of the mountains in Monongalia county, now West Virginia, about six or seven miles from the Pennsylvania line; here he remained until 1810, when he moved eighteen miles up the river, in the upper edge of the county, and selecting a two hundred acre tract of land from woodlands, in course of time made himself a beautiful farm, whereon he ended his days, his aged partner having passed away from earth ten months before him.

He seems to have been a man of unusual push, enterprise and industry. Henry Boggess, their eldest son, born in

Fairfax county, November 24, 1793, married twice, and had thirteen children. First wife was Nancy Dragoo of West Virginia; his second, Catherine Pitzer of Maryland. He is still living, and a remarkable specimen, I am told, of longevity and preserved mental brightness; although growing less active of body, he still stands wonderfully erect, and his face keeps firm and handsome, and his eye bright. He and his aged wife reside with his youngest daughter, Mary Catherine, Mrs. M. N. Clayton of Rievesville, Marion county, West Virginia. He is now in his ninety-fifth year. These are his children: I. John Lindsay Boggess (deceased). II. Elvira Ann Boggess (see further notice), deceased. III. Hezekiah Hanson Boggess (deceased). IV. Henry Milton Boggess (deceased). V. Felix Riley Boggess, minister, Knoxville, Knox county, Illinois; two sons, also ministers. VI. Harriet Janes Boggess, Mrs. Cunningham, lives with her married daughter in Ohio. VII. Thomas Price Boggess (deceased). VIII. Elizabeth Jane Boggess (deceased). IX. Milly Maria Boggess (deceased). X. Anthony Colman Boggess, minister, Irvine, Tama county, Iowa. XI. Martha Nancy Boggess (deceased). XII. Fletcher Henry Boggess, Belinda, Lucas county, Iowa. XIII. Mary Catherine Boggess, wife of Marshall N. Clayton, by whom she has four sons and one daughter, resident of Rievesville, West Virginia. Pare M. Boggess of Buckhannon, West Virginia, is a grandson of Mr. Henry Boggess.

The elder daughter of Mr. Henry Boggess, Elvira Ann, married in 1834, John Fletcher McDougal, a scion of the fine old Scotch clan McDougal, which, as the reader already may have noticed, the Lindsays seemed to have a decided partiality for, marrying, as they have, many of the name. A curious and thoroughly Scotch incident has been related to me by a descendant of Mr. and Mrs. John F. McDougal, in reference to the earliest ancestor of their family in Virginia;

an incident of the inherent pride and independence of the Scotch.

Some years before the Revolution, as the story goes, William McDougal, a Scotch Presbyterian clergyman, came over to Virginia, direct from the Highlands of Scotland, and soon afterward married a Miss Brand of the colony, by whom he had two children, a son John, and a daughter; his wife dying soon after these additions to the family, he returned to Scotland, leaving his infant son and daughter to strangers. He returned to America about 1790, married again, and settled at Danville, Kentucky, where he died at a ripe old age, still a preacher. A few years after his return, he hunted up his children in Virginia, and offered his son large tracts of land, negroes, etc., if the latter would go and live near him, whose reply was "no, when sister and I were mere babes, you left us to the care of strangers; both are now married and doing well; I have paddled my own canoe thus far, and am able to do so in the future; I would not go for all you are worth!" Thus they parted; pride kept them apart, and ended all communication between them. Elvira Ann Boggess married the son of that son who gave the above answer to his father. Nine children were born of her marriage, and all were born and raised in Marion county, West Virginia. Ere the terrible Civil war came to blast happy, peaceful homes and hearts in the beautiful sunny spots of the South, and set father against son, and brother against brother, her gentle and loving mother and wifely heart ceased to beat for human joy or care, longer on earth. In 1855, God took her unto himself. The war did to her family, what it did to hundreds of others, scattered them over the States. Before 1866, none were left in the old home; the father, about that period, emigrated to Bancroft, Daviss county, Missouri, where he is now a resident, in his seventy-fifth year. The following is a record of her children:

I. Martha McDougal married first, Mr. Dudley, by whom she had a son, Boyd Dudley, who was reared and educated to great advantage and purpose, by his gifted and clever uncle, Judge H. C. McDougal of Kansas City, Missouri, and is now in the real estate and farm loaning business in Gallatin, Missouri, doing a lucrative business. He is married to a charming and helpful little lady. Secondly, she married Dr. R. L. Green of Bancroft, Missouri, whom she now lives with.

II. Margaret, wife of David F. Megill, Ray, Sumner county, Kansas.

III. John Roger McDougal, died at Monmouth, Illinois, September, 1866.

IV. Delia McDougal, wife of Wesley Keplor, McPherson, McPherson county, Kausas.

V. Henry Clay McDougal (see below).

VI. Festus Hanson McDougal, Princeton, Missouri.

VII. Harriet Elizabeth McDougal, wife of John D. Sloan, Ray, Sumner county, Kansas.

VIII. Luther E. McDougal, McPherson, Kansas.

IX. Clara Elvira McDougal, wife of Dan W. Keath, McPherson, Kansas.

Her fifth child, Henry Clay McDougal, deserves more than a passing notice in my record. He is one of the noted and gifted men of our bustling, active money-making West. His career has been full of stirring adventure, trials, and success; a son of war from boyhood, having enlisted from his native town in Marion county, West Virginia, in the army of the blue, when but sixteen years of age, wherein he served with such merit and valor, that at the close of this memorable Rebellion, he was acting quartermaster, with the rank of major, at the head-quarters of his regiment. He thence began the life of a civilian, and had many a tug with fortune, studying for the bar, and earning his daily bread at one and the same time, and often, at the close of a week, wondering if he would have enough to pay his board with. By degrees he rose above all this; the people of his town elected him to an official position, which he filled to their entire satisfaction. He kept constantly studying and diving into books—book-lore being the great oasis in his business life. He also traveled much through the vast West, and made use of all his mental faculties in his wanderings; he came East as well; he believed one cannot know too much of the country they live in. For many years he resided, as a lawyer, in Gallatin, Missouri. He is now a member of one of the leading law firms of Kansas City, Missouri, "Crittenden, McDougal & Stiles," Mr. Crittenden being the late Governor Crittenden of Kentucky.

Judge McDougal is also a director of the National Exchange Bank of Kansas City; capital, $250,000. He is a man of eloquent tongue, as well as a glowing and graceful writer; he is sympathetic and generous; on his well-defined, thoroughly Highland-Scotch face we can discern pluck, energy, and unusual foresight, as well as in his keen eyes, which study you attentively while he listens. In November, 1869, he married, in Gallipolis, Ohio, where she was born and raised, Emma Florence Chapdu, a descendant of a highly distinguished Franco-American family of that name, by whom he has these children: Mabel, Genevieve, Henry Clay, Jr., Edmond, and Emma Florence, the eldest of whom is in her seventeenth year.

The other children of Lindsay Boggess were: II. Matilda Boggess, born 1796. III. Thomas Lindsay Boggess, born 1798; his surviving children are Maria, wife of Judge Alpheus F. Haymond, and Caroline, wife of Thomas Hough; all of Fairmont, West Virginia. IV. Hillory Boggess, born 1800. V. Mary Ann Lindsay Boggess, born 1803. VI. Lindsay Boggess, born 1805. VII. Julia Boggess, born

1807. VIII. John Boggess, born 1809. IX. Milly Boggess, born 1812, wife of Mr. Duke Hoult, Fairmont, Marion county, West Virginia. She has two sons, Captain Alpheus Hoult of Peoria, Illinois, and Neil M. Hoult of Baltimore, address, 329 Snider avenue, Baltimore, Maryland. She, with her aged brother, already recorded, are the only surviving members of her parents' family.

Children of Mary Ann Lindsay, Mrs. Henry Boggess, continued:

IV. Henry Boggess, born May 3, 1774. Died single.

V. Nancy Boggess, born April 28, 1776; married John Reese, by whom she had thirteen children.

VI. Susanna Boggess, born February 3, 1778; married John Fry, by whom she had nine children.

VII. William Boggess, born October 16, 1780; married Abigail Llewellen, by whom he had five children.

VIII. Elizabeth Boggess, born February 8, 1783; married George Atkinson, by whom she had two children.

IX. Sarah A. Boggess, born November 29, 1785; became the wife of Henry Pruner and had three children.

X. Verlinda Boggess, born February 15, 1788; married James Atkinson, brother of her sister Elizabeth's husband, both of whom were Englishmen recently arrived in Alexandria, Virginia. She had eight children. The eldest, James William Atkinson, is married and has five children. Another, Emmett Frances, is the wife of Richard Stonnell, of Alexandria, Virginia, has no family. The youngest, Mary Ann Newton, is the wife of James Grigg of Alexandria, Virginia, and has three refined and agreeable young daughters, and two married sons living away from home. The daughters are the Misses Mary F., Verlinda Adelaide, or Ada, as she is called, and Ann Newton, or Eva Grigg, as she is called, who reside with their parents at 9 Columbus street, Alexandria, Virginia. The sons' names are Samuel A.

Grigg of Denver, Colorado, and James Richard Grigg of Mobile, Tennessee. Mrs. James Grigg is a well-preserved, sweet-mannered and handsome lady of middle age.

ADDENDA.

It is not improbable that the following Henry Lindley or Lindsey, whose inventory of personal estate is here given, was a collateral ancestor of our family in Northumberland county.

He appears to have been cotemporary with Opie Lindsay of Northumberland.

No record has evidently been kept of any of the younger sons or of the daughters which may have been born to these forefathers of ours on the lower Potomac, and judging by the usual prolificacy of the race we may suppose one or another had at the least three or four children. Our line being from elder son to elder son, the collateral branches have not been observed, or, let us say, recorded by our elder relatives.

Inventory of the personal Estate of Henry Lindley (also spelled Lindsey in the index of old Court Record wherein this inventory is recorded) of Northumberland, Virginia April 20 1726.

Pursuant to an order of this County Court wherein appraisers were appointed to appraise the Estate of Henry Lindley (or Lindsey) dec^{d} in obedience to the said order, we the subscribers accordingly met at the house of Isaac Baysie adm^{r} to the said dec^{d}, and being first sworn by Mr George Ball we have appraised the said dec^{d} Estate in money as followeth,

	£.	*S.*	*D.*
To a parcel of old Books....................	2	05	00
To " " " new cotton stockings	0	03	06
To $8\frac{3}{4}$ yards of white Linen at 8^{d} p^{d}..........	0	05	10
" $6\frac{3}{4}$ of narrow fine Lin' a 12^{d}	0	06	09
" 14 yards of Dow lace a 14^{d} p............	0	16	04
" $14\frac{5}{8}$ y^{rs} of White Lin' at 11^{d}..............	0	13	05
" 9 y^{rs} of fine White Lin' at 16^{d}	0	12	00

	£.	S.	D.
To 26¼ yrs checked Lin at 14[d]	1	10	07½
" 1¾ yrs of fine white Lin' at 18[d]	0	02	07½
" 9 yrs of Holland made up in sheats part Lacking at 18[d]	0	13	06
" ⅞ of Curting	0	02	00
" 24 ¼ and ½ of Sprig Lin' at 9[d]	0	18	03¼
" 19 yrs of com' Twil[d] Lin' a 10[d]	0	15	10
" 12 " & ⅞ of Cotton Sattin	1	05	09
" 22½ of Silk Crape a 12[d]	1	02	06
" 9¼ yrs of Bengalls a 2[d]	0	18	04½
" 7 " of Duray a 16[d]	0	09	04
" 7⅛ y[rs] of Strip[t] Holl Tick a 4[d]	0	08	05½
" Two Silk Hankerchiefs at 3/6	0	07	00
" Three coarse Silk Do a 20	0	05	00
" Four fine Silk Do a 2/6	0	10	00
" 8y[rs] Silk fring for Curtains	0	05	00
" 1 Muslin Neck Cloth	0	02	06
" Old Towels and 2 old Napkins	0	01	06
" 2 y[rs] of White Ribbon at 9[d]	0	01	06
" 1 Campaign Periwigg	0	15	00
" Some Thread and Silk	0	00	06
" 1 old fine hatt	0	02	06
" 1 great coat	0	14	00
" 1 old Lock and key	0	00	06
" 1 small old box wth Drawers	0	02	06
" 2 old rasors	0	01	00
" 1 old feather bed old boulster & pillows	2	15	00
" 1 Sett of very old Curtains & Vallens'	0	04	00
" 1 Lathing Hammer	0	00	10
" 1 old watch much out of order	1	10	00

LAZARUS TAYLOR
THO[S] PITMAN
W[M] TAYLOR

ISAAC BAYSIE
April 20, 1726.

This Inventory of the Estate of Henry Lindley or Lindsey dec[d] was presented to the Court by Isaac Baysie adm[r] of said dec[d] and is admitted to court.

A copy teste WM S CRALLÉ C. C.
Northumberland Court House
Virginia, Aug 22 1888.

APPENDIX.

[Further notice of the Lindsays of America, whose records have been furnished me, beginning with those of the Northern States; also a few notices of the Lindsays gleaned from historical and genealogical works.]

MAINE.

Welles.

A family of Lindsays, spelled Lindsey, are settled in this place, and deduce their descent from Matthew Lindsey of Yorke, Maine; the said Matthew left six sons and three daughters; Charles, one of the sons, is the representative of the Lindseys of Welles. They believe their early ancestor came from Scotland.

Bath.

Owin Lindsey (the name also spelled with an e) settled in this town in 1842, and became a farmer; he was born in Rehobeth, Massachusetts, January 23, 1796, and died in Bath, April 24, 1881, aged eighty-five, leaving children by adoption only. Owin's father, Benjamin Lindsey, was supposed to have emigrated from England to Massachusetts; he lived and died in Attleboro', Massachusetts, aged eighty-six. His other sons were, Benjamin and William, and his daughters, Sally, Betsey, Sophia and Mary Ann. Owin had two uncles, one named John Lindsey, and another whose name is not known, who emigrated to Maine and was lost sight of. The second Benjamin, brother of Owin, left two daughters, Mary Ann and Clara. William (also brother of Owin) left two sons, Stephen and Benjamin, and a daughter, Emiline.

Am indebted for the above to Mr. O. S. Lindsey of Bath, whose father was the adopted son of Owin Lindsey.

NEW HAMPSHIRE.

Durham.

Baptized by the Reverend Hugh Adams, James Lindsay, January 26, 1728–9, at Oyster River parish, now Durham.

"New England H. & G. Register."

MASSACHUSETTS.

Salem.

The Lindseys of Salem have a tradition in their family to this effect: About the year 1680, or thereabout, an English war vessel came unto the American coast, whose commander was a Lindsay, a Scotchman, from the east side of the Cheviot hills,* and who had sons on this vessel holding office under him. He had put into Salem for some repairs to his ship, that being the only port of that day where such repairs could be made; and while so delayed in port his elder son became acquainted with and married a Miss Moutton, daughter of the captain of the port, who had permitted the match under the arrangement that the groom, on his return to England, was to resign his position on the vessel and return and settle in Salem; the ship sailed away and ere reaching England had an engagement in the Bay of Biscay, was blown up, and all on board perished. The widow of this young Lindsay became in time the mother of a son, who grew up, married, and had a son, and for two or

* Probably from either a Berwickshire, Roxburghshire or Edinburghshire family of Lindsays.

three succeeding generations only one son likewise came into the family.

The earliest existing record of this family is the marriage of one Habakuk Lindsey to Mary Green, October 6, 1741: he resided in North Danvers, then a part of Salem, and died young, leaving three children, Samuel, Hannah and Habakuk. The first, when a young man, sailed to the island of Jamaica on business, and was said to have died there; there is no record of Hannah; and Habakuk the second became the perpetuator of the family; he was born in North Danvers, April 10, 1753; served during the Revolution as a minute-man in the battles of Lexington and Still Water. His wife was Joanna, daughter of Captain Gidion Gowing of Lynnfield, Massachusetts. In 1790 he moved to New Salem, where he died, January 12, 1835; his wife on March 31, 1831. They left the following two daughters and five sons, the latter of whom became the more recent founders of the name and family in different parts of New England. I believe that the earlier members of the family spelled the name after the old Scotch way, *Lindsay*. It has also been spelled Lyndsay, Lyndesay and Lindesay in olden times in Scotland, as we see by old charters, books, etc.

Mary, born March 26, 1777. Died ——.
Anna, born May 20, 1779. Died ——.
Samuel, born January 4, 1782. Died 1845.
Stacy, born May 12, 1786. Died 1855.
Isaac, born March 4, 1790. Died 185–.
Daniel, born April 11, 1794. Died 1887.
Ebenezer, born August 18, 1799. Died 1877.

Mary married John Oaks of New Salem, and had sons and daughters. Anna married Rufus Stacy of New Salem, and had sons and daughters. Samuel married Nancy Butler of Danvers, Massachusetts; they had six sons and four daughters, viz.:

Eliza, born ——. Died ——.
Horace, born 1811. Died 1838.
Abigail, born ——. Died ——.
Asa G., born 1813. Died 1882.
Daniel, born 1816. Died 1845.
Jane, born ——. Died ——.
Richard B., born 1821. Died 1863.
Silas F., born 1824. Died 1887.
Sumner P., born 1827. Died 1851.
Harriet M., born ——.

Eliza married Benjamin Thompson of New Salem, Massachusetts; they had no children. Horace H. married Eliza Stone of Fitzwilliam, New Hampshire; they had no children. Abigail married Franklin Vaughan of Prescott, Massachusetts; they had six children, four sons and two daughters; the sons were George, Harfield, Howard and Collis; the daughters, Abbie and Emma. Asa G. married Mary Sanborn of Springfield, Massachusetts; they had six children, four sons and two daughters:

Henry, born 1841; resides in ———, Massachusetts.
Samuel S., born 1850 (deceased).
Benjamin W., born 1852; resides in Ware, Massachusetts.
Albert R., born 1862; resides in Orange, Massachusetts.
Ellen.
Emma.

Daniel married Irene Gleason of Hardwick, Massachusetts; they had two sons, Horace D., born 1839, resides in ——, Massachusetts, and Farnam W., born 1846 (deceased).

Jane married Samuel Lemon of Ware, Massachusetts; they had no children.

Richard B. married Abigail Stone of Dana, Massachusetts; they had two daughters, Abbie and Rosella.

Silas F. married Maria Hale of Dana, Massachusetts; they had one son and two daughters; the son, Francis H., born 1848, resides in Dana, Massachusetts; the daughters were Hattie and Emma.

Sumner P. married Mary Atkinson of Prescott, Massachusetts; they had one son, John S., born 1849; he resides in Putnam, Connecticut.

Harriet M. married Calvin W. Richards of Hardwick, Massachusetts; they have one son and one daughter; their son, Emerson J., married Ida Taylor of Orange, Massachusetts; they have a son. The daughter, Edna B., married Charles A. Holland of Ninsdale, New Hampshire, and have a son.

Stacy Lindsey, son of Hab, married Haley Wilder of Sterling, Massachusetts, in 1816; they had seven children, all of whom are living at this date, February 25, 1888.

Augusta H., born January 8, 1817; resides at ——, Massachusetts.

Catherine J., born April 22, 1819; resides Cleveland, Ohio.

Theodore S., born July 9, 1822; resides Cleveland, Ohio.

Francis W., born July 23, 1824; resides Cleveland, Ohio.

Harriet F., born June 23, 1828; resides ——, Massachusetts.

George W., born March 29, 1831; resides Boston, Massachusetts.

Mary E., born September 28, 1835; resides Louisville, Kentucky.

Augusta H. married Josiah Miller; they have one son and one daughter; the son, Frank D., born September 25, 1845, is married; has no children. The daughter, Lillian, born December 8, 1859. Catherine J. married Lemuel G. Mason in 1845, who died in 1882; they had two sons; George L. Mason, born 1848, married Mary E. Lowe of Cincinnati, Ohio, who died in Nashville, Tennessee, in 1887; they had one son, named Fred T. Theodore S. Mason, born 1854, married Lulu Hanley in Chicago, Illinois, in 1881; they have one daughter, Grace E., born 1883, in Topeka, Kansas.

Theodore S. Lindsey married Rebeckah Dane of West Brookfield, Massachusetts, in 1849, who died in Cleveland, Ohio, in 1879; they had one son and one daughter; the son, Theodore D., born March, 1857, in Cleveland, married Nellie Almond of Cleveland, in 1881; they have a daughter Theo, born July 4, 1887. Nellie F., born December, 1860; married Charles W. Johnson of Cleveland, Ohio, in 1880; he died February 1, 1888, leaving a daughter, Anna R., born February 28, 1882. Mr. Theodore S. Lindsey, Sr., is paymaster of the Lake Shore and Michigan Southern Railroad Company in Cleveland, Ohio.

Francis W. Lindsey married Mary S. Brooks in Peru, Indiana, in 1853; they had four children, three sons and one daughter.

Frank B., born 1854; died 1873.

Mary, born 1857.

Fred, born 1864; resides in Chicago.

Charles, born 1870; resides in Cleveland.

Mary married James M. Reyburn of Peru, Indiana; they reside in Peoria, Illinois; they have three sons, Lindsey, born October, 1884; Walter, born 1886; and Charles, born 1887.

Harriet F. married Reverend G. H. Newhan in 1851, who died in Walpole, Massachusetts, in 1853, leaving one daughter, Mary Hattie, who was married to Bernadotte Bancroft in 1876, and died in 1878. Mrs. Newhan married Alexander R. Holmes, M. D., of New Bedford, Massachusetts, in 1858; they have one daughter, Grace L., born 1870.

George W. Lindsey married Mary Lowe in 1861, who died in 1884, leaving one daughter, Anna Louise, born 1875.

Mary E. Lindsey married O. G. Holt of Wittington, Connecticut, in 1863; they have one daughter, Katie Mitchel, born 1870; they reside in Louisville, Kentucky.

Isaac Lindsey, third son of Hab, married Susan Lincoln of Greenwich, Massachusetts; they had three children, two sons and a daughter. Susan, the eldest, married a Mr. Norcross of Phillipston, Massachusetts. Joseph married Abbie Packard of Greenwich, Massachusetts; they had one son. Charles, son of Isaac, married Martha Rich of Phillipston, Massachusetts; had four daughters, Emma, Ella, Alice, and Addie. Emma married George Gleason of Dana, Massachusetts. Ella married Frank Gleason of Dana, Massachusetts. Alice married a Mr. Randall of Petersham, Massachusetts.

Daniel, fourth son of Hab, was a physician in Swansea, New Hampshire, and Petersham and Athol, Massachusetts; he married Chloe Vaughan of New Salem, Massachusetts, in 1818; they lived together sixty-eight years; he died in 1887, at the age of ninety-three; she still survives; they had one son and five daughters.

Mary Ann, born 1819, married to Joseph J. Woodbury, who died in 1885; they had seven children.

J. Daniel, born 1844; resides at Chicopee Falls, Massachusetts.

Mary C., born 1846; resides at Worcester, Massachusetts.

Jerry J., born 1848; resides at Turner's Falls, Massachusetts.

Adele L., born 1850; resides at Worcester, Massachusetts.

Maria F., born 1852; resides at Southampton, Massachusetts.

Ida E., born 1854; resides at Turner's Falls, Massachusetts.

Stillman F., born 1856; resides at Miller's Falls, Massachusetts.

Phœbe E. Lindsey, born 1821; married George W. Green in 1840, who died in 1863; she died in 1874; they had one son, George W., born 1844; resides in Worcester, Massachusetts.

Esther M. Lindsey, born 1824; married Charles J. Shattuck in 1843; they reside at Barre, Massachusetts; they have three children. C. Wesley, born 1843; resides at Prescott, Massachusetts. Eugene, born 1854; resides at Barre, Massachusetts. Etta Olive, born 1857; resides at Turner's Falls, Massachusetts.

Calista A. Lindsey, born 1828; married Dexter Hale in 1848; they reside at Southampton, Massachusetts; they have one son, Charles M., born 1854; he resides at Southampton.

Marshall L. Lindsey, born 1831; married Lulu M. Sly of Webster, Massachusetts, in 1878; is a physician at Athol, Massachusetts; they have a son, Norman Marshall, born March 22, 1884.

L. Louisa Lindsey, born 1833; married Henry H. Olds in 1853; resides at Athol, Massachusetts; they had two children, Francis L., born 1859; resides at Taunton, Massachusetts. Nellie L., born 1866; died 1880.

Ebenezer Lindsey, the youngest son of Hab, married Susan Pickering Foster of Petersham, Massachusetts; he practiced medicine in Petersham, in Union, Connecticut, and in Dudley, Massachusetts, where he died in 1877; his widow died in 1886; they had one son, Silas Foster Lindsey, born 1827; married Salome Maria Chapman of Westford, Connecticut, in 1851; practiced medicine in Dudley, Massachusetts, thirty-four years, and died 1885; they had one son and one daughter. The son, Eben Foster Lindsey, born 1855; married Alice Witherell of Burke, New York, in 1880, who died in 1882, leaving a daughter, Alice W., born 1882. Minnie Jane Lindsey, daughter of Silas F., born 1862; married in 1886 to Edward Merle Frissell, M. D., of Dudley, Massachusetts.

Lynn.

According to the family record the founder of this family was Christopher Lindsay, who emigrated from Scotland about 1630 and settled upon a large tract of land on what is now part, if not all, of the celebrated town of Lynn; his patent for land is, I believe, still on record. Doubtless he was a Scotch gentleman of means and good family. He died April 19, 1669, leaving a widow, Margaret Lindsay, who died in December, 1669; their children were John and Eleazer. Christopher Lindsay had, 'tis said, a brother, Daniel Lindsay, who arrived from Scotland in 1637, and founded another branch of this family, of which all knowledge seems lost.

John, elder son of Christopher, inherited a portion of his father's estate; he left a grandson, Daniel, who had two sons, John and William, and three daughters, Deborah, Sally and Lydia. The elder son, William, died childless. The second, John, had six children, four of whom are living; the Reverend John W. Lindsay, late dean of the Boston University, Boston; James N. and Dr. William F. Lindsay of New York, and Miss Mary H. Lindsay of Lynn, are descendants of this family.

Later Data.

John, elder son of Christopher, married Mary Ally, 1667, by whom he had issue, John, born 1668; Samuel, 1669; Eleazer, 1671; Nathaniel, 1672; Sarah, 1675; Mary, 1677; Margaret, 1680, and Benoni, 1681. His second wife was Amy Richardson, married in 1682.

Eleazer, second son of Christopher, married Sarah Ally, in 1669, and had issue, Eleazer, born 1671; Mary, 1673; John, 1675; Abigail, 1677; Mary, 1680, and Ralph, 1684.

Fall River.

I believe the following family of Lindseys to be descended from William, fourth son of John and Elizabeth Monro Lindsey of Bristol, Rhode Island, 1694, and that owing to the early founder of it leaving home young, to settle in Rehobeth, Rhode Island, his record was lost to his family in Bristol. The genealogy of this family runs thus: John Lindsey of Bristol, Rhode Island, but latterly of Rehobeth, Rhode Island, born August 14, 1752, died January 17, 1829, and was married to Mary Bliss, August 2, 1778, who was born January 29, 1758, and died June 5, 1819, and had the following children:

Mary B., born April 7, 1779. Died August 17, 1851.

John, born April 2, 1781. Died April 28, 1862.

Nancy, born February 21, 1783. Died June 2, 1786.

Cyrus W., born May 28, 1785. Died January 25, 1836.

Zelotes, born September 20, 1787. Died October 14, 1787.

Samuel D., born January 23, 1789. Died February 13, 1876.

Charlotte, born April 9, 1791. Died December 20, 1820.

William H., born June 23, 1793. Died June 20, 1864.

John Lindsey the second married Ruth Sandford, by whom he had the following children:

John B., born ——.

William LeB., born ——.

Pliny, born 1822. Died 1845.

Charlotte, born 1823. Died 1871; married Henry Eldridge; no issue.

Mary, born 1825. Died 1848.

Thomas, born 1827. Died 1868; married Sarah Pocket; no issue.

Almanza, born 1829. Died ——; married, first, Abbie Snell, by whom he had a daughter, Letitia; married, secondly, Clotilda Trask, by whom he had two children, Edward and Fanny.

Charity, born 1833. Died 1885; married Henry Comstock.

Cyrus, born 1836; married Philomelia Hall; no issue.

Louisa, born 1839; married Horace Manchester; child, Horace.

Cyrus W. Lindsey, the second son of the first John, married Sarah Sabin, and had one child:

Sarah, born August 31, 1828. Died August 13, 1852.

Samuel D. Lindsey, the third son of the first John, married Temperance Ide, and had the following children:

Harriet T., born December 27, 1815. Died January 22, 1816.

Harriet, born March 5, 1817. Died October 12, 1841.

William H., born 1821. Died 1838.

Samuel A., born ——. Died April 21, 1858; married Rebecca Stuart.

John F.

Edward P., born ——. Died 1880; married Jenny Simpson.

Joseph F. Lindsey, the younger son of the first John, married three times: 1. Susan M. Ide; 2. Mehitable Paine; 3. Pamela A. Bullock, and had the following children:

Susan, born May 25, 1833; married Chester Smith, and has issue — Harriet Smith, Emma Smith (deceased), Annie Smith and Charles Smith.

John (by second wife), born June 10, 1827. Died July 27, 1838.

Joseph F. (by third wife), born October 4, 1849, who is a physician in high standing at Boston Highlands, Fall River. Joseph F. Lindsey, Sr., died at his residence on High street, Fall River, March 18, 1888, at the ripe old age of eighty-five and a little over. "For more than half a century he was associated with the growth of that city. He was the first teacher employed by the town who was paid by the year, somewhere in the early thirties, and he taught school in the vestry of the Baptist church. He subsequently became a dry goods dealer in a three-story wooden block where the City Hall now stands. In 1836 he was elected treasurer of the Fall River Savings Bank. To it he gave the best years and efforts of his life, and for more than forty years he was its respected and honored custodian.

"He was a gentleman of the old school of business men, distinguished alike for honesty, ability and courtesy; all those associated with him in business, especially the clerks around him, were warmly attached to him. He retired from business at his own desire in 1877, and had been passing down the hill of life in a quiet way, respected and honored by all. He served the town for six years on the school committee."

Huntington.

(Formerly Blandford.)

Robert Lindsay, the first of this family, emigrated from the north of Ireland,* was, in all probability, a Scotch-Irish Lindsay, and arrived here during, or just after the Revolution; he settled first at Dracut, Massachusetts, then removed to Blandford, which is now called Huntington; here he married and had the following children:

I. Joseph, who had issue—Samuel, Polly, Sallie, Dollie, and Lydia. *Samuel* married and had issue — Henry, Charles, Frank, and Eunice Lindsay.

II. William, who had issue—Jane, Sophia, Esther, Fanny, and John. The last married and has issue — John, Isabel, and Esther Lindsay.

III. John, who had issue — James, William, Olive, and Nancy. William married and had issue — Martha, William, Andrew Jackson, and Miranda Lindsay.

IV. Moses, who had issue — Betsey, Isabel, Robert, Heman, Electa, and Maria. *Robert* married and had issue — George Merrick, James Franklin, Maria and Frances; these two last, died young. James Franklin married, and had

---

* Was doubtless a descendant of the House of Loughry, or Cahoo of county Tyrone, Ireland.

issue — Susan M., Grace, and Robert Lindsay; the first of whom furnishes this record of her family.

V. Molly, who married Jonathan Welles.

VI. Isabel.

ANDOVER.

Samuel Lindsay, of this place, married Rachel Hardy in Branford, Massachusetts, March 2, 1773.

New England Historical and Genealogical Register.

NEW BEDFORD.

Benjamin Lindsay, Sr., publisher of the New Bedford *Mercury*, which appeared August 7, 1807, was born 1757, and died June 2, 1820. Children:—Hannah, who married Timothy F. Spooner, December 7, 1780, was the widow Bassett at the time; and Margaret, who married John Armstrong, January 10, 1834, at East Sandwich, Massachusetts.

New England Historical and Genealogical Register.

PEMBROKE.

Married December 1, 1771, by the Reverend Thomas Smith, Ephriam Lindsay to Ann Bonny.

New England Historical and Genealogical Register.

WEST BRIDGEWATER.

Thomas Lindsay, of this place, married Elizabeth, daughter of William Turner, 1745, and had issue — William, born 1747; Mary, 1749; Hannah, 1752; James, 1755; Thomas, 1758. *James* married, but had no children. *Thomas* married Thankful Bailey, 1786. *Mary* married Nathaniel Ames, 1734; Laurencia, another daughter, married Martin Howe, 1820; Betsey, another daughter, died 1815; John, another son, married Abigail Washburn.

History of Bridgewater.

Another family of Lindsays in this State, but who spell their name Linzee, descend, according to the family tradition, from one Captain John Linzee or Lindsay, who commanded the British sloop-of-war Falcon, at the battle of Bunker Hill. He married in Boston in 1772, Miss Susanna Inman, of a well-known New England family, and has numerous descendants, it is said, in America.

Captain John Linzee descended from the Lindsays of Kirkfortha, Scotland, and his family are thus a branch of the Scottish Lindsays. The family have a coat of arms.

America Heraldica.

Hannah Rowe Linzee, daughter of Captain John Linzee, married Thomas C. Dexter, in 1795. Captain Linzee was in the West Indies September 20, 1781. He also had a daughter Susan.

New England Historical and Genealogical Register.

RHODE ISLAND.

Bristol.

It is stated of this family of Lindseys, settled since 1694, in Bristol, that their earliest ancestor, John Linsey or Lindsey, came, it is supposed, with a brother from Scotland, a long while before the Revolution. In the old town records of Bristol his marriage is recorded, John Linsey (perhaps the name was spelled so by the recorder) to Elizabeth Monro, August 29, 1694. The following are the names of their eight children:

I. Samuel, born August 8, 1697, and married to Keziah Joslin, October 14, 1718, in Situate, Rhode Island; the former died December 18, 1775, and the latter October 29, 1740. The issue of the marriage were Sarah, born September 17, 1719; John, born November 10, 1721; Mary, born, December 20, 1723; Samuel, born February 29, 1727; and Jemima, born March 21, 1730–1.

II. Mary, born January 15, 1699.

III. John, born 1702; died April 1, 1761, aged fifty-eight years; he married Hannah Hoar November 23, 1723, by whom he had issue — Hannah, born August 20, 1724; Elizabeth, born 1726; Lydia, born January 9, 1732; John, born May 15, 1733; Benjamin, born June 12, 1735; William, born June 11, 1738; died of small-pox at Dartmouth, England, April 1, 1761, aged twenty; and Mary, born August 26, 1741. Mrs. Hannah Hoar Lindsey, their mother, died November 11, 1765, aged sixty-six.

IV. Elizabeth, born December 19, 1705.

V. Benjamin, born March 11, 1709–10, and married Elizabeth Church February 7, 1733, by whom he had one son, Joseph, born 1740; died September 4, 1797; married Debora Church August 10, 1771, and had fifteen children. Elizabeth, November 15, 1772; Debora, April 2, 1775; Sarah, July 25, 1776; Lydia, February 26, 1778; Joseph, December 27, 1779, and who left home at an early age, and was lost knowledge of; Martha, December 3, 1783; died March 25, 1784; Thomas, February 14, 1785; Jemima, January 14, 1787; Anne, November 14, 1788; died August 27, 1791; Twins, 15th September; died in a few days; Martha, August 29, 1791; Rebecca, July 1, 1793; married Samuel Vickery; Nancy, about 1795, married Perry Peckham March, 1814; Daniel B., April 11, 1797, who married Mary Monro, and had issue — Mary, born April 28, 1820; died 1821; Benjamin, 1882; Mary E., 1824, and who married Mathias Frederick; died November 12, 1852; Martha, 1826; Daniel, B., 1827; Samuel M., March 18, 1830; married May 20, 1852; Martha F. Blake and had issue — 1. Mary E., born March 30, 1853; died April 12, 1856. 2. Benjamin F., October 3, 1857, and who became a resident of Attleboro, Massachusetts, is a jeweler there, and married November 3, 1885, Harriet E. W. Hall, by whom he has issue — one son, Samuel H., born July 26, 1886. 3. George H., November 10,

1861; married May 26, 1885, Alice Mansir. Martha D., May 20, 1832; married May 5, 1852, Seabury Manchester; died January 17, 1877; Abby, January 20, 1836; died October 12, 1837; Abby A., May 20, 1839; married June 25, 1863, to George Curien; died February 11, 1869.

VI. William, born July 2, 1713, and was married to Mary Wardwell October 15, 1737, by whom he had the following issue: 1. Mary, born November 13, 1738. 2. Rebecca, born March 23, 1739. 3. Martha, born October 16, 1741. 4. William, born March 1, 1745; died young. 5. William, born March 24, 17—. 6. Benjamin, born May 2, 1753.

William Lindsey, their fifth child, married Catherine Woodbury, daughter of Jonathan Woodbury of Bristol, 26th of April, 1772; by whom he had issue — (1) Mary, of whom a romantic tradition is handed down, of her losing her lover at fifteen by his going to sea; his loss thereon, and her mourning for him till her death at the ripe old age of eighty-four. (2) Catherine, born December 3, 1776. (3) Jonathan Woodbury, born June 18, 1778, and who married Hannah Easterbrooks. The said Jonathan W. was a sea captain; their issue were: [1]Sarah, born July 12, 1798. [2]Hannah, August 5, 1800. [3]Martha, June 24, 1802. [4]Mary, August 18, 1804. [5]Lydia, April 2, 1807. [6]Jonathan, March 10, 1809; died July 2, 1853. [7]Catherine, August 4, 1811. [8]Abby, September 20, 1813. [9]William, 1816, who married Miss ———, and had the following five children: Crawford Easterbrooks (not long since Mayor of Fall River, Massachusetts), Charles Bradford, William J., John Hathaway and Eliza, all residents of Fall River, Massachusetts. [10]Nancy, born December 14, 1819. [11]Nathaniel, May 10, 1823, who married and had issue — Jonathan Woodbury Lindsay. (4) William (brother of Jonathan Woodbury Lindsay who married Hannah Easterbrooks), born August 23, 178–; died on his voyage home from Guinea; no issue. (5) Martha, born October 30, 1782. (6) Sarah, born October 24, 1787. (7) Nathaniel, born April 14, 1790; died young. (8) Allen, born June 20, 1793; lost at sea; left two sons; one Allen Lindsay, was last known to have resided as a merchant in Boston. (9) Nathaniel, born July 9, 1796, and also died young.

VII. Lydia, daughter of John and Elizabeth Monro Lindsey, born December 2, 1715.

VIII. Jemima, daughter of John and Elizabeth Monro Lindsay, born May 20, 1719.

Providence.

Misses Sarah and Catherine Lindsay of Wickenden and East streets, have been some years in America, and according to their family record, descended from the Crawford Lindsays of Balcarres, in Scotland. Their father (name not given me) was a native of Bunaw, but they were brought up in Oban, Argyleshire, Scotland, coming to Providence about thirty-five years ago. They have one brother and his son living in America (names not given me), whom, along with themselves, constitute this family.

CONNECTICUT.

Stamford.

A family of Lindseys settled in the above place, deduce their descent from Benjamin Lindsay of Marblehead, latterly New Bedford, Massachusetts. The representative of this branch in Stamford is Mr. Edward Delano Lindsey, a well-known architect of New York. He has an only daughter, Ellen Lindsey. He, with a few other surviving relatives, are all of this branch. I am unable to give the names of his relatives, as he did not furnish me further "data" than the above. They used the "e" in the spelling of the name.

Wethersfield.

Susannah Lindsay married Jonathan Hollister March 17, 1743, and had issue — Jacob, born 1743.

New England Historical and Genealogical Register.

NEW YORK.

Middletown.

A family of two brothers, Frank J. Lindsey and Arthur R. Lindsey, manufacturers, contractors, and builders, reside here, whose father was English, and grandfather Scotch-English. They were to furnish me further data respecting their family, but I did not receive it, and as they asked to be noticed herein, I have complied as well as in my power.

Albany.

A gentleman residing here, Mr. J. Halley Lindsay, and connected with the "*Albany Express*," one of the Albany daily papers, promised to furnish me some history of his branch, but up to sending my book to my publisher, I have not had the pleasure of receiving the same.

Bath.

(Steuben County.)

The first of this family was James Lindsay (son of George Lindsay), who was born in the North of Ireland in 1799, and came to America in 1825, and settled in Bath, where he died in 1884. Mr. Lindsay was a magistrate in Bath for the last thirty years of his life; he had three sons. George W., the eldest, born in 1838, was a member of the One Hundred and Seventh Regiment, New York Volunteers, and died in hospital at Annapolis, Maryland, of disease contracted in a Southern military prison. John R., the second son, was captain in the One Hundred and Seventh Regiment, New York Volunteers, and acting assistant adjutant-general of

Second Brigade, First Division, Twentieth Army Corps, and is now a resident of Hoboken, New Jersey. The third son, Charles H., born in 1846, removed to Scranton, Pennsylvania, where he now resides; he is secretary and treasurer of the Scranton Consumers' Powder Company — large manufacturers. This is probably another American branch of the Lindsays of Laughry or Cahoo, in county Tyrone, Ireland.

Attica.

(Wyoming County.)

The first of this family in Attica of the above county was Archibald Lindsey, who removed from South Hadley, Hampshire county, Massachusetts, sometime during the last century, to settle a home in this locality. Here he lived until his death in 1835, at the good old age of ninety-one. One member of this family think they are of Irish descent, probably Scotch-Irish; others say the early ancestor came direct from Scotland, was aged on his arrival and accompanied by brothers; he lived in Warren county, New York.

Archibald Lindsey married three times and left a numerous family behind him, who gradually became scattered through our different States. One son came into possession of the old homestead and died there, and was buried, like his wife, beside his father in the family burying-ground, in 1875, aged eighty-nine.

The names of Archibald Lindsey's sons and daughters are: Benjamin, Cyrus, Kiliab, Eliakim, Luke, E. Galloway, Isabel, Polly, Achseh and Nancy Lindsey.

I. Benjamin, the eldest, settled in Ohio, where he died some years since. No account given me of his family, if he left any.

II. Cyrus settled and died in Galena, Wisconsin; no account of him given me.

III. Kiliab was the son who succeeded to the old homestead; he came to it from Luzerne, New York. He had, like his father, a very large family; ten grew to manhood and womanhood. The youngest of his children, a son, Carmi Van Rensselaer Lindsey, now owns the ancient farmstead, a fine piece of land of about two hundred and ten acres, nearly all under cultivation. Mr. Lindsey has a quantity of thoroughbred cows and fifty-four colonies of bees, and is a very industrious farmer, highly respected and thought of by all in his vicinity. Four of his sisters and two of his brothers reside near him; another brother lives in Wisconsin.

IV. Eliakim, the fourth son, settled near Corry, Pennsylvania, where his two sons, Perry and Orson Lindsey, reside.

V. Luke, the fifth son, settled at Luzerne, New York, and died there. He has a son, W. Henry Lindsey, living at South Corinth, New York (Saratoga county), and a daughter, Martha, living in Attica, New York.

VI. E. Galloway married Amerilla Skinner of Glens Falls, New York, January 27, 1828; he deserted her, and she moved with her family to Norwalk, Ohio, in 1844. Issue, W. I. Lindsey, born Hudson, New York, 1832; residence, Norwalk, Ohio; Isabel, the eldest daughter, married a Mr. Church; Polly married Mr. Elijah Buttles; Nancy married Mr. Thomas Orton; Achseh married Mr. Ebenezer Beebe; Peggy married Mr. Randall.

Issue of Polly Lindsey by Mr. Buttles: Harrol, Carroll, Augusta and another daughter.

Luzerne Township.

(Warren County.)

A branch of Lindseys settled in this place for a while and belonging to the Lindsey family of Attica, descended from Eliphat Lindsey, brother to Jeduthan, Eliab and Archibald Lindsey. Eliphat married and had issue, Jelpah, Sally,

Roxana, Hannah, Chloe and Polly. Jelpah was the first wife of Elijah Buttles; Sally married a Mr. Mills; Roxana married a Mr. Lake; Hannah married a Mr. Allen; Chloe married a Mr. B. Colson of Bennington, Vermont, April 6, 1806, and had issue, Henry W. Colson, Mary Ann Colson, Sophia Colson, Melvin Colson and W. B. Colson, now of Norwalk, Ohio.

New York City.

The following family is another of recent settlement in America. The founder, John Lindsay, with his wife, who was a Miss Elizabeth Hunter of Aberfeldy, Scotland (daughter to Duncan Hunter of Aberfeldy and Belle Monroe of Inverness), and his children came from Glasgow, Scotland, to this country before the Civil war, and became residents of the metropolis. His father was John Lindsay of Glasgow, Scotland. His mother was a Miss Margaret Lockhart. The rest of his brothers and sisters of Glasgow, excepting one, James, who also came to America, were: Jane, Mary, Margaret (Mary and Margaret were twins), Elizabeth, David and Agnes Lindsay.

Jane married a Mr. John Morton and left four children, viz.: James, Willie, Thomas and Maggie Morton, residents of Scotland.

Mary married Mr. Daniel McMichael, and left some children, who live in Scotland.

Margaret married Mr. William Morton, brother of John Morton, and also has children in Scotland.

David died single.

Agnes still unmarried and lives in Scotland.

The children of John and Elizabeth Hunter Lindsay, who were born in Glasgow, Scotland, and now reside in America, are: Isabella Monroe, born March 26, 1841; John, born June 25, 1843; William, born January, 1845; Elizabeth, born October 13, 1847.

Isabella Monroe Lindsay was married June 27, 1860, in New York city, to Alexander Christie, of the firm of "Shaen & Christie," well established manufacturers' agents, who have branch agencies at Berlin, Germany, and Manchester, England. Children: Marion McA., Elizabeth H., Janet H., Isabella M., George A., Bertha and Lindsay Robert Christie.

Mr. and Mrs. Christie reside at Bayonne, New Jersey, a short distance from the city of New York.

John Lindsay practises law in New York city; is not married.

William Lindsay of the law firm of "Lindsay & Flammer," 7 Beekman street, Temple Court, New York city, is personally known to me. He is an intelligent gentleman, of very agreeable manners, considerable ability, shrewd discernment, and is a prosperous and successful attorney at law. And served in the Civil war with credit to himself. He has a refined and pretty wife and a most interesting little family. His wife was a Miss Jenny McAdam. Children's names: Sadie, Mary E., Adah, Edwin R. B. Mr. and Mrs. William Lindsay with their family reside in New York city.

Elizabeth Lindsay married William S. Rawlinson, by whom she has the following children: William S., Libbie, Minnie, and Nellie Rawlinson.

The brother, who, like John Lindsay, came from Glasgow, Scotland, to America, was James Lindsay, and probably he left the mother country about the same time. He settled in Detroit, Michigan. His widow resides there with some of her children; she was Miss Jane Ward of Stirling, Scotland. Their children's names are: William W., Jane, Margaret, and James Lockhart Lindsay. The two elder reside with their mother. Margaret is the only married one; her husband is William G. McCrea of New York city, by whom she has one child, William Grant McCrea. James L. resides in Denver, Colorado, as paying teller of the First National Bank of that city.

Mr. Robert Lindsay of this city, who is in business (data 1881) with George Bruce's Sons & Co., 13 Chambers street, traces his ancestry to Glasgow, Scotland.

There are other Lindsays in this city, but have not been able to ascertain any thing of their families beyond what is here recorded.

Early marriages of Lindsays here.

October 4, 1763, Elizabeth Lindsay to Hugh Phillips. 1763, William Lindsay to Elizabeth Pell.

May 26, 1779, Grace Lindsay to John Megger. 1772, Hugh Lindsay to Sarah Delaplain. 1783, Margaret Lindsay to John King.

---

*The early forefather of the following family was William Lindsay of Stirling, Scotland (son of one Alexander Lindsay of Scotland), who emigrated to America directly from Scotland, and landed in New York somewhere in 1800 or 1799; he kept a journal, but it is now lost to his descendants, who would thus have had more knowledge of him and his ancestry. His wife, who accompanied him to America, was Miss Agnes Walker of Edinburgh. He claimed descent from Lord Lindsay, of the time of Queen Mary of Scotland. There were born in Scotland to himself and wife two daughters, Agnes and Christina, and in New York city, in 1801, Gilbert Robertson (now deceased), and William; William died unmarried in New York city, also Christina, and they are both buried in old Trinity Churchyard of that city. Agnes married James Stevenson, by whom she had a numerous family, nearly all of New York city; one son, William L. Stevenson, resides in New Brunswick, New Jersey.

*Am indebted to the courtesy of Mr. Gilbert R. Lindsay of Rahway, for the above record.

The elder son, Gilbert Robertson Lindsay, married Susanna Brown of New York city, who survives her husband, aged eighty-two years. By this marriage they had issue — Gilbert Robertson Lindsay, counselor at law, Rahway, New Jersey; William (deceased), and John Brown Lindsay, who died in infancy.

Robert Richardson Lindesay, captain of the Seventh Regiment, N. B., New York National Guard, died in that city in 1873. He was a descendant of the Reverend Alexander Lindsay, Rector of Kilmac, county Monaghan, Ireland.—See *America Heraldica.*

Mr. Lindsay may possibly have left a family in New York.

Another Lindsay in this city is Robert Lindsay, type founder; place of business, corner of Fulton and Gold streets. Am not furnished with any data of his family.

Another, B. A. Lindsay, physician, 343 West Twenty-third street.

Another, Landy A. Lindsay, lawyer, 186 William street.

Another, David A. Lindsay, merchant, 50 White street.

Another, Frank E. Lindsay, secretary, 177 Broadway.

NEW YORK CITY AND BROOKLYN.

This family are a recent settlement in the States. In 1821, the founders of it, George Lindsay, with his wife Isabella, came out to Canada from Edinburgh, Scotland; they were accompanied by their two elder children. After a residence in Canada of about ten years, where three other children were born to them, they removed to the city of New York. Here Mr. Lindsay died some years ago. His aged widow still survives him. Their children were named Hugh, James,

Ellen, Isabella, and George Lindsay. The family have no record of the first son, except as to his death.

James Lindsay married Miss Lucie Bussaniah of River Head, North Carolina, by whom he had two sons; William B., the eldest, is a resident of Brooklyn, New York, and general passenger agent for the New York, Lake Erie and Western Railroad Company, in Brooklyn. The youngest, George W., is a widower with one child, and the Long Island Express Railroad Company have his services as their assistant superintendent.

Ellen Lindsay, single.

Isabella Lindsay married a Mr. Miller of New York city, where they reside.

George Lindsay, deceased.

James Lindsay served in the Civil war, and like many of the name, died fighting for his country.

Another Brooklyn family of Lindsay is that of John J. Lindsay, of the firm of John J. Lindsay & Co., manufacturers of wall papers, of that city. Mr. Lindsay's grandfather was George Lindsay of Drumnascamph, Ireland, where he died in 1848. His seven children were Thomas, John, Stewart, George, Archibald, Mary and Rachel Lindsay.

Thomas Lindsay, the elder, came to America and settled in Jeffersonville, Indiana, where he lived for thirty-five years, and died there a few years since, leaving a large family of girls.

John Lindsay came from Ireland in 1841, and settled in Kensington, the north-eastern part of Philadelphia, where he died September 22, 1852, leaving two children, Jane D. Lindsay, born in Philadelphia March 20, 1843, now Mrs. John McClintock of that city, and John Jones Lindsay, born in Philadelphia August 28, 1845; married, in Philadelphia, April 17, 1865, Miss E. Cordelia Baker, and moved to Brooklyn, his present place of residence and business, in

1869. Their children are Frederick Baker Lindsay, born in Philadelphia January 29, 1868, and Edna Lindsay, born in Brooklyn February 23, 1885.

Otsego.

(Cherry Valley.)

The earliest Lindsay supposed to have settled in New York was John Lindsay, a Scotch gentleman of means and good family, who made the following settlement and received the following honors:

"John Lindsay, founder of Cherry Valley settlement, in county of Otsego, N. Y., was a native of Scotland, and in Dec., 1730, received from his countryman, Governor Montgomerie, the commission of Naval Officer of the Port of New York. In 1732 he was appointed Sheriff of Albany, which office he filled until October, 1739. He acquired nearly 20,000 acres of the public lands located in different parts of the Province by patents dated from 1736 to 1741. He removed to Cherry Valley in 1740, with his wife, Lieutenant Congreve, his father-in-law, and servants, and gave to his new home the name of Lindsays Bush or New Wormestone, but being unacquainted with practical farming, and the French war breaking out, he was obliged to abandon his enterprise. Reinforcements being ordered to the Western frontier, Lieutenant Congreve resigned his commission in favor of Mr. Lindsay, who proceeded to Oswego in 1744. He was in Schenectady in the Winter of 1746–7. On the 14th of October of the last mentioned year, the Council taking into consideration several petitions of the Oswego traders praying His Excellency the Governor, to continue Lieutenant Lindsay in the command of the garrison at Oswego, and the request of the Indians of the Six Nations to the same purpose, and being also of opinion from their own knowledge of Mr. Lindsay, that he is well qualified for that command, and the more so, on account of his engaging address to the Indians, unanimously resolved to recommend His Excellency to order Lieutenant Lindsay to repair to Oswego to take command of the garrison there. He was commandant at that post until February 49, when he was appointed Indian Commissary and Agent there. He retained the latter situation until his death, which occurred in 1751. His widow, Penelope Lindsay, surviving him, but they had no children. At the time of his death Mr. Lindsay was a Lieutenant in Captain Clark's company of Independent Fuzileers."

Later data seems, however, to show they *had* children, but probably they died young or left no issue. Lieutenant Lindsay was an ancestor of the Lindsays of the Byres and Wormestone in Scotland, which ancient Lindsay family is now represented by Sir John Trotter B. Lindsay, Earl of Lindsay, Kilconquhar Fife.

From Campbell's History of Tyron County, 23. New York Book of Patents. New York Council Minutes, XXI, 277. Commissions, III, 300, 368, 481. Johnson's Manuscript, I.

ARGYLE.

(Washington County.)

The record furnished of this family by four or five painstaking and energetic members of it, who have devoted much time and patience to tracing out their early ancestry, and who are Messrs. James E. and Ralph E. Lindsay of Davenport, Iowa, Mrs. Hannah Howard *née* Lindsay, and A. H. Howard of Chicago, and others, shows every probability, I think, that their first ancestor in America was a Donald Lindsay who came over with other emigrants from Scotland about 1739, in company with Captain Laughlin Campbell, from the Isle of Isla in Argyleshire, and was one of those who participated in the Argyle patent or grant. (See letters.)

ALBANY, N. Y., *Jan.* 7, 1888.

Mr. J. E. LINDSAY:

Dear Sir — Yours of the 3[d] received, and on reading the correspondence to Mr. Melius, he felt very much annoyed because your matter has been delayed until this late day. In a general way, he informed me of what you wanted ; I then went to the Secretary of State Office and from his instructions readily found the Argyle Patent; and find as follows: that among about 136 others, I find the name of Donald Lindsey, one son and two daughters, and also find the name of Donald Lindsey in the Duplicate of

Argyle Patent in Book or Volume 17, Page 63, and Volume 17, Page 64, respectively.

In the other Books and Pages in relation to Petitions for grants of land, I do not find Donald Lindsey, or any name of Lindsey. In the Petition of Donald, George, and James Campbell, and their three sisters, Rose Graham, Margaret Eustace, and Lilly Murray, I find the others are John Campbell, Sr., James Calder, & John Campbell, Jr., and Allen Campbell, granted 10,000 acres May 18, 1763; 1,000 to each petitioner. In the Petition of May 2, 1763, for 47,450 acres, Volume 16, Page 167, I find the name of Duncan Lindsey. Yours, &c.,

EUG. J. O'NEILL,
Co. Clerk's Office.

Notes from Judge Gibson's letter to Mr. Melius, clerk of the Court, Albany, N. Y., and loaned by Mr. Melius:

"In 1739, in the company that came with Laughlin Campbell from the Isle of Isla in Argyleshire, Scotland, was Donald Lindsay and his wife, Mary McQuarrie, of the Clan McQuarrie, and four children. They landed in the City of New York early in the Summer of that year. In 1764 he participated in the grant of the Argyle Patent, and received a lot on which he lived and died, coming and settling on the lot in 1765."

Donald Lindsay was accompanied to America, as Judge Gibson's letter mentions, by his wife, Mary McQuarrie, and four children, whose names were Richard, Duncan, Effie, and Christian. The genealogy continues—this Donald Lindsay came to America as an emigrant, under Captain Laughlin Campbell, and was perhaps a relative of Lieutenant John Lindsay, the settler in Otsego county, Cherry Valley. Tradition says of this family, that Duncan was a second son, and that their early ancestor settled in Argyle, New York. As Donald Lindsay came to America under Captain Laughlin Campbell, and as emigrants who came with Captain Campbell founded the settlement in Argyle, they believed Donald was the father of their Duncan, as Duncan lived in Argyle long before the Revolutionary war.

The Province of New York promised grants of land to Protestant settlers, and Captain Campbell seeing this promise, which was made in 1734, and extensively advertised, visited New York and made an agreement with the Governor and Council, which provided that he should bring to New York one hundred families; each family to have from a hundred and fifty to five hundred acres of land, and Captain Campbell should receive one thousand acres of land for each family brought; doubtless it was the promise of land which induced Donald Lindsay to bring his family to America; when the emigrants arrived, however, the grants were refused, and the homeless emigrants underwent many hardships. Many enlisted in the Carthagenian expedition to earn enough to prevent themselves and families from starving. In 1763, twenty-five years after the arrival of the emigrants, the sons and daughters of Captain Campbell, and four others (see Eug. J. O'Neill's letter), received a ten thousand acre grant of land, and the year following, several families, who were either the original emigrants or their descendants, received grants. So, partial justice was done, but not until after many, who should have been grantees, had passed away.

The genealogy of this New York branch of Lindsays begins as follows:

First Generation.

Donald Lindsay, born probably in Argyleshire or Fifeshire, Scotland, married Mary McQuarrie, and emigrated to America with his wife and family in 1739, and settled in Argyle, where he died some time after 1765, being one hundred and four years of age.

Second Generation.

(Issue of Donald Lindsay and Mary McQuarrie, his wife.)

I. Richard Lindsay, born in Scotland, or in Argyle, New York, history unknown, but he probably settled in Vermont.

II. Duncan Lindsay, born either in Scotland, or in Argyle, New York; married twice, first Anna McDougal, secondly Mrs. Agnes McCoy, *nee* McIntyre; he lived in Argyle, New York, until his death, about 1785.

III. Effie Lindsay, history unknown.

IV. Christian Lindsay, history unknown.

Third Generation.

(Issue of Duncan Lindsay, Anna McDougal and Agnes McCoy.)

I. John Lindsay, born near Argyle, New York, about 1762, married Hannah Hennegen, a lady of German descent, in Argyle, New York. After his marriage he settled near Coburg, Upper Canada, and afterward near Hemingsford, Lower Canada. He died near Coburg in 1846, aged eighty-four years. He was always engaged in farming.

II. David Lindsay, born near Argyle, New York, about 1766, married Betsy McDowall (Betsy McDowall, and Martha McDowall, wife of Daniel, were daughters of John McDowall and Euphamy Smith, his wife, who came from Scotland and settled in Northumberland, New York), and lived after his marriage near Saratoga Springs, and afterward settled near Paradox Lake. He was a farmer and lumberman, and was drowned when fifty-one years of age, while driving logs in the North river (now Hudson). His wife survived him, dying in April, 1854.

III. Daniel Lindsay, born near Argyle, New York, August 14, 1773, was a farmer and lumberman. He married Eleanor, usually called "Polly" McIntyre. She died soon after their marriage, and he afterward married Martha McDowall, a sister to Betsy McDowall, who married David Lindsay. From the time of his second marriage until 1820 or 1822, he lived on a farm in Northumberland, New York. At the above-mentioned date he moved to North Hudson, Essex county, New York; moved from there to Addison, Vermont, and died there August 12, 1840. His wife died in Malone, New York, in 1862, aged eighty years. Daniel Lindsay was not a large man, weighing about one hundred and sixty-five pounds, but was splendidly developed, physically. He was a Mason of high degree, and his Masonic apron is in the possession of his daughter, Hannah M. Howard; she also has a Royal Arch Jewell bearing date 5800, which he owned. He belonged to a Lodge and a Chapter in Fort Edward, New York.

IV. Allen Lindsay, born in Argyle, New York, in 1772, was a farmer. He married in Rhode Island, Amy Brown, in 1792; settled in North Hudson, New York, and lived in Canada a short time previous to 1806. His wife died in North Hudson, New York, and he afterward married Sally Culver, near Albany, New York. He died in Caton, New York, January 12, 1872, being nearly one hundred years of age. His second wife is living with her daughter Harriet Rose, in Corning, New York.

V. Mary Lindsay, married John Smith, and lived in Canada.

VI. Effie Lindsay, married Nathan Durgee; lived in Northumberland, New York, until the time of her death, 1817 or 1820.

VII. Betsy Lindsay, married John Hennegen; lived twelve to fourteen miles from Shadagee Falls, Province of Hinchenbooke, Canada.

VIII. Nancy Lindsay, married Nathan Peterson; lived for a time in Fort Miller, New York, afterward near Coburg, Upper Canada, and from there moved to Canada Corners or Campton, Illinois, where she and her husband both died.

IX. Margaret Lindsay, born about 1756; married Francis De Long; lived near Coburg, Canada.

Fourth Generation.

(Issue of John Lindsay and Hannah Hennegen.)

I. Richard Lindsay, born near Coburg, Canada, January 23, 1789; married Nancy Wood, a New York lady, in Mooers, Clinton county, New York, July 18, 1811. He fought against the British, as a private, at the battle of Plattsburg, in the war of 1812. He was by trade a cooper. He lived in Coburg, Canada, Woodville, New York, Kane county, Illinois, and died in Courtland, De Kalb county, Illinois, August 7, 1861. His wife was born November 15, 1791, and died December 28, 1863.

II. John Lindsay, born probably in Coburg, Upper Canada, in 1791; married Polly Dewey, born in St. Pierre, Lower Canada. They lived in Hemmingsford, Lower Canada, until after the birth of their son Henry, and daughter Hannah; then settled near Coburg, Upper Canada, where Ezekiel, Harriet, and Betsy were born; afterward moved to Ellis' Scenery, where George and Charity were born; then settled in Hopkinton, St. Lawrence county, New York. He fought against the British, as a private, at the battle of Plattsburg, in the war of 1812. He was a farmer and lumberman, and died in Hopkinton, New York, in 1871.

III. Joseph Lindsay, born probably near Coburg, Upper Canada, about 1793; married Olive Wolcott in Upper Canada; lived in Canada a short time after his marriage, and then moved to Campton, Illinois, where he lived for twenty years, and then settled in Sycamore, Illinois, to be with his son. He died in November, 1874, and his wife died in April, 1874.

IV. David Lindsay, born in Upper Canada, probably in 1795; married Nancy Williams in Canada; remained in Canada for a time; then removed to Illinois, and died in Sycamore, Illinois, about 1861. His wife survived him three or four years, and died in Courtland, Illinois, at the residence of her daughter, Mrs. Pengegast.

V. Duncan Lindsay, born in Upper Canada about 1797; married Katie McCarty; lived in Clark, Upper Canada, and afterward near Sycamore, Illinois, where he died. He was a farmer. His wife died in the Winter of 1878, at the residence of her son William.

VI. Allen Lindsay, born near Coburg, Upper Canada, about 1801; married Miss McCarty, a sister to Katie; lived near Coburg, afterward near Sycamore, Illinois, and died at the latter place in 1861; was a farmer; wife lives at Hambleton, near Coburg, Upper Canada.

VII. Alexander Lindsay, born near Coburg, Upper Canada, about 1803; married Eunice Lewis; lived in Canada, Cleveland, Ohio, Illinois, Wisconsin, Eastern Kansas, and now lives in Fellsburg, Kansas.

VIII. Rachel Lindsay, born near Coburg, Upper Canada, about 1805; married Joseph Brisbin, a Canadian; lived in Canada, on a farm, near Sycamore, Illinois, and died in Sycamore, Illinois, about 1866.

IX. Effie Lindsay, born near Coburg, Upper Canada, about 1807; married John Gordon; lived in Clark, Upper Canada, until her death, 1844–5; husband a farmer.

X. Margaret Lindsay, born near Coburg, Upper Canada, about 1809; married John Brisbin (not a brother to Joseph Brisbin); lived near Coburg, where her husband farmed extensively; died in Hambleton, Upper Canada, in 1839.

XI. Mary Lindsay, born near Coburg, Upper Canada, about 1811; married William Ellsworth; lived many years in Canada, afterward in De Kalb, Illinois, and is now living in Michigan.

XII. Daniel Lindsay, born in Upper Canada, near Coburg, about 1813; married a Miss McCarty, a sister to Katie McCarty; lived in Upper Canada until 1840; afterward in

De Kalb county, Illinois, until 1861, at which time he returned to Canada, where his wife died in 1864–5; again married; had no children.

(Issue of David Lindsay and Betsy McDowell.)

I. Euphemy Lindsay, born near Saratoga Springs, New York; married Albert De Garmo; died in Taylor, Cortland county, New York, in 1844.

II. Anna Lindsay, born near Saratoga New York; married William Holmes; lived in Dryden, Tompkins county, New York; died about 1870.

III. Margaret Lindsay, born near Northumberland, Saratoga county, New York; married Henry Griffin; moved to Dryden, New York; died about 1875.

IV. Martha Lindsay, born near Northumberland, New York, in 1805; married Peter McDonald; lived in Athol, New York, and now lives in Taylor, Cortland county, New York.

V. Mary Lindsay, born in Saratoga county, New York, near Northumberland; married a Mr. Holmes; died in Baraboo, Wisconsin, in 1875.

VI. Jane Lindsay, born near Northumberland, New York, December 29, 1806, twin sister to James; married Amasa Holmes in 1826; lives at Rogers Park, Illinois; her husband died April 3, 1885, in his eighty-third year.

VII. James Lindsay, twin brother to Jane, born December 29, 1806; married Elizabeth J. McMillan in Athol, New York; lived in Northumberland, New York, in 1855; was a millwright and builder; is now living on a farm near Oshkosh, Wisconsin.

(Issue of Daniel Lindsay and Martha McDowell.)

I. Eleanor, commonly called Nellie, born in Northumberland, New York, September 14, 1799; married Robert Cook De Long; lived in North Hudson, New York, about 1850;

husband died there, and September 14, 1864, she went to live in Malone, New York, with her children; died in 1874, aged seventy-five years; husband born March 2, 1796.

II. John D. Lindsay, born in Northumberland, New York, about 1799; married Eliza Palmer, who died, and he afterward married Hannah Bois; died on a farm near Eiizabethtown, New York, about 1880.

III. Anna Lindsay, born near Northumberland, New York, in 1801; married Asaph Billings Totman; lived in North Hudson, New York, afterward in Keeseville, New York, and finally removed to Peru, New York, where she died about 1865. Her husband moved to Saratoga Springs, New York, and lived there until his death, 1880–1885, with his daughter, Helen Jackson.

IV. Daniel Lindsay; died in infancy.

V. Robert D. Lindsay, born in Northumberland, New York, April 16, 1804; married Elizabeth Churchill about 1824; she was born January 12, 1809; they lived in Schroon, Essex county, New York, until 1868, when they moved to Crown Point, New York, where he died April 9, 1873, and his wife died June 17, 1875; was a farmer and lumberman, and at one time a major in New York State Militia.

VI. Euphemy Lindsay, born December 28, 1806, in Northumberland, New York; married William Johnson, November 7, 1824; died September 14, 1840.

VII. Daniel Lindsay, born March 19, 1810; never married; a painter; died in Malone, New York.

VIII. Hannah Maria Lindsay, born May 30, 1812, in Northumberland, New York; lived with her father until her marriage to Ira Howard, January 21, 1836. Her husband was born in Unity, New Hampshire, March 15, 1808, the son of Ira Howard and Mabel Stoddard; he was a miller by trade, and lived successively in Keeseville, New York, 1836–1839; on a farm near Plattsburg, New York, 1840; Schuyler

Falls, New York; Peru, New York; Westport, New York, Addison, Vermont, 1841–1848; North Hudson, New York, 1848–1851; Crown Point, New York, 1851–1854; Neenah, Wisconsin, 1854–1859; Oshkosh, Wisconsin, 1861–1878; Onero, Wisconsin, 1878–1879, and died aged seventy, in Onero, Wisconsin. After her husband's death Mrs. Howard went to live in Neenah, Wisconsin, and remained there until the Fall of 1879, when she moved to Chicago to be with her children; lives 2458 Dearborn street, Chicago, Illinois.

IX. Eliza Doanda Lindsay, born in Northumberland, New York, April 15, 1814; married Tabor Corey Innis in August, 1831; born about 1808; they lived at different times in North Hudson, New York; Addison, Vermont; Rosendale, Winnebago county, Wisconsin. In Wisconsin Mr. Innis was a farmer; in New York in the iron and lumber business. About 1870, she with her husband went to Bingham Lake, Minnesota, where she died in 1873. After the death of Mrs. Innis, Mr. Innis again married, and is now living near Bingham Lake, on a farm.

X. Alexander Lindsay, born near Northumberland, New York, August 30, 1816; married Harriet Hazzard in Peru, New York. His wife died and he afterward married Sarah A. Keeler, born June 30, 1817, in Malone, New York; she was a daughter of one of the early settlers of Malone. Their marriage took place June 21, 1842. He died in 1873, from the effects of disease contracted while serving as captain of Company H, One Hundred and Forty-second New York Volunteer Infantry, in the war of the Rebellion. He served under Gencral Curtis, and at the time of his enlistment was exempt from military duty on account of his age. He was a marble manufacturer and farmer, and patented a process for polishing glass, which was received with high favor by the English, whose country he visited in 1856 and 1858, while introducing his patent. His wife still survives him, and lives with her children in Woodland, California.

XI. David, died aged six years and eight months.

(Issue of Allen Lindsay and Amy Brown.)

I. Polly Lindsay, born in Canada in 1794; married Thomas Harrington, a farmer, lived in Dryden, Tompkins county, New York, and died there about 1882.

II. Betsy Lindsay, born in Saratoga county, New York, in 1796; married Jonathan Quinby; lived in Corning, New York; died in Alpine, Schuyler county, New York, in 1873; her husband was a farmer.

III. John Lindsay, born in 1798; married Susan Stickler; lived in Michigan until his death, about 1847; was a farmer.

IV. Susan Lindsay, born in Tompkins county, New York, in 1806; married Joseph Smith; lived in Corning and Caton, New York; husband was a blacksmith and farmer; she now lives in Minneapolis, Minnesota.

V. Allen Lindsay, born in Tompkins county, New York, in 1810; married Hannah Snyder; lives on a farm near Corning, New York; wife died in November, 1846, and he afterward married Harriet Benson in Roseville, Pennsylvania, in 1847.

VI. Rachel Lindsay, born in 1812, in Dryden, Tompkins county, New York; married Samuel Mitchell; lives in Dryden, New York; husband was a mason.

VII. Zepheniah Lindsay, born near Dryden, New York, in 1814; married Eve Stickler; died in Michigan.

VIII. Ann Lindsay, born in Tompkins county, New York, in 1816; married Levi Force; died in Caton, Steuben county, New York.

IX. Merritt Lindsay, born in Tompkins county, New York, in 1820; married Emeline Abgar; lives near Big Flats, New York; is a farmer and tobacco raiser.

X. Amy Lindsay, born in Tompkins county, New York, in 1822; married —— Snyder; moved to Minnesota.

(Issue of Allen Lindsay and Sally Culver.)

XI. Daniel Lindsay, born in Tompkins county, New York; married Lorena Decker; was a private in the war of the Rebellion; returned home on a furlough and died while home in 1863; was a farmer.

XII. Loretta Lindsay, born in Tompkins county, New York; married John Vero. He left her because she would not become a Catholic; she afterward married Oliver Smith; lived and died in Corning, New York.

XIII. William Lindsay, born in Tompkins county, New York; married Adeline Stickler; enlisted to serve in the war of the Rebellion; supposed he died, as he never returned home; his widow afterward married Levi Lindsay, and after his death married Mr. Howard; lives in Towanda, New York.

XIV. James Lindsay, born in Tompkins county, New York; married Alice Decker; was a soldier in the war of the Rebellion.

XV. Harriet Lindsay, born in Tompkins county, New York; married Henry Grant; he died in the army; she afterward married Ira Rose, overseer of the poor in Corning, New York.

XVI. C. W. Lindsay, born in Tompkins county, New York; married —— ———; is a railroad bridge watchman in Rocky Strain, Yates county, New York.

XVII. Lydia Lindsay, born in Tompkins county, New York; married William Vogal of Corning, New York; lives in Corning.

XVIII. Almeda Lindsay, born in Tompkins county, New York; married James Pudney; lives in Cortland county, New York.

(Issue of Effie Lindsay and Nathan Durgee.)

I. Nathan Durgee.
II. Peggy Durgee.
III. Effie Durgee.
IV. Deborah Durgee.
V. Elizabeth Durgee.

(Issue of Betsy Lindsay and John Hennegen.)

I. David Hennegen married Polly Petersen; died in Clark, Upper Canada, in 1838; wife moved to Elgin, Illinois, where she died.

II. Joseph Hennegen died in Hemmingsford, Lower Canada.

III. John Hennegen died in Lower Canada.

IV. Daniel Hennegen died when an old man, in Clark, Upper Canada.

V. Allen Hennegen married Betsy ——.

(Issue of Nancy Lindsay and Nathan Petersen.)

I. Amelia Petersen, born near Fort Miller, New York, September 1, 1792; married Truman Cleveland; he died in Bonhead, Canada West, November 21, 1839; July 30, 1866, she died at Lilly Lake, Kane county, Illinois.

II. Duncan Petersen married —— ——; moved to Kane county, Illinois, where he died.

III. Jonathan Petersen died in Iowa; never married.

IV. Nancy Petersen married Benjamin Brown, and lived in Canada West; afterward in Campton, Illinois, where she died; her family moved to Iowa.

V. Sally A. Petersen married Gilbert Brown; lived in Coburg, Upper Canada; family probably lives in Iowa.

VI. Nathan Petersen married Emily Hall; lived in Upper Canada; moved to Iowa, where he and his wife died.

VII. Isabel Petersen; lived for a time in Upper Canada;

married Benjamin Hall; moved from Canada to Wisconsin, and from there to Chautauqua, New York.

VIII. Elizabeth Petersen married Thomas Hall, a brother to Benjamin Hall, who married Isabel Petersen, and Emily Hall, who married Nathan Petersen.

IX. Polly Petersen married David Hennegen; lived near Coburg, Upper Canada, and died there.

(Issue of Margaret Lindsay and Francis De Long.)

I. Alexander De Long never married.

II. Francis De Long married —— ——; was poisoned in De Kalb, Illinois.

III. Dean De Long never married.

IV. Maria De Long married William Patterson; was bitten by a mad dog.

V. Betsy De Long is supposed to be the mother of Robert (Cook) De Long, who was brought up by his grandfather, and took his name; she afterward married Gideon Wolcott, and died in De Kalb, Illinois.

VI. Abbie De Long married Otis Baldwin.

VII. Margaret De Long.

VIII. John De Long married —— ——.

IX. Jene De Long.

X. Effie De Long.

Fifth Generation.

(Issue of Richard Lindsay and Nancy Wood.)

I. Parathena Lindsay, born October 15, 1812, in Upper Canada; died in infancy.

II. Rachel Lindsay, born April 7, 1815, in Upper Canada; married February 12, 1830, Francis Youngs, born 1807; he is a farmer, and they live in Gothenburg, Dawson county, Nebraska.

III. Tyler Lindsay, born February 20, 1817, in Upper Canada; married Maria Blackman February 22, 1851; wife died in 1883; lives in Chester, Fair county, Kansas.

IV. Amasa Lindsay, born December 26, 1818, in Woodville, New York; married Maria Patterson in 1849; wife died in De Kalb, Illinois, in 1857; afterward married Samantha Collier in 1859; lives in Sherman county, Nebraska.

V. Clark Lindsay, born September 7, 1820, in Upper Canada, near Coburg; married Sarah Glenn in Ripley, Brown county, Illinois; she was born September 12, 1828; they were married April 10, 1850; he is a potter by trade; wife died in April, 1886; he lives in Ripley, Illinois.

VI. Lewis Lindsay, born January 4, 1823, near Coburg; married Sabra Lewis, sister to Alexander Lindsay's wife, about 1843; wife died about two years after marriage; afterward married Isabel Cole about 1851; she died in 1884; he is a miner, and lives in Sacramento, California.

VII. Louise Lindsay, born January 4, 1823, twin sister to Lewis; died when two years of age.

VIII. Alexander Lindsay, born August 2, 1826, near Coburg, Canada; married Amy Carpenter of New York State, about 1843; he is a cheese dealer in Plymouth, Sheboygan county, Wisconsin.

IX. Sarah A. Lindsay, born December 8, 1827, near Coburg, Upper Canada; married February 2, 1848; George Walker, born in Clark Township, Upper Canada, June 15, 1825; he died December 6, 1880; October 3, 1883, she married Ezekiel Lindsay, and lives in Oshkosh, Wisconsin.

X. Margaret Lindsay, born January 22, 1831, near Coburg, Canada; married Elisha Badger January 1, 1852; he is a farmer, and lives near Smithfield, in Fayette county, Iowa.

XI. William W. Lindsay, born May 6, 1835, in Clinton county, New York; married Emeline Calhoun February 20, 1865; is a railroad contractor; lives in Chester, Kansas.

(Issue of John Lindsay and Polly Dewey.)

I. Henry Lindsay, born in Upper Canada, near Coburg, about 1813; married Eda Blanchard in December, 1842; is a wagon and carriage manufacturer in Hopkinton, New York.

II. Hannah Lindsay, born near Hemmingsford, Lower Canada, about 1815; never married; died in Hopkinton, New York, aged eighteen.

III. Hiram Lindsay, born in Upper Canada about December, 1817; married Octava Witherell in June, 1843; is a farmer and lumberman; has lived fifty-two years in Hopkinton, New York.

IV. Betsy Lindsay, born near Coburg, Upper Canada, about 1819; died in infancy.

V. Ezekiel Lindsay, born near Coburg, Upper Canada, July 6, 1823; married Lorinda Barnes, January 29, 1843, in Dickinson, New York; April 9, 1844, they moved to Campton, Illinois, on a farm; from there moved to Burlington on a farm; afterward lived near Plato, Illinois; from Plato moved to Waupaca county, Wisconsin; from there to Washaura, Wisconsin; remained in the latter place eleven years, and in May, 1877, settled in Oshkosh, Wisconsin, which is still his home; he has been a farmer and lumberman; February 16, 1848, his wife died, and November 11, 1850, he married Emeretta Barnes; October 3, 1883, he married Mrs. George Walker (Sarah A. Lindsay); Mr. Lindsay enlisted March 22, 1863, to serve three years in the war of the Rebellion; he was in but one battle, the battle of the Wilderness, and there received a wound, a compound fracture of the left thigh, which left him maimed for life. After receiving his wound he was thirty days inside the Rebel lines, and his experience would make an interesting narrative. He served as a private in Company I, of the Seventh Wisconsin Infantry, which belonged to the famous "Iron Brigade."

VI. Harriet Lindsay, born in Upper Canada about 1825; married Nelson Witherell about 1843; lived in Hopkinton, New York, until 1861, then moved to Sun Prairie, Wisconsin, and died in Sun Prairie about 1873; her husband is a farmer in Northern Kansas.

VII. John Lindsay, born in Upper Canada, December 30, 1829; married Jane S. Parker, born February 21, 1833, in Canada; married in St. Lawrence county, New York; lived in Hopkinton, New York, until his death, June 19, 1887; wife still lives in Hopkinton.

VIII. Charity Lindsay, born in St. Pierre, Lower Canada, about 1835; married William Prince in September, 1853; he was born in England in 1829; is a saddler by trade, and lives in Hopkinton, New York.

IX. George Lindsay, born in Lower Canada about 1831; married Fanny Hayden about 1857; farms the old John Lindsay farm in Hopkinton, New York; wife died about 1875.

(Issue of Joseph Lindsay and Olive Wolcott.)

I. William A. Lindsay, born near Coburg, Upper Canada, about 1824; married Betsy J. Collins in Campton, Illinois, about 1850; owns and operates a grist-mill in Philandro, Dakota.

II. Mary Lindsay, born about 1828; married Hiram Eddy in Campton, Illinois; died in 1877; husband is a capitalist, living in De Kalb, Illinois.

III. Elisha Lindsay, born near Coburg, Upper Canada, about 1829; married Louise Powers in St. Charles, Illinois, about 1851; he is a butcher in Philandro, Dakota.

IV. Savilla Lindsay, born May 10, 1830, in Hamilton Township, Canada West; married Horace Powers, a brother to Louise Powers, in St. Charles, Illinois, in 1852; he is a capitalist in Denver, Colorado.

V. Sabrina Lindsay, born about 1834, near Coburg, Upper Canada; married Edmund Eddy, a brother to Hiram Eddy, about 1857; he is an organ and sewing machine agent in St. Charles, Illinois.

VI. Richard Lindsay, born about 1836, near Coburg; married Susannah Petersen about 1857; he lives in St. Charles, Illinois.

(Issue of David Lindsay and Nancy Williams.)

I. John Lindsay, born about 1820, near Coburg; died unmarried.

II. Noble Lindsay, born about 1822, near Coburg; died unmarried.

III. Oliver Lindsay, born about 1824, near Coburg; died unmarried.

IV. Hannah Lindsay, born about 1826, near Coburg, Upper Canada.

V. Jane Lindsay, born about 1828, near Coburg, Upper Canada; married —— King; lived in Clark, Upper Canada, where he died; he was a carpenter; she probably lives near Clark, Upper Canada.

VI. Caroline Lindsay, born about 1830, near Coburg; married Richard Pendegast, a carpenter and joiner in Malta, Illinois.

VII. Lucretia Lindsay, born about 1832, near Coburg; married Joseph Hennegen; lived in Cortland, Illinois.

(Issue of Duncan Lindsay and Katie McCarty.)

I. Robert Lindsay, born near Coburg, Upper Canada, about 1823; married Amanda Locey in Clark, Upper Canada, about 1842; is a farmer near Rudd, Orange county, Iowa.

II. Jeremiah Lindsay, born near Coburg, about 1825; married Amy Walters in Canada; is a carpenter and joiner, and probably lives in Clark, Upper Canada.

III. Lyman Lindsay, born near Coburg, about 1827; married Margaret Ellsworth in De Kalb, Illinois, about 1852; lives in ———, Iowa.

IV. William Lindsay, born near Coburg, Upper Canada, about 1829; married in Iowa, Jessie ———.

V. Daniel Lindsay, born near Coburg, Upper Canada, about 1831; married near Campton, Illinois, Mary Hamilton; is a barber in De Kalb, Illinois.

VI. Betsy Lindsay, born about 1833, near Coburg; married O'Callanan McCarty, a nephew to Katie McCarty; she died in Genoa, Illinois, in 1875; Mr. McCarty afterward married in Canada —— ———; she died; he is now principal of the Genoa High School in Genoa, Illinois.

(Issue of Allen Lindsay and —— McCarty.)

I. George Lindsay, born near Hambleton, Upper Canada, about 1831; probably lives in Canada.

II. Matlin Lindsay, born near Hambleton, Upper Canada.

III. Charles Lindsay.

IV. Duncan Lindsay.

V. Jonas Lindsay.

VI. Betsy Lindsay.

VII. "Tamma" Lindsay.

VIII. Malinda Lindsay.

(Issue of Alexander Lindsay and Eunice Lewis.)

I. Rachel Lindsay, born about 1837.

II. William Lindsay.

III. Richard Lindsay.

IV. Edwin Lindsay.

(Issue of Rachel Lindsay and Joseph Brisbin.)

I. Hannah Brisbin, married Joseph Roseberry; lives in ———, California.

II. Effie Brisbin, married —— Robeseer.

III. Daniel Brisbin, married Louise ———.

IV. Harriet Brisbin, married —— Barney.

V. Samuel Brisbin, married ———.

VI. Margaret Brisbin, married William Brisbin.
VII. Allen Brisbin, married ——.

(Issue of Mary Lindsay and William Ellsworth.)

I. John Ellsworth.
II. Aaron Ellsworth.
III. Maria Ellsworth, married William Linton.
IV. Hannah Ellsworth.
V. Rachel Ellsworth.
VI. Lucinda Ellsworth.

(Issue of Euphemy Lindsay and Albert De Garneo.)

I. James De Garneo; died in the army.

(Issue of Margaret Lindsay and Harry Griffin.)

I. Alexander Griffin.

II. Catherine Griffin, married Newton Aldrich, a lumberman in Gouverneur, New York.

III. Elizabeth Griffin, married —— Broughton; died leaving two children.

IV. Martha Griffin, married Daniel Dean; lived in Fort Edward, New York, and died in Waupun, Wisconsin.

(Issue of Mary Lindsay and Linus Holmes.)

I. Jane E. Holmes, married for first husband, Amasa Rogers; second husband, William Andrews.

II. Sarah Holmes, married Adam Goodyear; lives in Portage City, Wisconsin.

III. Martha A. Holmes, married —— Quimby; died in Dryden, New York.

(Issue of Martha Lindsay and Peter McDonald.)

I. James L. McDonald lives in Taylor, Cortland county, New York.

II. George McDonald.

III. Williams McDonald, married —— ——; lives in Taylor, Cortland county, New York.

IV. Jennie McDonald, married Cyrus Graves; is a widow living in Taylor, Cortland county, New York.

(Issue of Jane Lindsay and Amasa Holmes.)

I. Margaret Holmes, born January 26, 1827, in Homer, Cortland county, New York; married December 31, 1855, W. H. Gardner in Cortland county, New York; lives at Rogers Park, Illinois; husband a printer by trade; she died March 2, 1888; body taken to Nunda, New York.

II. Louise Holmes, born April 16, 1830; married Samuel C. Graves in Homer, Cortland county, New York, April 6, 1868; husband was a lawyer; lives in Nunda, New York.

III. Mary J. Holmes, born October 28, 1836, in Cortland county, New York; married William J. Leake in Cortland county, New York; lives in Rippey, Iowa.

(Issue of James Lindsay and M. Elizabeth McMillan.)

I. Martha J. Lindsay, born Stony Creek, New York, January 9, 1843; married March 11, 1862, C. H. Fuller; he was born April 27, 1843, near Stony Creek; they live in East Galway, New York. Have one child, a daughter, Nellie, Mrs. Smith Hubbell of Lake George, New York.

II. Mary Elizabeth Lindsay, born at Stony Creek, New York, June 20, 1848; died October 6, 1849.

III. Mary Ellen Lindsay, born at Stony Creek, New York, October 24, 1854; married February 11, 1874, William J. Morris, born in England; lives in Oshkosh, Wisconsin, where her husband is in the employ of a sash, door and blind company.

IV. Daniel Arthur Lindsay, born at Stony Creek, New York, May 20, 1858; is a provision merchant in Oshkosh, Wisconsin.

(Issue of Nellie Lindsay and Robert Cook De Long and Francis De Long.)

I. Evidney De Long, born in 1820; married James Van Wert about 1844; he served in the Twenty-second New

York Volunteers, afterward in the Fifth New York Cavalry, and died in a hospital on Long Island Sound in 1864; she died July 22, 1854.

II. John De Long, born in 1823; married Celestia Jordan; is a marble manufacturer in Elizabethtown, New York.

III. Sarah A. De Long, born in 1827, in North Hudson, New York; married William Johnson; husband died in Green Bay, Wisconsin, November 16, 1886; she lives at East Beekmanton, New York.

IV. Charlotte De Long married Seth Sumner, February 14, 1876; he was a soldier in a Wisconsin regiment in the war of the Rebellion; he is now a lumberman in Brillion, Wisconsin.

V. Eliza De Long, born August 31, 1832, in North Hudson; married Lyman Brownell in Peru, New York, August 31, 1853; lives in San Jose, California, where he is in the marble business.

VI. Robert De Long, born November 14, 1834; married Sabra Dewey April 19, 1859; she died November 20, 1872, and he married Mrs. Eugene Collins, June 10, 1874; he is a marble manufacturer in Malone, New York.

VII. Alexander De Long, born in January, 1834; married Carrie Salone; lives in California on a sheep ranch.

VIII. Harriet De Long, born in 1836; married Leo Lee in Lewis, Essex county, New York, in 1860; lives in San Jose, California, on Ninth street.

IX. Martha De Long, born in 1840; married Horace W. Brownell in Essex Junction, Vermont; he was a lieutenant in the Sixth Vermont Volunteers, and fought in every battle in which his regiment was engaged. In the last April of the war he received a wound which maimed him for life; is a butcher in Milwaukee, Wisconsin.

X. Daniel De Long, born in 1840; twin brother of Martha; married Hattie Boyce; lived in Spencer, Wisconsin, and is now living in Donley's Mills, Kings county, Washington Territory, near Seatle.

(Issue of John D. Lindsay and Eliza Palmer.)

I. Charlotte Lindsay, born in Northumberland, New York, about 1826; married Hiram Baker in Addison, Vermont, in 1848; they bought and lived in the old Daniel Lindsay place in Northumberland, New York; in 1867 she married Richard Osborn, a Presbyterian minister, for her second husband; lives in Saratoga Springs, New York.

(Issue of John D. Lindsay and Hannah Boies.)

II. Marvin Lindsay, married —— ———; died ——.

III. Adelia Lindsay, married —— Stacy; lives in Vergennes, Vermont.

IV. Daniel Lindsay.

V. Abbie Lindsay.

VI. Martha Lindsay; married in Elizabethtown, New York; died.

VII. Charles Lindsay.

VIII. John Lindsay; died young.

IX. Anna M. Lindsay; died young.

(Issue of Anna Lindsay and A. B. Totman.)

I. Henry Totman, born at Keeseville, New York, about 1826; married Elizabeth Jackson; was a saw-mill foreman; died in Green Bay, Wisconsin; wife died about 1882.

II. Helen M. Totman, born at Keeseville, New York; married Daniel Jackson; he died in Saratoga Springs, and she still lives there; he was a carriage and car builder.

III. Maria Totman died young.

IV. Daniel Totman died when sixteen to eighteen years old.

(Issue of Robert D. Lindsay and Elizabeth Churchill.)

I. James Edwin Lindsay, born at Schroon, New York, April 12, 1826; married Mary H. Phelps of the same place;

born January 31, 1832; their marriage took place July 8, 1858; he has always been in the lumber business, but received a civil engineer's education. Previous to the drowning of his sister's husband, John Tompkins, he and Mr. Tompkins were partners in logging on Schroon river. In 1856 and 1857 Mr. Lindsay was engaged in locating pine timber in Wisconsin, on Black river and its tributaries. This work was only done partially for himself. In 1861, he with his wife, settled in Iowa, where he became the partner of Eliphalet Harris in buying and selling rafted lumber in Davenport. Mr. Harris retained his residence in Queensbury, Warren county, New York, and Mr. Lindsay conducted the business. In April, 1862, Mr. Lindsay's brother in-law, John B. Phelps, went to Davenport and purchased the interest of Mr. Harris. Lindsay and Phelps continued in the business of buying and selling rafted lumber until 1866, when they built a saw-mill in Davenport, which they still operate.

II. Henry E. Lindsay, born in Schroon, Essex county, New York; died young.

III. Margaret Lindsay, born in Schroon, New York, December 4, 1830; married in same place John Tompkins, born in 1823 in Stillwater, New York. Mr. Tompkins became the partner of James E. Lindsay, and was with him until the time of his death by drowning, while driving logs on Schroon river, near Elk lake, May 9, 1852. December 29, 1864, she married her present husband, James E. Pond, born March 31, 1842; is operating a saw-mill, and is also engaged in the manufacture of sash, doors and blinds in Crown Point, New York.

IV. Martha E. Lindsay, born March 14, 1833, in Schroon, New York; married Jones Tompkins, born June 2, 1826, a younger brother to John Tompkins, who married Margaret Lindsay; Martha E. Lindsay and Jones Tompkins were married in 1849. Just previous to the breaking out of the war Mr. Tompkins went West, and after the war went to Neillsville, Wisconsin, where for a few years he was engaged in lumbering with Freeman D. Lindsay; he afterward went to farming about ten miles north of Neillsville, and is still in that business; she died June 11, 1887.

V. Freeman De Witt Lindsay, born February 19, 1837, in Schroon, New York, enlisted in the One Hundred and Eighteenth New York Volunteer Infantry, and served three years, was mustered out as a sergeant June 13, 1860. His regiment was the first to enter Richmond after the surrender of General R. E. Lee, December 31, 1865. Mr. Lindsay settled in Wisconsin, where he has ever since been engaged in the lumber business. September 15, 1872, he married Clara B. Hubbell, born July 12, 1855, in Waymart, Pennsylvania; since his marriage he has made Neillsville his home; he has been Sheriff of his county, Mayor of Neillsville, and served one term in the Wisconsin Legislature.

VI. Emma Louise Lindsay, born in Schroon, New York, September 27, 1840; died in July, 1855.

(Issue of Euphemy Lindsay and William Johnson.)

I. Van Rensselaer Johnson, born September 2, 1825; married Cornelia Carpenter March 23, 1849.

II. Sarah A. Johnson, born May 9, 1827; married Amos Skidmore March 10, 1846; he died August 24, 1858; December 4, 1860, she married Jerome Boyce; he died May 4, 1864; she lives at Stockbridge, Michigan.

III. Aaron C. Johnson, born June 9, 1829; died October 11, 1849.

IV. Martha Elizabeth Johnson, born February 29, 1832; married Ira W. Howe October 28, 1850; he was born November 4, 1819; is a farmer; lives in Danville, Michigan.

V. Eliza J. Johnson, born June 20, 1834; married November 15, 1854, Elbridge G. Taylor, born January 4, 1826; he is a farmer near Lyndon, Washtenaw county, Michigan.

VI. Mary E. Johnson, born August 3, 1840; died February 28, 1841.

(Issue of Hannah Maria Lindsay and Ira Howard.)

I. Asoph Henry Howard, born in Keeseville, New York, December 31, 1836; married in Onero, Wisconsin, Maria A. Hichins in July, 1860; engaged in the milling business from 1861 to 1874, in Onero, Wisconsin; his wife died in July, 1875; he was a commercial traveler from 1875 to 1879, and afterward was engaged with a commission firm; is now financial secretary of Washington Camp No. 2, P. O. S. of A., and a prominent member of the Chosen Friends, and other orders; lives 2458 Dearborn street, Chicago, Illinois.

II. Julia Elma Howard, born in Addison, Vermont, May 7, 1847; married July 8, 1869, George A. Tyler in Onero, Wisconsin; they have lived in Winneconne, Wisconsin, Neenah, Wisconsin, Detroit, Michigan, and now live in Chicago, Illinois, where he has a barber shop in the Rialto Building; he served as a drummer in the late war.

III. Ira Edwin Howard, born in Addison, Vermont, July 21, 1849; was a student in the Chicago University in 1873; is now a fresco painter in Louisville, Kentucky; he married Carrie Helmerick in Louisville, Kentucky, December 21, 1887.

IV. Maria Josephine Howard, born in Crown Point, New York, April 1, 1852; is an elocutionist, and lives with her mother and brother in Chicago, Illinois.

V. Janette Everest Howard, died in infancy.

VI. Wallace Adelbert Howard, died in infancy.

(Issue of Eliza Doanda Lindsay and Tabor C. Innes.)

I. Harriet M. Innes, born in West Moriah, New York,

January 19, 1834; married John R. Ford March 23, 1858; lives in Neenah, Wisconsin.

II. Mary Helen Innes, born in West Moriah, New York, November 27, 1835; married John Cook in December, 1857; lives in Minneapolis, Minnesota; husband a painter.

III. Eliza A. Innes, born in West Moriah, New York, March 9, 1840; married William E. Ford in September, 1861; he died in Neenah, Wisconsin, in April, 1866; in March, 1875, she married William Servis of Sheboygan Falls, Wisconsin; she died May 11, 1875; husband is a carriage manufacturer.

IV. Charles H. Innes, born in Addison, Vermont, July 8, 1842; married Mary Hales July 4, 1862; died December 18, 1887, in Faulka, Dakota.

V. Wallace Innes, born in February, 1844, in North Hudson, New York; was in the Second Wisconsin Cavalry in the late war, and was drowned in the Gulf of Mexico, while being transported to New York, with other sick soldiers.

VI. Edward Innes, born in North Hudson, New York; married Hattie Hales in 1866; she was a sister to the wife of Charles H. Innes; he died at Lakeside, Minnesota, in 1878.

VII. Albert Innes, born about 1852, in North Hudson, New York; married —— ——; lives in Fargo, Dakota.

VIII. John F. Innes, born April 2, 1853; married —— ——; lives at Bingham Lake, Minnesota.

(Issue of Alexander Lindsay and Harriet Hazzard.)

I. Maria Howard Lindsay, died young.

(Issue of Alexander Lindsay and Sarah A. Keeler.)

II. Julius A. Lindsay, born February 22, 1851, in Malone, New York; married in Fresno, California, October 6, 1884, Nannie Williams; lives in Tulare, California; is cashier of the Bank of Tulare; graduated from the Milwaukee Business College, and is a book-keeping expert; settled in California in 1873. Issue — Edgar Alexander Lindsay, born October 2, 1885.

III. Janette C. Lindsay, died young.

IV. Martha Lindsay, born at Peru, New York, April 15, 1844; graduated from Temple Grove Seminary of Saratoga Springs, New York; in 1870 married Dr. Thomas Ross in San Jose, California, August 27, 1870; he was a graduate of Magill College, Montreal, Canada; she died at Woodland, California, December 19, 1881. Issue — Olita R. Ross, born at Woodland, California, February 12, 1877.

V. Fred. G. Lindsay, born February 5, 1861, in Malone, New York; graduated from the San Francisco School of Pharmacy, November 19, 1883; is a druggist in Tulare, California.

VI. Minnie Lindsay, born in Malone, New York, August 5, 1859; lives in Woodland, California; is a graduate from the schools of Buffalo, New York.

(Issue of Polly Lindsay and Thomas Harrington.)

I. Julia Harrington, born in Dryden; married Leonard Fitch, a farmer, near Dryden, New York.

II. Amanda Harrington.

III. Henrietta Harrington.

IV. Henry Harrington, born near Dryden, New York; married —— ——; is a farmer near Dryden, New York.

(Issue of Betsy Lindsay and Jonathan Quimby.)

I. John W. Quimby, born in Tompkins county, New York; married Mary J. Whitlock of Corning, New York; is a lumberman.

II. Charles Quimby.

III. Allen Quimby.

IV. Sylvester Quimby, born in Tompkins county, New York, is dead.

V. Harriet Quimby, born in Tompkins county, New York married James Shaffer, a farmer in Michigan.

VI. William Quimby, born in Tompkins county, New York; married; lives in Corning, New York.

(Issue of John Lindsay and Susan Stickler.)

I. Libbie Lindsay, born in Caton, New York; married —— ——; lives in Michigan.

(Issue of Susan Lindsay and Joseph Smith.)

I. Alph. Smith, born in Dryden, New York, in 1837; married Ada Howard of Caton, New York; is a farmer near Caton.

II. Emma Smith, born in 1839, near Dryden, New York; married Albert Lawrence; lives in Minneapolis, Minnesota.

III. Sarah Smith, born in 1841, in Dryden, New York; married Levi Force in Caton, New York; husband was a farmer, and died in 1881 in Corning; she still lives in Corning.

IV. Frank Smith, born in 1843, in Dryden, New York; married Sarah Cole of Caton, New York; is a tobacco raiser near Painted Post, New York.

V. Sophia Smith, born in Dryden, New York, in 1845; lives in Corning, New York.

VI. Melvina Smith, born in Dryden, New York, in 1847; married —— ——; lives in Minnesota.

VII. Mary Smith, born in 1849, in Dryden, New York; died when thirteen years of age.

VIII. Augusta Smith, born in 1851, in Dryden, New York; married Snieral F. Thrawl, a farmer in Corning, New York.

IX. Elmira Smith, born in Dryden in 1853; lives in Corning, New York.

(Issue of Allen Lindsay and Hannah Snyder.)

I. Horace Lindsay, born January 22, 1837, in Dryden, New York; married Clarissa Simonds in Caton, New York,

April, 1859; he was a farmer, and died in Caton February 22, 1871.

II. Levi Lindsay, born November 15, 1839, in Corning, New York; married Adeline Stickler in Big Flatts, New York, in May, 1867; was a farmer, and died August 19, 1876.

III. Charlotte H. Lindsay, born December 10, 1844, in Caton, New York; married Alphonzo Craus October 12, 1862, in Addison, New York; he is a farmer near Muscoda, Wisconsin.

IV. Hannah Lindsay, born November 30, 1846, in Corning, New York; died when sixteen years of age.

(Issue of Allen Lindsay and Harriet Benson.)

V. Helen Lindsay, born in Caton, New York, August 30, 1849; married William Rogers December 20, 1875, in Caton, New York; he is a farmer near Caton.

(Issue of Rachel Lindsay and Samuel Mitchell.)

I. Rachel Mitchell, born in Tompkins county, New York; married Mr. Beard, and lives in Ohio.

II. Helen Mitchell, born in Tompkins county, New York; lives in Ohio.

III. Eliza Mitchell, born in Tompkins county, New York.

(Issue of Ann Lindsay and Levi Force.)

I. Oscar Force, born in Caton, New York; married Francis Wolcott of Caton; is a farmer, and lives near Caton, New York.

II. Edwin Force, born in Caton, New York; married Charlotte Bidler; was drowned; was twin brother to Edward.

III. Edward Force, born in Caton, New York; twin brother to Edwin; married Julia Conklin; is a farmer near Caton, New York.

IV. Artemus Ford, born in Caton, Steuben county, New York; married Hattie Burt of Corning, New York; is a farmer near Caton.

V. Alice Force, born in Caton, New York; married Joseph Thurber of Caton; husband is a farmer near Caton, New York.

(Issue of Merritt Lindsay and Emeline Abgar.)

I. Adeline Lindsay, born in Caton, New York; married William Vandmark of Mottville, New York; husband is a manufacturer of woolen goods in Mottville, New York.

II. Amelia Lindsay, born in Caton, New York; married Wilson Pierce, a farmer, and lives in Cattaraugus county, New York.

III. Justus Lindsay, born in Caton, New York; married —— ———; is a farmer near Big Flatts, New York.

IV. Mary Lindsay, born in Caton, New York; married William Smork of Corning, New York; died in 1886, and her husband still lives in Corning.

(Issue of Daniel Lindsay and Lorena Decker.)

I. Ed. Lindsay, born in Corning, New York; lives in Dean's Corners, New York.

II. El. Lindsay, born in Corning, New York; lives in Dean's Corners, New York.

(Issue of Loretta Lindsay and John Vero.)

I. Eliza Vero, born in Corning, New York; lives in Woodhull, New York.

II. Elizabeth Vero, born in Corning, New York; lives in Woodhull, New York.

III. John Vero, born in Corning, New York; lives in Woodhull, New York.

(Issue of Loretta Lindsay and Oliver Smith.)

IV. Emma Smith, born in Corning, New York; married; lives in Corning, New York.

(Issue of William Lindsay and Adeline Stickler.)

I. Agnes Lindsay, born in Corning, New York, in 1857; married Henry Stickler of Big Flatts, New York; now a tobacco raiser near Cameron Mills, New York.

II. Della Lindsay, born in 1859 in Corning, New York; married Leroy Rogers of Tompkins county, New York; lives in Towanda, New York.

(Issue of James Lindsay and Alice Decker.)

I. Ella Lindsay, born in Corning, New York; married —— ——; lives in ——, New York.

(Issue of Harriet Lindsay and Henry Grant.)

I. Ida Grant, born in Corning, New York; married —— ——; lives in Corning, New York.

(Issue of Harriet Lindsay and Isaac Rose.)

II. Ezra Rose, born in Corning, New York.

III. Polly Rose, born in Corning, New York.

IV. Nettie Rose, born in Corning, New York.

(Issue of Lydia Lindsay and William Vogal.)

I. Mina Vogal, born in Cortland county, New York; married —— ——; lives in Corning, New York.

II. Edith Vogal, born in Cortland county, New York; lives in Corning, New York.

III. Harriet Vogal, born in Corning, New York; lives in Corning, New York.

(Issue of David Hennegen and Polly Peterson.)

I. Alpheus Hennegen, married Sally A. Peterson in 1837, in Upper Canada; died in Elgin, Illinois.

II. Isabel Hennegen, married Samuel Adams of Chautauqua, New York.

III. Betsy Hennegen, married David Folsom.

IV. Manly Hennegen, married —— Brown of Maple Park, Illinois; died in De Kalb county, Illinois.

V. Joseph Hennegen, married —— Kelleby; lives in Sycamore, Illinois.

VI. Jonathan Hennegen, married —— ——; lives in Elgin, Illinois.

VII. Nancy Hennegen, married John Kelleby in Upper Canada.

(Issue of Amelia Peterson and Truman Cleveland.)

I. Reuben Cleveland, born April 13, 1814; married Julia Slausen in Chazy, Clinton county, New York; moved to Chicago, Illinois; was by trade a builder, but held a position in the United States Custom House for several years; died about 1883.

II. Truman Cleveland, died young.

III. Sally A. Cleveland, born April 9, 18—; married —— Denham in Hemmingsford, Lower Canada; from there moved to Coburg, Upper Canada.

IV. Jesse Cleveland, died young.

V. Amelia Cleveland, born August 1, 1823; married William Brophy of Bonhead, Canada West; moved to Chicago about 1847; now living on a farm near McCauleyville, Minnesota.

VI. Susan Cleveland, born September 29, 1824; married James E. Palen of Oswego, New York, in Canada West; lived for ten years in Oswego, and afterward removed to Chicago, where Mr. Palen is a blacksmith; she died in 1862, and is buried in Rose Hill Cemetery.

VII. Truman Cleveland, born in 1826; married Mrs. —— Brisbin; lived and died in Kane county, Illinois.

VIII. Lansing Cleveland, born 1829; died young; never married.

(Issue of Duncan Petersen and —— ——.)

I. Dorothy Petersen.

II. Harriet Petersen, married Zelostus De Long; lives in St. Charles, Illinois.

III. Julia Petersen, married —— ——; lives in Iowa.

IV. Jesse Petersen.

(Issue of Nancy Petersen and Benjamin Brown.)

I. Melissa Brown.

II. Hester Brown.

III. Alonzo Brown.

IV. Joseph Brown.

V. Isaac Brown.

VI. Reuben Brown, married —— Hammond at Campton, Illinois.

VII. Lucretia Brown, married Joseph Bellby.

VIII. Henrietta Brown.

IX. William Brown.

(Issue of Sally A. Petersen and Gilbert Brown.)

I. Nathan F. Petersen; lives in Elgin, Illinois; used to be in the Chicago post-office, and several others.

(Issue of Nathan Petersen and Emily Hall.)

I. Permilla Petersen.

II. Amy Petersen, married John Barker in Genoa, Illinois.

III. Cleveland Petersen, married Miss Quaif; lives in Cherokee, Iowa.

IV. Nicholas Petersen.

V. Sophy Petersen.

VI. Solomon Petersen.

(Issue of Isabel Petersen and Benjamin Hall.)

I. Betsy Hall, married —— Craig.

II. Mary Hall, married —— Penny; lives in Milwaukee, Wisconsin.

III. Phimela Hall.
IV. Evidney Hall.
V. Johiah Hall.
VI. Benjamin Hall.
VII. Henrietta Hall, married —— Bull.
VIII. Peter Hall, married Elmira ———; lives in Chautauqua, New York; died leaving no children.
IX. Polly Hall, married Hiram Rust of Chautauqua, New York.
X. Maria Hall, married Daniel Mitchell of Chautauqua, New York.

(Issue of Elizabeth Petersen and Thomas Hall.)

I. Nicholas Hall, married —— ——.
II. Firilly Hall, married —— Hosford; kept hotel in Malone, New York.
III. Truman Hall.
IV. Delia Hall, married John Gregg; moved to Milwaukee, Wisconsin, where her husband kept hotel.
V. Johiel Hall.
VI. Betsy Hall, married —— Gleason, a ship-carpenter; went to live in Milwaukee, Wisconsin.
VII. Isabella Hall.
VIII. Evidney Hall.
IX. Benjamin Hall.
X. William Hall.

(Issue of Polly Petersen and David Hennegen.)
(See issue of David Hennegen and Polly Petersen.)

Sixth Generation.

(Issue of Rachel Lindsay and Francis Youngs.)

I. Richard Youngs, born near Coburg, Upper Canada; married Fannie Brown in Kearney, Nebraska; wife died and he married afterward Mary —— in Kearney, Nebraska; is a farmer near Gothenburg, Nebraska.

II. Mary Youngs, born near Coburg, Upper Canada; married George Renwick, a Scotchman, who died in 1875, near Sycamore, Illinois; he was a farmer; she lives near Sycamore, Illinois.

III. Nancy Youngs, born near Coburg; married John Croinese, a gentleman of German descent, born in New York State; they live near Gothenburg, Nebraska.

IV. Katie Youngs, born near Coburg, Upper Canada; married Hambleton Hickox, a farmer in Malta, Illinois; they live in Kearney, Nebraska.

V. Elizabeth Youngs, born in Kane county, Illinois; married Eugene Hickox, a brother to Hambleton Hickox.

VI. Walter Youngs, born in Kane county, Illinois; married in Springfield, Illinois; is a druggist in Springfield, Illinois.

VII. Jane Youngs, born in Kane county, Illinois; married Marion Jacox, a farmer; lives in Gothenburg, Nebraska.

VIII. Alonzo Youngs, born in Kane county, Illinois; never married; lives near Gothenburg, Nebraska.

(Issue of Amasa Lindsay and Samantha Collier.)

I. Edwin Lindsay; lives in Sherman county, Nebraska.

(Issue of Clark Lindsay and Sarah Glenn.)

I. Julia A. Lindsay, born May 28, 1851; married D. C. Hetrick in February, 1874; lives in Ripley, Illinois.

II. Richard H. Lindsay, born August 31, 1854, at Mound Station, Illinois; lives in Ripley, Illinois.

III. Genevieve A. Lindsay, born August 25, 1858, in Adams county, Illinois; married Henry Hetrick, now dead, March 5, 1875.

IV. William A. Lindsay, born April 24, 1860, near Mound Station, Illinois; lives at Ripley, Illinois.

V. Mary E. Lindsay, born July 15, 1864, near Mound Station; lives at Ripley, Illinois.

VI. Charles F. Lindsay, born May 29, 1868, near Mound Station; lives at Ripley, Illinois.

VII. Frederick L. Lindsay, born April 5, 1871, near Mound Station, Illinois; lives at Ripley, Illinois.

(Issue of Lewis Lindsay and Isabel Cole.)

I. Chester Lindsay, married in California; a miner; lives in Sacramento, California.

II. Hiram Lindsay; a miner; lives in Sacramento, California.

(Issue of Alexander Lindsay and Amy Carpenter.)

I. Louise Lindsay, born in Kane county, Illinois; married Seth Conover; lives in Plymouth, Wisconsin, where her husband is in the cheese business.

II. Imogene Lindsay, born in Plymouth, Wisconsin; married Edwin Gardiner, a farmer near Plymouth, Wisconsin.

III. Jacob Lindsay, born near Plymouth, Wisconsin; married —— Cady; she died, and he afterward married —— ——; is a cheese dealer in Sheboygan, Wisconsin.

IV. Lydia Lindsay, born near Plymouth, Wisconsin; married Asa Cady; he died in Plymouth, Wisconsin.

V. Mary Lindsay, born near Plymouth, Wisconsin; married Frank Eastman; he is a gardener near Sheboygan Falls, Wisconsin.

(Issue of Margaret Lindsay and Elisha Badger.)

I. Anna Badger, born in De Kalb county, Illinois, at Mayfield; married George Price, a farmer; lives in Fayette county, Iowa.

II. Horace Badger, born in De Kalb county, Illinois, near Mayfield; married Libby Ross; he is a farmer near Smithfield, Iowa, and is about to embark in the flour and feed business in Kansas city, Missouri.

III. Josephine Badger, born near Mayfield, De Kalb county, Illinois ; married Lafayette Ross, a farmer in Kansas.

IV. Mary Badger, born in De Kalb county, Illinois ; married George Wilkinson in Fayette county, Iowa ; her husband is a butcher in Olwin, Iowa.

V. Maude Badger, born in De Kalb county, Illinois ; lives with her parents.

VI. Ettie Badger, born in De Kalb county, Illinois ; lives with her parents.

VII. Albert Badger, born in De Kalb county, Illinois ; lives with her parents.

(Issue of William W. Lindsay and Emeline Calhoun.)

I. George Lindsay, born May 18, 1870, in Mayfield, Illinois.

(Issue of Henry Lindsay and Eda Blanchard.)

I. Susan Lindsay, born in Hopkinton, New York, about 1845 ; married —— ——— ; lives in Hopkinton, New York.

(Issue of Hiram Lindsay and Octava Witherell.)

I. Laurena Lindsay, born in Hopkinton, New York, about 1844 ; married Nelson Parker, a farmer near Hopkinton, New York.

II. Eleanor Lindsay, born in Hopkinton, New York, about 1846 ; married John Parker, a farmer near Wrightstown, Wisconsin.

III. George Lindsay, born in Hopkinton, New York, about 1848 ; married —— ———; farmer.

IV. Nelson Lindsay, born in Hopkinton, New York, about 1850 ; married —— ——— ; lives in Hopkinton, New York.

V. Morton Lindsay, born about 1869, near Hopkinton, New York ; lives with her parents.

(Issue of Ezekiel Lindsay and Lorinda Barnes.)

I. Parmelia Lindsay, born February 23, 1845 ; died February 16, 18— ; young.

II. Henry B. Lindsay, born November 1, 1846, near Burlington, Illinois; served three years in the war of the Rebellion, in Company I of the First Wisconsin Cavalry; married Sarah House, a Virginia lady, and lives in Clay Center, Kansas.

III. Melvina M. Lindsay, born April 16, 1848, near Burlington, Illinois; married Torrence Brisbin about 1864, a farmer near Sycamore, Illinois.

IV. Edward E. Lindsay, died young.

(Issue of Ezekiel Lindsay and Emeretta Barnes.)

V. Minard B. Lindsay, born October 10, 1851; drowned when two years and a half old.

VI. George Milford Lindsay, born December 27, 1852; married in 1875, Sarah A. Therman; is a farmer near Greenfield, Iowa.

VII. Milan Sandford Lindsay, born April 15, 1854, near Plato, Illinois; married Emma Myers in Vindland, Wisconsin, December 24, 1880; is an attorney at law and president of the Omaha, Nebraka, Loan and Savings Association.

VIII. Willard Freeman Lindsay, born June 14, 1856, near Bloomfield, Wisconsin; married Nellie Starks in Evanswood, Wisconsin, April 15, 1883; wife died April 13, 1885; he is a farmer near Menlo, Iowa.

IX. Wallace Truman Lindsay, born February 16, 1857, in Bloomfield, Wisconsin; lives in Red Bluff, California.

X. Emma D. Lindsay, born June 28, 1861, in Bloomfield, Wisconsin; married Frank Madel in Oshkosh, Wisconsin; died September 1, 1882; husband is again married and lives in Centreville, Wisconsin.

XI. Cora A. Lindsay, born February 21, 1864, in Bloomfield, Wisconsin; died young.

XII. Dora M. Lindsay, born March 16, 1867, near Bloomfield, Wisconsin; died September 12, 1886, in Oshkosh, Wisconsin.

(Issue of Harriet Lindsay and Nelson Witherell.)

I. Hannah Witherell, born near Hopkinton, New York; married George Wood, a farmer; they live in Northern Kansas.

II. Henry Witherell, born in Hopkinton, New York; married Mary Clark in Sun Prairie, Wisconsin; is a farmer near Sun Prairie.

III. Maria Witherell, born in Hopkinton, New York; lives with her parents.

(Issue of John Lindsay and Jane Parker.)

I. Mary J. Lindsay, born in Stockholm, New York, March 4, 1854; died in Hopkinton, New York, October 9, 1865.

II. Katie E. Lindsay, born in Hopkinton, New York, November 26, 1855; married January 11, 1873, Philo G. Henderson, a mechanic; he died in Hopkinton, February 17, 1886; she lives in Lowell, Massachusetts.

III. Ella C. Lindsay, born in Hopkinton, New York, August 14, 1857; married July 4, 1883, Levi S. Whitcomb, an overseer in a thread mill in Holyoke, Massachusetts.

IV. John F. Lindsay, born in Hopkinton, New York, June 16, 1860; married in Hopkinton, New York, in 1882, Vesta D. Livermore of Hopkinton; she died in 1883; October 19, 1886, he married Hattie M. Smith of Hopkinton; is a farmer.

V. Fred. D. Lindsay, born in Hopkinton, New York, June 3, 1853; married Nellie M. Ring of Boston, Massachusetts, June 29, 1886; he is in the employ of the American Express Company in Holyoke, Massachusetts.

VI. Carrie M. Lindsay, born in Hopkinton, New York, June 15, 1865; is a school teacher in Portland, Oregon.

VII. Jennie I. Lindsay, born in Hopkinton, New York, December 10, 1871, and is now attending the State Normal and Training School at Potsdam, New York.

VIII. Mabel R. Lindsay, born in Hopkinton, New York, March 12, 1874; lives with her mother.

IX. Madie D. Lindsay, born in Hopkinton, New York, March 18, 1876; lives with her mother.

(Issue of Charity Lindsay and William Prince.)

I. John Prince, born near Hopkinton, New York, September 17, 1855; married Sarah A. Miller July 3, 1883; lives near Hopkinton, New York, on a farm.

II. Hiram Prince, born in Hopkinton, New York, May 30, 1858; died in November, 1870.

(Issue of George Lindsay and Fannie Hayden.)

I. Eva Lindsay, born in Hopkinton, New York; married Nelson Parker; lives in Cleveland, Ohio.

II. —— ——.

III. —— ——.

IV. —— ——.

(Issue of Savilla Lindsay and Horace Powers.)

I. Frank Forrest Powers, born August 12, 1857, in De Kalb, Illinois; married in Denver, Colorado, September 22, 1884; is a farmer in Weld county, Colorado.

(Issue of Richard Lindsay and Susannah Petersen.)

Willard Lindsay, born in Campton, Illinois, —, ——; married — — ———; is a farmer near Campton.

(Issue of Caroline Lindsay and Richard Pendegast.)

I. George Pendegast, born near Clark, Upper Canada; married in Chicago; is a hardware merchant in Chicago, Illinois.

II. —— ——.

III. —— ——.

(Issue of Robert Lindsay and Amanda Locey.)

I. John Lindsay, married —— Orchard; is a farmer near Rudd, Iowa.

III. —— Lindsay, lives near Rudd, Iowa.
IV. Robert Lindsay, lives near Rudd, Iowa.

(Issue of William Lindsay and Jessie.)

I. —— ——.
II. —— ——.
III. —— ——.
IV. —— ——.

(Issue of Betsy Lindsay and O'Callahan McCarty.)

I. —— ——.
II. —— ——.

(Issue of Hannah Brisbin and Joseph Roseberry.)

I. Joseph Roseberry, married —— ——; lives in California.

II. Daniel Roseberry, married —— Sammas; is a blacksmith in Iowa.

III. Alexander Roseberry, married —— ——; is a grocer in Hampshire, Illinois.

IV. Jane Roseberry, married —— Westgarth, an Englishman, a farmer; he died; she lives in Denver, Colorado.

V. James Roseberry.
VI. Rachel Roseberry.
VII. —— ——.
VIII. —— ——.

(Issue of Daniel Brisbin and Louise.)

I. Levi Brisbin, married —— ——; lives in Lodi, Illinois; a fine musician.

II. George Brisbin, lives in Lodi, Illinois; a fine musician.

III. Sylva Brisbin, married —— ——; lives in Lodi, Illinois; dressmaker.

IV. Savilla Brisbin, married —— Smith; lives in Lodi, Illinois.

V. Belle Brisbin, died 1886.

(Issue of Margaret Brisbin and William Brisbin.)

I. Charles Brisbin, born in Hamilton Township, Northumberland, Ontario, Canada; married Jane Lapp; lives on a farm in Upper Canada; is a farmer.

II. Fields Brisbin, born in Hamilton Township, Northumberland, Ontario, Canada; married Sylvia Staunton; died aged fifty-one, in Kane county, Illinois; wife lives in Sunset, Illinois, where she afterward married Mr. Gage.

III. Ira Brisbin, married Betsy Berkel; lives in Baltimore, near Coburg, Upper Canada, on a farm.

IV. Emily Brisbin, born in Hamilton Township, Northumberland county, Ontario, Canada; married David Smith, a farmer; died aged twenty.

V. Allen Brisbin, born in Hamilton, Northumberland county, Ontario, Canada; married Ann Gallagher; lives in Lansing, Michigan.

VI. Margaret Brisbin, born in Hamilton, Northumberland county, Ontario, Canada; married Thomas Slater, a farmer; lives in Strathray, Ontario, Canada.

VII. William Brisbin, born in Hamilton, Northumberland county, Ontario, Canada; married Ellen Plues; is a farmer in Allenwick, Ontario.

(Issue of Martha Ann Holmes and Quimby.)

I. —— ———, daughter; married; lives in Yankton, Dakota.

(Issue of Jennie McDonald and Cyrus Graves.)

I. —— ———, daughter.

II. —— ———, daughter.

(Issue of Margaret H. Holmes and W. H. Gardner.)

I. Fanny Gardner, born in Homer, Cortland county, New York, December 17, 1861; is an accomplished musician, and teaches in Kindergarten schools.

(Issue of Mary J. Holmes and William J. Leake.)

I. Georgie A. Leake, born in Bloomington, Illinois.
II. Alice L. Leake, born in Bloomington, Illinois.
III. Amasa J. Leake, born in Bloomington, Illinois.
IV. Willis S. Leake, born in Bloomington, Illinois.

(Issue of Martha Lindsay and C. H. Fuller.)

I. Mary Louise Fuller, born April 3, 1863; died March 14, 1864.

II. Nellie Fuller, born August 14, 1864; married Smith Hubbell May 27, 1883; her husband is a lumberman living in Lake George.

(Issue of Mary Ellen Lindsay and William J. Morris.)

I. Nina Morris, born March 29, 1875.
II. Pearl Morris, born July 29, 1879.

(Issue of Evidney De Long and James Van Wert.)

I. James Edgar Van Wert, born in August, 1845; married Libby Lawrence in North Hudson, New York, in 1865.

II. Mary H. Van Wert, died in 1848.

III. Martha Van Wert, married in Malone, New York, Clinton Ladd of Duane, New York, in 1868; died in 1869 in Duane, New York.

IV. Anna Maria Van Wert, born in March, 1857; died in 1858.

V. Frances M. Van Wert, born in March, 1852; married Thomas W. Wing of Burlington, Vermont, in 1872; lived in South Pueblo, Colorado.

VI. Albert Van Wert, born in 1854; married Jennie Ladd of Duane, New York, in 1878; he is a marble cutter by trade, and is farming near Duane, New York.

(Issue of John De Long and Celestia Jordan.)

I. Wilbur De Long, born in North Hudson, New York; lives in Grand Rapids, Michigan.

II. Helen Imogene De Long, born in North Hudson, New York; married in California, Henry Barr, school teacher.

III. Lillian De Long, married Mr. Racraft, and lives in Alma, Michigan.

IV. James M. De Long, born in North Hudson, New York; was in 1887 a student in college in Poughkeepsie, New York.

(Issue of Sarah A. De Long and William Johnson.)

I. A. Wallace Johnson, born at Black Brook, New York, in September, 1853; married Anna F. Claussen January 7, 1885; is a marble manufacturer in Port Howard, Wisconsin.

II. Ida Nellie Johnson, born in March, 1850; married in Beekmanton, New York, Andrew C. Ray; her husband is in the iron business in Beekmanton, New York.

(Issue of Eliza De Long and Lyman Brownell.)

I. Arthur Brownell, born in Malone, New York, in 1856; married in San Jose, California, where he still lives.

II. Died in infancy.

III. Elmer Brownell, born in 1865; school teacher and a member of the San Jose, California, school board.

(Issue of Robert De Long and Sabra Dewey.)

I. Herbert De Long, born in July, 1862, in Malone, New York, and is in the marble business in Malone, New York.

II. Addie May, died aged five years.

III. Dela J., born in Malone in November, 1863; lives in Malone, New York.

IV. Lola Belle De Long, born in 1865; died in 1866.

V. Jennie Sabra De Long, born May 10, 1872.

(Issue of Alexander De Long and Carrie Salone.)

I. Cora De Long, born in Lewis, New York, in 1864.

II. Carrie De Long, born 1868, and died 1870.

III. Robert De Long, born 1870, in Lewis, New York.

IV. Lesslie De Long, born 1873; died in San Jose, California, in 1876.

V. Jene Rachel, born in San Jose, California, in 1876.

(Issue of Martha De Long and Horace Brownell.)

I. Nellie Brownell, born at Essex Junction, Vermont, in 1867.

II. Genevieve Brownell, born at Essex Junction, Vermont, in ——.

III. Myron S. Brownell, born at Essex Junction, Ver mont, in 1877.

IV. Gertrude Brownell, born in 1869; died in 1872.

(Issue of Daniel De Long and Hattie Boyce.)

I. Daniel De Long, born in 1866.

II. Robert De Long, born in 1868, in Hilbert, Wisconsin.

III. Carrie De Long, born in 1870, in Hilbert, Wisconsin.

IV. Ira De Long, born in 1873, in Hilbert, Wisconsin.

V. Nellie De Long, born 1875.

VI. Hattie De Long, born in 1878, in Hilbert, Wisconsin; died in 1879.

VII. Mattie De Long, born in 1882, in Spencer, Wisconsin; died in October, 1884.

(Issue of Helen M. Totman and Daniel Jackson.)

I. Anna Jackson, married Dr. J. L. Fuller of North Creek, Warren county, New York.

(Issue of Henry Totman and Eliza Jackson.)

I. J. E. Totman, married —— ———; lives in La Crosse, Wisconsin.

(Issue of James E. Lindsay and Mary H. Phelps.)

I. Ralph E. Lindsay, born in Davenport, Iowa, August 20, 1861; lives in Davenport, and is in the employ of "Lindsay & Phelps."

II. Millie Lindsay, born in Davenport, Iowa, March 14, 1863; married in February, 1887, Fred Wyman, who is employed by Lindsay & Phelps in Davenport, Iowa.

III. George F. Lindsay, born in Davenport, Iowa, February 27, 1871; lives in Davenport.

(Issue of Margaret Lindsay and John Tompkins.)

I. James R. Tompkins, born November 6, 1849; died October 16, 1852.

II. J. Mott Tompkins, born October 16, 1851; married in Moriah, New York, Manie Farr; he is a farmer near Maple Works, Wisconsin.

(Issue of Margaret Lindsay and James E. Pond.)

III. Freeman C. Pond, born in North Hudson, New York, April 28, 1870; lives with his parents.

(Issue of Martha E. Lindsay and Jones Tompkins.)

I. James E. Tompkins, born July 15, 1850; married in Neillsville, Wisconsin, Frank Raymond, July 4, 1875; is a farmer near Neillsville, Wisconsin.

II. Elias Tompkins, born July 14, 1852; died April 15, 1861.

III. Fred Tompkins, born September 8, 1855; died October 11, 1857.

IV. Ella Tompkins, born October 27, 1857; died December 11, 1857.

(Issue of F. D. Lindsay and Clara B. Hubbell.)

I. Lulu May Lindsay, born July 7, 1873; died February 1, 1878.

II. Elizabeth J., born October 14, 1875; lives with her parents.

III. Nina Joe, born December 29, 1879.

(Issue of Van Rensselaer Johnson and Cornelia Carpenter.)

I. Aaron Churchill Johnson, born July 17, 1850; died April 3, 1882; married Etta Pierce at Leslie, Michigan, March 7, 1877; was a dentist.

(Issue of Sarah A. Johnson and Amos Skidmore.)

I. Josephine E. Skidmore, born July 11, 1848; married John A. Collins, a farmer, October 26, 1867.

II. Clinton Amos Skidmore, born February 18, 1856; is married and lives on a farm in Stockbridge, Ingham county, Michigan.

(Issue of Martha Elizabeth Johnson and Ira W. Howe.)

I. Odel N. Howe, born March 4, 1855; a printer.

II. Edward Everett Howe, born February 23, 1862; a teacher.

III. Carrie E. Howe, born April 24, 1864; a teacher.

IV. Anna E. Howe, born January 30, 1872.

V. Ira W. Howe, born January 1, 1874.

(Issue of Eliza J. Johnson and Elbridge Taylor.)

I. Stephen Taylor, born February 6, 1858; died February 16, 1858.

II. Inez May Taylor, born May 27, 1859; married —— Yocum, a grocer in Jackson, Michigan.

III. Jennie Taylor, born November 15, 1861.

IV. Amos E. Taylor, born May 3, 1864.

V. Susan E. Taylor, born January 14, 1867; died May 11, 1883.

VI. Louise E. Taylor, born May 5, 1869.

VII. Libbie S. Taylor, born February 20, 1873.

(Issue of Harriet M. Innes and John R. Ford.)

I. Mary Eliza Ford, always called Mamie, born April 5, 1860; died October 6, 1887; previous to her death was a stenographer in Minneapolis, Minnesota.

II. Albert Edward Ford, born June 3, 1862; lives in Neenah, Wisconsin.

III. Jessie Richie Ford, born April 28, 1864; died December 18, 1887, in Neenah, Wisconsin.

IV. Hattie Ellen Ford, born August 27, 1866; died October 11, 1875.

(Issue of Mary Helen Innes and John B. Cook.)

I. Helen A. Cook, born in Rosendale, Wisconsin, September, 1863.

II. Wallace Jay Cook, born June, 1865.

(Issue of Eliza A. Innes and William Ford.)

I. Carrie Janet Ford, died September 25, 1875.

II. Anna E. Ford, born August 20, 1866; died in December, 1866.

(Issue of Charles H. Innes and Mary Hales.)

I. Martha Leake Innes, born September, 1863.

II. Tabor C. Innes, born ——, 1865.

III. John F. Innes, born ——, 1868.

IV. William Ford Innes, born ——, 1875.

V. Florence Innes, born ——.

VI. —— ——.

(Issue of Edward C. Innes and Hattie Hales.)

I. Edward C. Innes, born in Minnesota.

(Issue of Albert C. Innes and —— ——.)

I. —— Innes.

II. —— Innes.

(Issue of John F. Innes and —— ——.)

I. —— Innes.

(Issue of Julius A. Lindsay and Nannie Williams.)

I. Edgar Alexander Lindsay, born October 2, 1885, in Fresno, California.

(Issue of Martha Lindsay and Thomas Ross.)

I. Died young.

II. Died young.

III. Died young.

IV. Olita Ross, born February 12, 1877, in Woodland, California; lives with her father, Dr. Thomas Ross.

V. Died young.

(Issue of Julia Harrington and Leonard Fitch.)

I. Charles Fitch, born in Dryden, New York; married —— ———; lives in Dryden, New York.

II. Henry Fitch, born in Dryden, New York; married; lives in Dryden, New York.

III. Mary Fitch, born in Dryden, New York; married; lives in Dryden, New York.

(Issue of John W. Quimby and Mary J. Whitlock.)

I. Elnora Quimby, born in Corning, New York; married —— ———; lives in Cattaraugus county, New York.

II. Elmer Quimby, born in Corning, New York; lives in Cattaraugus county, New York.

III. Adelbert Quimby, born in Corning, New York; lives in Cattaraugus county, New York.

IV. Albert Quimby, born in Corning, New York; twin brother to Adelbert; dead.

V. Elizabeth Quimby, born ———; married —— ———; lives in Cattaraugus county, New York.

VI. Hattie Quimby, born in Corning, New York; married —— ———; lives in Cattaraugus county, New York.

VII. Cora Quimby, born in Corning, New York; married —— Miller, and lives in Corning, New York.

(Issue of Harriet Quimby and James Shaffer.)

I. Libbie Shaffer, born in Michigan, and lives in Michigan.

II. Hattie Shaffer, born in Michigan, and lives in Michigan.

(Issue of William Quimby and —— ——.)

I. Alma Quimby, born in Corning, New York; lives in Corning, New York.

II. Elma Quimby, born in Corning, New York; lives in Corning, New York; twin to Alma.

(Issue of Emma Smith and Albert Lawrence.)

Not known.

(Issue of Frank Smith and Sarah Cral.)

I. Edward Smith, born near Corning, New York; lives at Painted Post, New York.

II. Albert Smith, born near Corning, New York; lives near Painted Post, New York.

(Issue of Augusta Smith and S. Thrawl.)

I. Jessie Thrawl, born in Corning, New York; lives near Corning, New York.

(Issue of Horace Lindsay and Clarissa Simonds.)

I. Edward Lindsay, born in Caton, New York, in 1860; is a carpenter in Caton, New York.

II. Cora Lindsay, born in 1867, in Caton, New York; lives in Corning, New York.

III. Anna Lindsay, born ——; died ——.

(Issue of Levi Lindsay and Adeline Stickler [Lindsay].)

I. Frederick Lindsay, born in Caton, New York, in 1866; married —— ——; lives in Towanda, New York.

II. Maynard Lindsay, died ——.

III. Joseph Lindsay, died ——.

IV. Charles Lindsay.

V. Died in infancy.

VI. Avery Lindsay, born in 1873, in Caton, New York; lives in Towanda, New York.

(Issue of Charlotte Lindsay and Alphonzo Craus.)

I. Flora Craus, born December 10, 1865; married Frank Collins, a farmer, in January, 1881; lives near Twin Bluffs, New York.

II. Frank Craus, born November 9, 1870; lives in Muscoda, Wisconsin; born in Caton, New York.

III. Ada B. Craus, born September 22, 1872, in Addison, New York; lives in Muscoda, Wisconsin.

IV. Mary M. Craus, born in Caton, New York, March 29, 1875; lives in Muscoda, Wisconsin.

V. Myrtle May Craus, born October 12, 1878, in Tompkins county, New York; lives in Muscoda, Wisconsin.

VI. Nellie L. Craus, born June 1, 1880, in Tompkins county, New York; lives in Muscoda, Wisconsin.

VII. Eugene Craus, died ——.

(Issue of Helen Lindsay and William Rogers.)

I. Louis Rogers.

II. Albert Rogers, born in Caton, New York, in 1882.

III. William Rogers, twin brother to Wilbur, born in Caton, New York, in 1883.

IV. Wilbur Rogers, twin brother to William.

(Issue of Oscar Force and Frances Wolcott.)

I. Archibald Force, born in Caton, New York; lives in Caton, New York.

II. Levi Force, born in Caton, New York; lives in Caton, New York.

(Issue of Edward Force and Julia Conklin.)

I. Jennie Force, born in Caton, New York; lives in ——.

II. Edward Force, born in Caton, New York; lives in Caton, New York.

(Issue of Alice Force and Joseph Thurber.)

I. Herbert Thurber, born in Caton, New York; lives in Caton, New York.

II. Edward Thurber, born in Caton, New York; lives in Caton, New York.

III. Martha Thurber, born in Caton, New York; lives in Caton, New York.

(Issue of Artemus Force and Harriet Burt.)

I. Fred Force, born in Caton, New York; lives in Caton, New York.

II. Artemus Force, born in Caton, New York; lives in Caton, New York.

(Issue of Agnes Lindsay and Henry Stickler.)

I. Edward Stickler, born in 1884, in Steuben county, New York.

(Issue of Reuben Cleveland and —— ——.)

I. Amelia Cleveland, born November 12, 1833, in ———; married Lawrence B. Waterman, now dead; married for her second husband —— Wheelon; lives at 263 Florney street, Chicago, Illinois.

II. Esther Cleveland, born December 22, 1835; married George D. Buckley; lives in Oneonta, New York.

III. Silas Ezra Cleveland, born March 16, 1838; married Mary Patrick, and carries on livery business with his son, at 962 West Madison street; has served in the Chicago city council, and is now deputy sheriff of Cook county, Illinois.

IV. Truman D. Cleveland, born January 15, 1840; lives corner of Congress street and Campbell avenue, Chicago, Illinois; is in the paving business; married Jennie Vaughn.

V. Willard Willis Cleveland, born January 16, 1842, and died young.

VI. Reuben F. Cleveland, born February 25, 1844, and died young.

(Issue of Sally A. Cleveland and —— Denham.)

I. Amelia Denham, married George Cook, and lives at Canada Corners, Kane county, Illinois.

II. Emeline Denham, married Frank Hall, who is an extensive farmer near Sycamore, Illinois.

III. Josephene Denham, died young.

(Issue of Amelia Cleveland and William Brophy.)

I. Charles Brophy, married —— Hubb in Picton, Canada, and lives corner of Western avenue and Monroe street, Chicago, Illinois, and is a commercial traveler.

II. Truman W. Brophy, born ——, in Chicago, Illinois, and married Emma Mason; is a dentist at 96 State street, Chicago, Illinois.

III. Reuben C. Brophy, born ——, in Chicago, Illinois; married —— ——; is a physician in Duluth, Minnesota.

IV. Emeretta Brophy, married —— Snell, and lives in Glyndon, Minnesota.

V. George Brophy.

VI. Fred Brophy, died young.

VII. Hattie Brophy, lives with her parents.

(Issue of Susan Cleveland and James E. Palen.)

I. Amelia Palen, born in Oswego, New York; married —— ——, and lives in Detroit, Michigan.

II. Eliza Palen, born in Oswego, New York; married —— Thurston, and lives on Lake street, Chicago, Illinois.

III. Cornelia Palen, born in Canada; married Simeon O. Vaughn, and lives in Chicago, Illinois.

IV. Charles E. Palen, born Oswego, New York, and lives in Iowa; unmarried.

(Issue of Truman Cleveland and Mrs. —— Brisbin.)

I. Armida Cleveland.

II. Lansing Cleveland.

III. Julia Cleveland.

(Issue of Mary Hall and —— Penny.)

I. Fred Penny.

Seventh Generation.

(Issue of Louise Lindsay and Seth Conover.)

I. Amy Conover.
II. Mabel Conover.
III. Frank Conover.
IV. John Conover.

(Issue of Imogene Lindsay and Edwin Gardner.)

I. Alec ——.
II. —— ——.

(Issue of Jacob Lindsay and Ola Cady.)

I. —— ——.
II. —— ——.

(Issue of Mary Lindsay and Frank Eastman.)

I. Seth Eastman.

(Issue of Eleanor Lindsay and John Parker.)

I. Nellie Parker, born at Hopkinton, New York, lives with parents in Wrightstown, Wisconsin.
II. Albert Parker.
III. Octava Parker.

(Issue of Henry Lindsay and Sarah House.)

I. Robert Lindsay.
II. Jane Lindsay.
III. —— ——.
IV. —— ——.

(Issue of Melvina Lindsay and Torrence Brisbin.)

I. John L. Brisbin, born in Sycamore, Illinois.
II. —— ——.
III. —— ——.

(Issue of George Milford Lindsay and Mary A. Therman.)

I. Mary A. Lindsay.
II. Alphonzo Lindsay.

(Issue of Belle Lindsay and Charles Walker.)

I. —— Walker.

(Issue of Edwin Lindsay and —— ——.)

I. —— Lindsay.

(Issue of Frank F. Powers and —— ——.)

I. Forrest Leslie Powers, born June 14, 1885.
II. —— ——, he was born August 4, 1887.

(Issue of Nellie Fuller and Smith Hubbell.)

I. Smith Hubbell, born June 23, 1886, died in infancy.
II. Susan Martha Hubbell, born July 22, 1887.

(Issue of James E. Van Wert and Libby Lawrence.)

I. Jessie Van Wert, born in Burlington, Vermont, in 1875.

II. Fred Van Wert, born ——, twin brother to Albert Van Wert.

III. Albert Van Wert, born ——, twin brother to Fred.

IV. Vance Van Wert.

V. —— ——.

(Issue of Albert Van Wert and Jennie Ladd.)

I. Ethel Lee Van Wert.
II. —— ——.

(Issue of A. Wallace Johnson and Anna Claussen.)

I. Wallace Rae Johnson, born in June, 1886, at Fort Howard, Wisconsin.

(Issue of Ida N. Johnson and Andrew C. Rae.)

I. Jennie W. Rae, born 1874.

(Issue of J. E. Totman and —— ——.)

I. —— Totman, born about 1877.

(Issue of Millie Lindsay and Fred Wyman.)

I. Edith Wyman was born January 5, 1888.

(Issue of J. Mott Tompkins and Manie Farr.)

I. Gracie Tompkins, born 1875.
II. Robert Tompkins, born 1877.
III. Fred Tompkins, born 1880.
IV. Frank Tompkins, born 1882.

(Issue of James E. Tompkins and Frank Raymond.)

I. Earl Tompkins, born 1885.

(Issue of Josephine E. Skidmore and John A. Collins.)

I. ——— ———.
II. ——— ———.

(Issue of Carrie E. Howe and —— Falcher.)

I. Roy Falcher, born 1887.

(Issue of Inez May Taylor and —— Yocum.)

I. Floyd Yocum, born in 1886.

(Issue of Flora Craus and Frank Collins.)

I. Wilbur Collins, born in Newfield, New York, March 10, 1882.

II. May Collins, born December 12, 1883, in Tompkins county, New York.

(Issue of Amelia Cleveland and L. B. Waterman.)

I. Frances Waterman, born March 7, 1882.

(Issue of Esther Cleveland and George D. Buckley.)

I. Blanch Buckley, born September 30, 1872.

(Issue of Silas E. Cleveland and Mary Patrick.)

I. Reuben Cleveland, born January 13, 1864.
II. Alice M. Cleveland, born May 10, 1865.
III. Carrie Cleveland, born July 11, 1867.
IV. Silas E. Cleveland, born September 10, 1874.

(Issue of Truman D. Cleveland and Jennie Vaughn.)

I. Mabel Cleveland, born May 16, 1873.

II. Russell Cleveland, born ——, 1875.
III. Julia Cleveland, born December 25, 1877.

(Issue of Charles Brophy and —— Hubb.)

I. Eva Brophy.
II. Jennie Brophy.
III. Minnie Brophy.
IV. Charles Brophy.
V. William Brophy.

(Issue of Truman W. Brophy and Emma Mason.)

I. Eugenia Brophy.
II. Florence Brophy.
III. Truman W. Brophy, Jr.

(Issue of Reuben C. Brophy and —— ——.)

I. —— ——, a daughter.

(Issue of Emeretta Brophy and —— Snell.)

I. —— ——, died young.

(Issue of Cornelia Palen and Simeon O. Vaughn.)

I. Frederick E. Vaughn, born March 21, 1862; married —— ——; lives 1429 West Jackson street, Chicago, Illinois; is in the employ of Western Division Chicago Railroad Company.
II. Amelia E. Vaughn.
III. Frank Estella Vaughn, married —— Whitney.
IV. Ida Vaughn, married —— ——.

(Issue of Fred. E. Vaughn and —— ——.)

I. —— ——.

(Issue of Ida Vaughn and —— ——.)

I. —— ——, daughter.

NEW JERSEY.

TENAFLY.

A family of the name, residents of this place, deduce their descent from one David Lindsay of Tullyhenan, County Down, Ireland, who came with Monroe from Scotland to Ireland in 1641 to help the Irish Protestants after the massacre of 1641, and obtained the estate of Tullyhenan, at Banbridge, County Down, which still remains in the family and is now the property of Mr. David Lindsay, a first cousin to Mr. Maurice Lindsay of Tenafly, New Jersey.

The family crest is a tent proper, semee of stars, ar, with the motto "astra, castra, numen, lumen, munimen," and the arms, "gules, a fesse chequy, arg, and azure, within a bordure of the third semee of stars," from which I infer that the family are descended from the Lindsays of Balcarres in Scotland, an offshoot of the Crawford Edzell Lindsays, now called the Edzell and Crawford Lindsay, and the present senior house of Lindsay.

David Lindsay the first, of Tullyhenan, had a son David Lindsay, of Tullyhenan, who married Isabella Johnston, daughter of Maurice Johnston, and they had a son Maurice Lindsay of Tullyhenan, who married a Mary Weir, he died in 1815, and he left a son, John Lindsay of Tullyhenan, who died 1858, his wife was a Catherine Crawford, he left a son, George Crawford Lindsay, born 1813, at Tullyhenan, and died at Moorlands, 1885; was justice of peace of Moorlands and Mount Ida, County Down, Ireland; his wife was Jane Woods; he came to America in 1838, but latterly returned to Ireland, where he died; it is not stated where he settled on coming to America. He had six children, Mary Lindsay (Mrs. George Godfrey, of Contrai, Belgium); John Lindsay, married; James Lindsay, who died in 1864; Katherine

Lindsay, who died in infancy; Katherine Lindsay, the second, unmarried; George Crawford Lindsay, married, and Maurice Lindsay, now of *Ercildun*, Tenefly, born in 1853, and who married the 2d of June, 1879, at Weisbaden, Germany, Adelaide Ela, eldest daughter of Hamilton Ela Towle, C. E., of New York, a descendant of the distinguished old Towle family of Rye, New Hampshire.

His children are Edith Lindsay, born October 5, 1880; Gertrude Ela Lindsay, born 10th of August, 1882, and Maurice Hamilton Lindsay, born 18th September, 1886. Maurice Lindsay the first, who married Mary Weir, had a brother David Lindsay, whose children, Mary or Margaret Lindsay and David and James Lindsay, came to America and settled. It is possible, therefore, that their descendants are now in some of our States.

The mother of these children of David Lindsay was a Miss Mullyan of Ireland.

Rahway.

A Mr. Andrew Lindsay from Scotland is a resident of this place. His family is connected by marriage with a member of the firm of W. L. Mershon & Co., printers and electrotypers, of this city.

Elizabeth.

A Mr. Seton C. Lindsay resides here.

PENNSYLVANIA.

Philadelphia.

The history furnished me of this family shows that its early ancestor was Andrew Lindsay, a native of Belfast, Ireland, whose wife's family name was either Lowery or Downing, and that the Lindsay and Lowery or Downing families were rich and flourishing linen manufacturers of that part of Ireland. A member of Andrew Lindsay's family was in Parliament. The said Andrew Lindsay was the youngest of his family, and on his marriage he received considerable aid from his parents; his wife also, from her parents, who sent them thus well provided for, to America. They probably arrived in America almost a century ago; settled in Philadelphia, where Mr. Lindsay opened a store for the sale of Irish linens, but it is said failed through the trickery of a smart Yankee. Three children were born to them in America, William R., Samuel, and Rebecca Lindsay. The first learned the trade of a printer, and became the local editor on the "Cincinnati Daily Commercial," when in its infancy. He died in Cincinnati about 1849, leaving a widow and young son, Joseph W., born January 18, 1846, and who has had a somewhat checkered career. When the Civil war broke out he tried to enlist, but was found too young; he finally went to West Virginia with teamsters, and enlisted for a few months under General G. Rosecrans, as special messenger, carrying messages through the mountains to different commands; after that he returned to Cincinnati, and being older, enlisted in the Thirty-ninth Regiment, Ohio Volunteer Infantry, and during the war was wounded and captured by forest bushwhackers on the Cumberland river, and left the army to recruit.

In September 27, 1865, he was married to Ruth Dennis in Cincinnati; has one child, a son, and is a practicing dentist of that city.

Samuel, second son of Andrew Lindsay, is married, and resides with his family at Edge Hill, Iron county, Missouri.

Rebecca, daughter of Andrew Lindsay, died about five years ago, in Allegheny City, Pennsylvania. Address of Mr. Joseph W. Lindsay, 276 Bremen street, Cincinnati, Ohio.

Data.—From the Pennsylvania Magazine of history and biography, which may prove interesting as a family link to this or other Lindsays, once of Philadelphia. Records of Christ Church, Philadelphia: William Lindsay, buried February 19, 1739-40; Sarah Lindsay, buried August 4, 1752. From the directory of this city I infer there are a good many families of Lindsay and Lindsey residents here, and regret that I have not been furnished with some knowledge respecting their branches of the clan Lindsay.

Riceville.

(Crawford County.)

There is a family of Lindsays living here, who is represented by Mr. Walter R. Lindsay; associate county commissioner and director of the poor of the county, whose parents I believe were or are Robert and Adeline Lindsay of Venango county. Mr. Lindsay has a brother, John M. Lindsay, in Franklin, Pennsylvania, and another, James Lindsay, living near Utica, Pennsylvania. At his suggestion I wrote for further information of the family, to his brother James Lindsay, but my letter brought no reply.

Guilford.

(Franklin County.)

In 1751-2 a James and John Lindsay resided here and owned land; also, in 1756, James, John, Fulton and Mary Lindsay.

History of Franklin county, Pennsylvania, page 153.

Chester.

A James Lindsey lived here with his family (said to be numerous) in 1725, and was of Irish descent, and owned considerable land.

Pennsylvania Magazine of History and Biography.

Cumberland and Blair Counties.

(Latterly of Ohio.)

The gentlemen of this branch who kindly furnished this record, regretted their inability to give a more complete history of their ancestors; many of their forefathers served in the Revolution, and died therein, and their families became scattered through our different States, South and West, and the wants of the rising generations, and locating their homes they said, made them attend little to the preservation of their family history; those who did, perhaps, preserve it, living in the old locality, passed away ere any of the younger members of the family in the far West met or spoke with them, but there has always been a strong tradition in the family that it descends from one of the Lord Lindsays of Scotland. The early ancestor of this branch, David Lindsay, came to America from the North of Ireland, about the time of the Revolution, and was, 'tis said, accompanied by several brothers; he served through the war, and then settled near Carlisle, in Cumberland county, and from this fact, I infer he may have been connected with the Chambersburgh and McConnellsburgh Lindsays, or possibly the Allegheny or Reading Lindsays, who were from the North of Ireland.

He married and had a numerous family, eight sons and seven or eight daughters. I have only been furnished with partial records of two of the sons, Jacob and James, who both served in the war of 1812–13. These sons settled homes in Hollidaysburgh, Blair county, Pennsylvania, where they each reared a numerous family. Two of Jacob Lindsay's sons live in Ohio, and to whose courtesy I am indebted for this brief history of their family — Mr. E. D. Lindsey (they use the "e" in the name) of Mansfield, Ohio, married and has a family, and Mr. J. F. Lindsey, unmarried, of Marion, Ohio.

The following data may be of interest and service to this branch: From history of Cumberland county, Pennsylvania. One of the settlers in Cumberland was Alexander Lindsay, of Scotch descent, and Eliza (Wilt) Lindsay, his wife, of English descent; he died in 1875, leaving eight grown up sons and daughters; one son, H. M. Lindsay, married Elmira Hartman, and now living in Cumberland county. Issue — Hartman (deceased) and Alice M. Another son of J. W. Lindsay married Mary Bell Dewalt in 1883, and lives in Cumberland county. Issue — Bessie Wilt.

Blairsville.

(Indiana County.)

The early ancestor of this family is supposed to have come from Scotland to America about 1785 to 1790, and settled a home near Blairsville; his name was Thomas Lindsay; he married, very likely, in Scotland; his issue were:

1. Sarah, who married a Mr. John Reed, of Indiana county. 2. Ellen, who married a Mr. John Long, and resided in Indiana county. 3. Thomas, who married Sarah A. McGuire (a descendant of the Wycliffes, one of the earliest colonial families of Maryland), and who was born 1791; died April 11, 1870. In 1835 he and his wife emigrated to and settled a home in Rock Island, Illinois. They had issue ten children. 4. James, who emigrated to Mifflin, Ohio, in early part of this century, and was lost knowledge of. 5. Esther, who married a Mr. Scott, and moved to Ohio.

Record of the children of Thomas and Sarah Lindsay, *nee* McGuire, of Rock Island, Illinois.

I. Susan, born 1815, and who married Adam Noel; they resided for a while in Blairsville, then moved to Davenport, Iowa, where she now lives a widow; her husband died in 1872. She has an only child, named Margaret Jane, who married Gillis Woeber, by whom she has issue five children,

William, born August 22, 1858; Ida, born February 10, 1861; Edward, born May 3, 1866; Nionia, born November 11, 1863; Alice, born November 15, 1869; Ida Noel, married Joseph Voly.

II. James, born 1817; he came to Rock Island with his father; married Catherine Murray, December 2, 1856, in St. Louis, and left her a widow in 1884 in Davenport, Iowa, where she lives on the old homestead. Issue, Andrew, born 1859; James A., born 1860; Charles S., born 1863, and now residing with his old mother.

III. Andrew, of him no record furnished.

IV. Ellen, married a Mr. H. Bradley, and issue all deceased.

V. Thomas, who married Mary Finch, and left issue an only child, named Clara, who married George Leonard, and died suddenly, leaving one child, named Belijah, who now resides with her grandparents, Mr. and Mrs. Leonard.

VI. Margaret, who married, first, Lucius Moss, by whom she had issue, one child, named Cornelia, who married, first, Samuel Call, by whom she had issue, Stella and Kittie, who died very young; secondly, O. P. Welch, by whom she had four children. Margaret's second husband was Mr. Mottle, by whom she had issue, Harley A. and Maggie Mottle, who is now a nun in one of the western convents.

VII. Sarah, who married Peter Dubuque, and had no issue.

VIII. Augustine, resides at Jamestown, Dakota; he married Laura Day, in 1856; issue, Addie, born 1857, who is married and has several children, William, Josephine (deceased), George E., who married Melissa Evans, Emma, who married William Lloyd, Augustine, Joseph, Minnie, Edwin, these last three of whom reside with their uncle, Horace Bradley, near Davenport, Iowa.

IX. Silvester, of whom no record.

X. Mary Ann, Mrs. Matthews, of Davenport, Iowa.

McConnellsburgh.

The first of the name and family in this place was Andrew Lindsay, who settled here in 1834; his early ancestor, with two or three brothers, came from Scotland along in the eighteenth century, and settled in the Cumberland valley, between Pennsylvania and Maryland. The brothers' names were Duncan and Renfrew Lindsay. Andrew, the early ancestor, founded a family in Chambersburgh, Pennsylvania. He left a son, John Thomas (who died in Chambersburgh), and Andrew the second, and Margaret. The said Andrew the second, of McConnellsburgh, was one of the first builders of the Philadelphia and Pittsburgh Turnpike Company, and died the president of the company. At the age of eighteen, he was made an adjutant of a Pennsylvania regiment at the battle of Baltimore, when General Ross was killed. He served his country well during the Revolution, and received large grants of land afterward for his valuable services; he died in 1834, leaving a widow, who was Jane Davison of Chambersburgh, and eleven children; in 1838 she and her family emigrated to Peoria, Illinois, where the branch has since flourished. The following is the family record or names of their children:

John T., who preceded the family one or two years to Peoria, practiced law there for a time, and was also an active politician on the side of the Democrats; becoming deaf, he retired to his extensive cattle ranch in Peoria, Knox county, Nebraska, which his sons now principally attend to. He is a gentleman of considerable intelligence, and has written some interesting novels, giving scenes of life and people in the far West and South. His novel, "French Exiles of Louisiana," published by W. B. Smith & Co., New York, and which he kindly sent to me, I read with great interest.

Davison, the second son, resides in McConnellsburgh, Pennsylvania.

James C., resident of Peoria, Illinois, married, and has children; one is Charles C. Lindsay of Des Moines, Iowa.

Hugh and Columbus also live in Illinois.

Joseph A., resides in Cincinnati, Ohio.

The daughters are, Elizabeth, who is married to a Mr. John A. McCoy of Illinois. Jane to a Mr. Isaac Mahan. Cynthia to a Mr. Joseph Barr, and Mary to a Mr. E. Bayden, all of Illinois.

CHAMBERSBURGH.

(In the Cumberland valley.)

The following branch of Lindsays are, in my opinion, a branch of the McConnellsburgh Lindsays, each having ancestors who settled in Chambersburgh, Pennsylvania. This branch knows less, even, of its ancestry than the one mentioned; John Lindsay was its earliest known ancestor; he resided in the above town, was married to Frances Crawford, who survived him many years (he having died comparatively young) and by whom he had eight children:

I. James of Weston, Missouri, deceased; sons, James C. and Edward, deceased.

II. John Vance, married Catharine E. Wolff, who survives him at Chambersburgh; children, John B., of Pittsburgh; Thomas C., William M., Mary E., and Frank. Thomas C. is in business with Joseph Horne & Co., Pittsburgh. William M., with E. A. Ford, Pittsburgh; Mary E. is Mrs. James G. Gordon of Philadelphia; Frank resides in Chambersburgh.

III. Edward, died young.

IV. Elizabeth, married David Bigham; they left three children, residence, Baltimore, viz.: Martha, Mrs. M. B. Clarke; Elizabeth, Mrs. John Reed, and John L. Bigham.

V. Sarah, married J. Smith Grier.*

---

*Omitted. Sarah, the fifth child, who married J. Smith Grier, left three children, John, L., Mary, and Thomas Grier.

VI. Jane, married Frederick Byers and left two children, viz.: Elizabeth, Mrs. John White, and Annie.

VII. Mary, married John D. Grier; children, E. Lindsay, Thomas, deceased, and George Grier of Pittsburgh.

VIII. Rebecca, married William G. Reed; children, William B., Fannie, Mary, Lindsay, Fred B., and Sarah. The first three married; Fannie to the Rev. Frank Newton of India, and Mary to a Mr. M. M. Gardner.

Am indebted for the above record to Mr. John B. Lindsay of Pittsburgh, son of John Vance Lindsay, deceased.

PITTSBURGH.

(Allegheny County.)

The founder of this branch of the Pennsylvania Lindsays was John Lindsay, who came to America, about 1831, from Armagh, County Tyrone, Ireland. Two of his brothers and six sisters preceded him. In all probability he was descended like many of the Lindsays of County Tyrone, from the Houses of Loughry or Cahoo, in that county, which is an offshoot of the Lindsays of the Byres, Scotland (see chart). The Loughry and Cahoo Lindsays were also descended from Thomas Lindsay, the famous Snowden Herald of Queen Mary's time. John Lindsay settled in Pittsburgh and there founded the first iron factory of that city, which he left in a flourishing condition at his death. He married twice; first, Mary Elkins; second, Jane McCause, and left one son to succeed him in his business, and three daughters.

I. James H. Lindsay, married Hannah Lighthill, and has five children, all young; he is a partner in the iron firm of Lindsay & McCutcheon, of Allegheny City, Pennsylvania; he resides in Allegheny City.

II. Martha Lindsay, married the Reverend James Prestley, D. D., a Presbyterian minister, by whom she has a son and daughter. She is a widow and resides with her young children in Ohio.

III. Rebecah Lindsay, married Lesley Orr of Pittsburgh, Pennsylvania, son of Mr. Orr of the old firm in Pittsburgh, "White, Orr & Company." Mr. Lesley Orr and family reside in Allegheny City, Pennsylvania. He has five children, still young.

IV. Mary Elkins Lindsay, married Reverend John R. Paxton, D. D., pastor of the Forty-second Street Presbyterian Church, New York city. She has one daughter and one son.

The following is a record of John Lindsay's two brothers, Thomas and James, and his six sisters, who they married, and their children:

I. Jane Lindsay, Mrs. Andrew Sloan, living in Rankin, Illinois, a lady of advanced years.

II. Thomas Lindsay, who married Mary Clemens, who lives, a widow now, in Allegheny City, Pennsylvania.

III. Mary Lindsay, Mrs. James McCauley, widow, resides with her son, James McCauley, in Illinois. The son is married and has one child.

IV. Rebecah Lindsay, Mrs. James McCutcheon, who resides in Allegheny City, and has one daughter and three sons. Her husband is senior partner of Lindsay & McCutcheon, iron factory, in Allegheny City.

V. Margaret Lindsay, Mrs. Hugh Watson, of Newark, Ohio; one son and one daughter. Her husband is a farmer.

VI. Eliza Lindsay, Mrs. Joseph Patterson, resident of Allegheny City, Pennsylvania. Her husband is a real estate agent. No family.

VII. Ellen Lindsay, Mrs. Parks Brown, resident of Allegheny City, Pennsylvania. Has one daughter and two sons. Her husband is a merchant in the above city.

VIII. James Lindsay (by the second wife), who married Mary Granger. His widow and only son live in Iowa City,

Iowa. Mary Granger was a daughter of Judge Granger of Ohio.

The parents of John Lindsay, who settled in Pittsburgh, Pennsylvania, in 1831, were James Lindsay, and Jane and Martha Osborough, his two wives. They lived and died in County Tyrone, Ireland.

James Lindsay, Sr., had brothers and sisters, some of whose children emigrated to America, viz.: William and John Lindsay, sons of his brother, Mitchel Lindsay, emigrated to Illinois, where likely they have descendants; and William Lindsay, son of his brother, Joseph Lindsay, emigrated to America; and a daughter of his brother, John Lindsay, emigrated to America; as also his uncle, Andrew Lindsay, whom tradition says came over before the Revolution and settled in or near Wheeling, West Virginia. Doubtless descendants of his are in existence in Virginia or elsewhere.

Near Pittsburgh.

(Allegheny County.)

Another family of Lindsays spelled, however, with the "e," trace their early ancestry to this locality, and are perhaps related to the preceding families I have written of who settled here. The tradition, however, in this family, is that their early ancestor came direct from Scotland before the Revolution, but this tradition may arise from the fact that being originally from Scotland ere their ancestor settled in Ireland, and the clan being so old a Scotch one, the elder members dwelt more on this point in their history, and in consequence, posterity has clung to it and so lost trace of their Irish identity. The genealogy of this branch as given to me by one of its members, now settled in Visalia, California, Tipton Lindsey, Esq. (and also by his daughter Kate, who has shown great interest in her family ancestry), who had it from his father in turn is, that David Lindsay (then spelled with the "a" he thinks), emigrated before the Revolutionary war direct from Scotland, and bought and settled a large farm near or where the city of Pittsburgh now is; that here he lived and died, and left four sons, viz.: Hezekiah, who settled in Ohio; David, Jr., of Kentucky (or as one member of this family says who settled in Virginia); Edward, of North Carolina, and William, who was killed in the Revolutionary war at the battle of Guilford Court House, having been under General Morgan, then commanding a branch of General Greene's army. William left two sons, viz.: John, who died in the wilds of Kentucky, or was killed at Boon's Lick, Missouri, unmarried; and William, who lived in Kentucky, and afterward in Indiana, where he died. These two Lindsays had a sister named Sallie, who married a Mr. Williams, and lived in North Carolina, near Guilford Court House; William, who died in Indiana, left sons, John, William, Joshua, Findla, and Boyde, and daughters. These sons, 'tis said, were always fond of relating to their families that they descended from Sir David Lindsay, of Mary Queen of Scots time.

The Lindsays were so numerous in Scotland at this time, and so favored at court, with not a few bearing this title, that it would be difficult to trace back to an ancestor without some territorial significance to guide one, as for instance, his home or estate, Sir David Lindsay of "The Mount," Lord-Lyon-King at Arms, whom you have seen mentioned herein, lived at this period, and was a descendant of the great family of Lindsays of the Byres, whom the Irish Lindsays of County Tyrone, as also mentioned, claim descent from. *He* was the most famous Sir David Lindsay of that day. The following is a record of William Lindsey's five sons:

I. John, of Indiana and Kentucky, who married and had issue, William, Joshua, John, Mark, Nathan, Tipton, and a daughter Elizabeth. William, the elder, married and had issue, George and Nathan Lindsey. Joshua, the second, also married and settled in Kentucky, and had issue, Wayne, Mark, John, Dora, Alice, Jane, Amanda and Lucy. John, the third son, left issue, Charles T., and Lelia Lindsey (now Mrs. Sisson), and Alma and Edwin K. Lindsey. Mark, the fourth son, left no issue. Nathan, the fifth son, left no issue. Tipton, the sixth son, resides in Visalia, California, and has two children, Charles T. and Kate Lindsey. Elizabeth, the daughter, married a Mr. Charles Cole of Indiana, and is a resident of Westville of that State; has two daughters, Adda B. and Ella L. Cole.

II. William, who left no issue.

III. Joshua, a minister of the Gospel, who married and had thirteen children; some were named John, Elizabeth, Mary, Sallie, and Martha Lindsey.

IV. Findla, left no issue.

V. Boyde, left no issue.

There were four daughters of this family, sisters to the above recorded five sons of William Lindsey, but their histories have not been furnished me.

Reading.

(Berks County.)

Another descendant of the Lindsay family of Loughry or Cahoo, County Tyrone, Ireland, is Ninian Lindsay, of County Tyrone, who emigrated to America in 1790, accompanied by three brothers, who, it is stated, moved in different directions South and West, some it is supposed founding families in the city of Philadelphia. Ninian Lindsay settled a home in Reading, Berks county, Pennsylvania, where he raised a large family, and lived to the remarkable age of ninety-two, dying in the year 1859. His sons' names were Robert (dead), George de B. of Pittsburgh, Pennsylvania; Oliver of Washington, Pennsylvania; Lewis of Allegheny City, Pennsylvania (dead), and William K. of Davenport, Iowa (dead).

The last-named gentleman, William K. Lindsay, who lived a while in Wheeling, Virginia, settled in Davenport, Iowa, with his family. He died in that city at an advanced age, April 15, 1885. His children are John B., Ann M., Elizabeth, Ninian, and William K. The eldest, John B. Lindsay, who is in business in Davenport, married in 1857, Adeliza Lewis, and has the following children: Ellinor M. (Mrs. Henry Spalding of Dentor, Texas, with two children), John B., Jr., Cornelia B., and Ninian, the latter residents of Davenport, like their father.

Ninian Lindsay, brother of John B., lives at Tonis River, New Jersey, has a son James, and his brother William K. Lindsay, wife and family, in Bronson, Florida. The sisters: Anna M. is a Mrs. Bryan of Davenport, Iowa, and Elizabeth L. is Mrs. Merrell of Des Moines, Iowa.

William K. Lindsay married in 1868, at Geneseo, Illinois, Miss Ella M. Campbell, by whom he has five children; before moving to Florida, he lived at Stuart, Iowa. The early record which has been furnished me of this family, is that Ninian Lindsay, who came from County Tyrone, Ireland, but born in St. Johnson, Scotland, settled at Reading, Pennsylvania, was the son of Robert Lindsay of County Tyrone, Ireland, who was the son of Hugh Lindsay; Hugh Lindsay being a descendant of Dr. Alexander Lindsay of Cahoo, in County Tyrone, Ireland, who was killed along with his daughter, by a cannon ball, during the siege of Derry, 1688, while looking from the ramparts. The family of Cahoo was a distinguished Irish branch of the Lindsay family; it had amongst its descendants some notable men, both of the bar, in the ministry, and army and navy. It was an offshoot of the Lindsay of Loughry of the same county, which was the senior Irish house of Lindsays; this being the first family of Lindsay planted in Ireland, the founder of which was Robert Lindsay, chief harbinger to James the First of England, and Sixth of Scotland, who obtained a grant of land in Ireland from this monarch. He was a son of the famous Snowden Herald of Scotland, who was Thomas Lindsay, and who held this important position under Queen Mary, and lived to a great age. The Cahoo and Loughry Lindsays descended from the noble house of Lindsays of the Byres, in Scotland, now represented by Sir John Trotter Bethune Lindsay, Earl of Lindsay.

The Lindsays of the Byres are a branch of the Great House of Crawford, the most Ancient House of the Lindsays.

Before ending this record, I must add that in several deeds in Ireland of the Loughry family, William, the third son of Robert, the founder of this family, is described as having gone to parts beyond the sea — to the Colonies, *and to America.* These deeds are of the period of 1667. Very likely his descendants are now in America, and perhaps ignorant of their early forefathers; so far, I cannot deduce any of the branches I know of, as descended from said William Lindsay.

The brothers of Ninian Lindsay of Reading were Robert, John, Hugh, William and Oliver. Three of these came to America with him, as before stated.

DELAWARE.

Newark.

About the early part of this century William, James and Sallie Lindsay emigrated either from Virginia or Maryland to this place, so some of the descendants think; efforts were made by one of this family, Mrs. James Gibson Lindsay, of Philadelphia, *nee* Theodora Jevois, to gain some information respecting its early ancestry, but unfortunately they were futile; despite her enterprise and energy she could find none to assist her in her laudable work; some of the aged relatives were either too old to be interviewed or too far removed to other States to hold conversation with and unable to write their thoughts or recollections down.

Mrs. Lindsay says the tradition in the family is that the early branch of the Clan in America claimed direct descent from the Earls of Balcarres in Scotland, that the family were distinctively Scotch in every way, and their alliances were generally with those of Scotch descent.

William Lindsay had issue an only child, William H. (engineer and architect), born in Newark, in 1819, and who married Cornelia Davis of Philadelphia, and lived for a time in Chester county, Pennsylvania, Wilmington, Delaware, and died at Columbia, South Carolina, January, 1880, leaving a wife and seven grown up children, who are here recorded.

I. William E., married, and has four children; residence, Wilmington, Delaware; in business with the Harland and Hollingsworth Company, ship and car builders of Wilmington.

II. James Gibson, in the iron and steel business, Philadelphia. He married Theodora Jevois, a Philadelphia lady of good old Scotch stock, by whom he has three sons, names not given, and a daughter, Eleanor; residence, 202 St. Mark's Place, West Philadelphia.

III. Mary Virginia, single; residence, 1518 Arch street, Philadelphia.

IV. Emma Cunningham, single; residence, 1518 Arch street, Philadelphia.

V. Albert Gillispie, single; residence, 1518 Arch street, Philadelphia.

VI. Edwin Durang; residence, Charleston, South Carolina.

VII. Cornelia Davis, single; residence, 1518 Arch street, Philadelphia.

Wilmington.

There are some Lindsays and Lindseys here, but I have failed to gather any information about them. The Reverend H. Lindsay was a resident here at one time, and to whom I wrote, but was not fortunate in receiving a reply to my letter.

MARYLAND.

Lindseyville.

(Worcester, formerly part of Somerset County.)

This branch of Maryland Lindsays who also use the "e" in the name, believe their early forefather in America came direct from England, although of Scotch descent; very probably he sailed from England for America, and so gave rise to this tradition in the family. His name was James, and a will supposed to be his, is recorded for probate in the Annapolis court-house, of date 1671. Another will here, is that of Elizabeth Lindsey of 1677, who was of Somerset county, Maryland. The next, that of David Lindsey of Somerset county, 1681. The next, Thomas Lindsey, same county, 1698; the next, David Lindsey, same county, 1720.

James Lindsey was the father of David Lindsey of Somerset county, who died in 1681 (see above), leaving a widow, Sarah, and two sons, one of whom was James Lindsey. This James Lindsey married a Miss Nicholes of Delaware; his will is filed in 1796, at the court-house of Worcester county, Maryland. By this lady he had three children, viz.: Mathias Nicholes, Major, Betsey. Mathias N. Lindsey married Nancy Bevins in 1797, and had issue, Betsey, Harriet, William, Mathias Nicholes. Betsey Lindsey died unmarried; Harriet married a gentleman named Leven Brettingham; William died unmarried; Mathias N. married Anna M. Slocomb of Virginia, by whom he had issue, Henry Clay, Thomas S., Cora Anna, George W., James A.

Henry Clay Lindsey resided in Accomac county, Virginia, and died in Baltimore February 3, 1886; his wife was Amanda Townsend, by whom he had nine children—Washington Irving, and eight others; his widow and children reside in that city. Thomas S. is the only member of the family in the old vicinity; he lives on a portion of the old family estate, which he farms. He married Mary T. F. Collins, by whom he has a daughter, married to Mr. W. D. T. Drummond, and residing in Baltimore.

Cora Anna Lindsey married Dr. George Bishop; died leaving no family.

George W. Lindsey married Eleanor Collins; died leaving no family.

James A. Lindsey, who was a physician, married Laura Meekins; he left a daughter who lives in Baltimore.

Major Lindsey, second son of James Lindsey, married Hetty Townsend, by whom he left three sons, viz.: James, Peter, and Zedok.

Betsey Lindsey, daughter of James Lindsey, and sister to Major Lindsey, married James Given, by whom she left two sons, James L. Givens and David Givens; the first died in Iowa; the other quite young.

Mathias Nicholes Lindsey, the second, who married Anna M. Slocomb of Virginia, was a man of large landed estate in Worcester county, inheriting, as he did, the home of his forefathers. This estate included about four thousand acres of the best land in the county, and had a small village upon it, which was called Lindseyville, having been incorporated by the county. He also owned mills, many vessels, and many negroes, and was in a flourishing condition until the late war, which ruined him, as many others. He became insolvent, lost heart and energy, being now over the prime of life, and gradually sank under his losses, dying about ten years after the war, and was laid to rest beside his fathers in the burying-ground of the old church where the family had long worshiped in, been married, christened, and had the last sad rites performed for them for generations.

The old homestead and land was purchased by the late banker, Mr. Joseph Drexel of New York or Philadelphia. The chart of portion of this land was given by Charles the Second to James Lindsey, or David, his son, September, 1685; said chart is still in possession of the family. Thomas S. Lindsey of Lindseyville, the sole surviving member of the family now in the old vicinity, is described to me as a man of fine personal appearance, about five feet ten, somewhat stout, erect and dignified, with gentle manners, but easily aroused in any just cause, and a favorite with all classes. He is a personal friend of the Hon. George Covington, the member of Congress from his county. He and his wife are sincere lovers of the old neighborhood, and all its Lindsey associations; and desire nothing more than to buy back the old homestead of their family if possible, and end their days here. He and his father used an "e" in the spelling of the name, but his ancestors used the "a." Postal address of Mr. and Mrs. Thomas S. Lindsey, "Kly Grange," Worcester county, Maryland.

Data.— In the last part of the seventeenth century, Worcester county, Maryland, was laid off from Somerset county, which was an immense tract, and included what is now Worcester county, Wicomico county, Sussex county, and Kent county, Delaware. Kent county being quite a large tract also. It is now divided, part in Maryland, part in Delaware.

Charles county, Maryland, is on the other side of the Chesapeake, opposite Fairfax county, Virginia.

Pope's Creek.

(St. Mary's County.)

The tradition in this family is that two brothers, John and Thomas Lindsay, came from England, either before or after the Revolution, and settled at Pope's Creek, Maryland; Thomas Lindsay married a Miss Frazier; his son, Noble Lindsay, settled in White House, Virginia, during the late war; then moved back to Maryland at its close, and there died; he married and left a family, a son, John Lindsay, who lived and died in Maryland; and a daughter, Rebecca Lindsay (Mrs. Smith), now a resident of Alexandria, Virginia; John Lindsay's widow and son Noble Lindsay, reside also in Alexandria, Virginia; the latter being a merchant there.

Unionville.

(Frederick County.)

The early settler of this family, I am told, came from Scotland. He had a son John Lindsay, who had a son Benjamin Lindsay, who died in 1861, and who left a son Hamilton Lindsay, residence at the above place. For lack of further information I can say nothing more of this branch.

Dublin.

(Hartford County.)

The first ancestor of this family was one Andrew Lindsay, who emigrated from Ireland to America, I am told, and settled in this county; he was drowned in Deer creek October 6, 1786, while returning from an election in Belair, Maryland; his wife was Elizabeth Smith, said to have been a beautiful, accomplished, and most pious woman, by whom he left five children.

I. William, who married a Miss Fisher, and left four sons and four daughters.

II. Andrew, who married a Miss Spedden, and left five sons and two daughters.

III. Robert, who emigrated South or West, and was lost knowledge of.

IV. Jane, who became the first wife of James McCauseland, a native of Ireland.

V. Elizabeth, who became the second wife of the said James McCauseland; there were two sons and eight daughters by these two marriages. One daughter is Miss Maria C. McCauseland of Dublin, who kindly furnished me this record of her family.

VIRGINIA.

Alexandria.

A family here, trace their Lindsay ancestry to one Delilah Lindsay — Mrs. Walter Penn, of Maryland, who came to Virginia and settled in 1829, when a young wife. Her husband was a descendant of the noted William Penn, the founder of Pennsylvania, and both, it is said, traced their ancestry to England. She had several brothers and sisters; one brother — who was very much older than herself — was a minister, the Reverend John Lindsay, who went to England or Scotland, and remained there. One sister married a Doctor Dunlap, another a Mr. Triplett. The family record was unfortunately destroyed in 1856, when Mrs. Delilah Lindsay Penn died of yellow fever. She has a daughter living in the above town with *her* daughter, Mrs. James L. Pettit; Mrs. Pettit's sister, Mrs. Ella Hubert Sanzio of Haymarket, Prince William county, Virginia, kindly furnished me the above fragments of her grandmother's family history, which I hoped she might have added to, but my letter asking for further information brought no reply, much to my regret.

BERRYVILLE.

(Clark County, formerly Frederick County.)

From the tradition in this family of its ancestry, I am strongly led to believe that it is connected in a collateral way with the Northumberland and Fairfax Lindsays. The tradition is that in 1740, two brothers, Thomas and John Lindsay, removed from some part of the lower Potomac, possibly Northumberland, and bought and settled here an immense tract of land known then, as now, as Longmarsh, and were called wealthy farmers of the Shenandoah valley, and that they had a sister who married a Hierome Lindsay Opie, an ancestor, probably, of the Hierome Lindsay Opie who owned a large and elegant farm near Berryville in 1850.

These said two brothers were cotemporary with Robert Lindsay of Northumberland, who removed from there and settled in Fairfax county about 1743, and it is barely possible that the three were brothers, sons of the one father, Opie Lindsay of Northumberland.

The elder of these two brothers, Thomas, married and had two sons named Thomas and John. Thomas Lindsay the second, married a Miss Mary Regan, a lady of considerable personal charms and wealth, by whom he had seven children, who were —

I. Lewis Lindsay, who was born and raised on Longmarsh, but latterly became a resident of Winchester, Virginia, where his fine character, means, and position made him a leading citizen for many years.

In 1860 Mr. Lindsay and family removed to Washington, where, being in poor health, he put himself under medical care, and where he died in 1863. His wife was a Miss Anna (commonly called Nancy) Harrison, a collateral descendant of General Harrison of Revolutionary fame, a lady of most endearing qualities, and who must have been handsome, tall, and queenly in youth, as she certainly bore undoubted evidence of good looks in her old age. She was dignified, yet gentle in her conversation and manners, and surrounded up to the last days of her life at the fine old age of eighty, by a circle of admiring relatives and friends. She passed peacefully away January 10, 1882, at her residence, 920 Fifteenth street, in Washington, D. C. The children of this marriage were, Lewis E., John Harrison, Sidney Carter, Lydia A., Helen Pendleton, and Emma Gould. The sons died unmarried. Sidney Carter, married a surgeon of Baltimore, named Doctor Joseph E. Claggett, by whom she has a daughter, Miss Rose Claggett; the family are residents of Baltimore. Lydia A., not married, and a resident of Washington, D. C. Helen Pendleton married a Mr. Minor Bawsel, and soon afterward removed to Texas, where they were both stricken down with yellow fever and died, leaving three infant children named Edward Everett, Charles M. and Lewis Lindsay Bawsel, who were carefully raised by their aunt, Miss Lydia A. Lindsay, and their grandmother Lindsay, in Washington. Emma Gould, noted for considerable personal attractions, and a married belle for a brief season in Washington, as the wife of General George Peabody Este, died suddenly in the second year of her marriage, October 8, 1870.

II. Hugh Lindsay, died unmarried.

III. Alban Lindsay, died unmarried.

IV. Abraham Lindsay, died unmarried.

V. Mildred Stuart, who married a Mr. Samuel Lauck, a descendant of General Lauck, of the Revolution, by whom she had issue, Peter (who now resides in Culpeper, Culpeper county, Virginia), Lewis, Emily and Rebecca Lauck.

VI. Martha Douglas, who married a Mr. McWilliams and had issue, one son, who died leaving no issue.

VII. Thomas Lindsay, who emigrated with his wife and little family to Kentucky, and was lost knowledge of by his relatives.

John Lindsay, brother of Thomas, who married Miss Mary Regan, and younger son of Thomas Lindsay, the early settler on Longmarsh, married a Miss Sarah Ahriel of Virginia, and had issue, John, who became a captain of the Winchester militia, commanded by Lord Fairfax, and who married and had issue, one child, Sarah Anne, who married a Mr. Showers of Virginia, by whom she had the following children : James, Margaret Anne, Samuel, Charles and Sarah Showers. Post-office of this family is Millwood, Clark county, Virginia.

The history of the first John Lindsay, who was brother to the early settler, is lost to the family. It is supposed he moved to other parts of the country. In this lost branch it is said was preserved the family crest or coat of arms. These Berryville Lindsays use the " e " in the name, owing to the fact that it had for many years been thus corrupted by the clerks of the court in entering wills and other records of the family, and the later members of the family had not paid much attention to the change.

Berry's Ferry.

(Clark County.)

Another family of Lindsays or Lindseys in this county, and residents of Berry's Ferry, a short distance from Berryville, was that of Doctor James Lindsay, a physician, born here in 1809, and who died in March, 1864; by his wife Sarah Lindsey *nee* —— —— of Virginia, he had issue, three sons, Joseph B., John and James Madison, and a daughter; Joseph B. Lindsay became an M. D., like his father, and is, I am told, a fine specimen mentally and physically (even now in his seventieth year), of the clan Lindsay.

In consequence of his abilities and fine character, Governor Thayer of Oregon, during the Indian wars in that State some years since, commissioned him a surgeon with the rank of major, on the staff of Brigadier-General James H. Turner. He also served four years as a surgeon in the Confederate army. He is now a resident and practicing physician of Berry's Ferry, and a widower without children.

John Lindsay married a Miss Yerbey of Virginia, is also a resident of Berry's Ferry, and of the oldest Berry homestead, which was built some hundred years ago, and is yet a marvel of strength and solid beauty of style; has no family. His wife, noted for her loveliness in youth, is even now, in her old age, a lovely-looking lady, and makes a most charming and gracious hostess.

James Madison Lindsay also became an M. D.; he married an heiress, Miss Berry, whose ancestors had possession of nearly the major part of this land around Berryville and Berry's Ferry, by whom he had issue, James W., who was killed at the battle of Upperville, Fauquier county, Virginia, June 23, 1863, while in his twenty-third year (Company D, Stewart's Cavalry); John T., who died of yellow fever in Central America, August 9, 1878, in his twentieth year, while acting as supercargo on board a merchant ship; both unmarried. Josephine Lindsay, who died in childhood in 1862, aged seven years. Sarah M., who is married and lives in Georgia, and George W. Lindsay, who is married and lives occasionally in Baltimore and Berry's Ferry.

These Lindsays, although unable to trace the connection, believe they are allied to the Berryville Lindsays.

Port Royal.

(Caroline County.)

The early forefather of this branch of Virginia Lindsays came over from Scotland to Jamaica, West Indies, about 1720 to 1730, and settled a large plantation in Jamaica. He was a gentleman of means and position, holding for a time during his life, an important official position on that island;

but it is said that he finally lost it owing to a charge of cruelty brought against him, and proven, that of hunting the maroons with bloodhounds, trained for that purpose. Some of the elder members of this family believed that they were connected with the Lindsays of Northumberland and Fairfax counties, and desirous of discovering if this were so, I made search for the affiliation, but failed to discover any connecting link; but I think I have found the connecting chain of the family in this country with that in Scotland.

In volume I, appendix, page 430, of "The Lives of the Lindsays," Lord Lindsay's history of our Scottish ancestors, it appears that the last Lindsay of Blacksolme, or Blackholm in Renfrewshire, also of Balquharrage, Stirling (who were descended from the famous Lindsays of Dunrod), whose name was William Lindsay, was in possession of the above estate in Scotland till 1728, and who finally selling his estate, emigrated to and settled in Jamaica, West Indies.

William's father was named Alexander. From the names, dates, and coincident of settlement in the West Indies, I feel sure that the Jamaica Lindsay and the Lindsay of Blackholm in Scotland were one and the same, and on giving my opinion on the subject to some of this family, they shared in it fully with me. Also see further on, stronger reasons for this supposition. Perhaps character is as true a guide, for the somewhat harsh nature tradition has given to the Jamaica Lindsay, points to his origin from the great but cruel House of Dunrod. It would thus seem that the ferocious spirit of his ancestor, the notorious Sir James Lindsay, the accomplice in the murder of the Red Comyn, still beat through his veins. I insert here a passage in "The Lives of the Lindsays," volume ii, page 290, in reference to the Lindsays of Dunrod;

"The House of Dunrod derived, as before stated, from a younger son of the Lindsays of Cragie and Thurston, maintained for many ages a high station in the west of Scotland, but was doomed ultimately to succumb. Descended from Sir James Lindsay, the accomplice in the murder of the Red Comyn, the 'curse of Caerlaverock' seems to have pursued them for centuries. Their sun set, as it rose, in blood. Their original residence was the Castle of Dunrod, in Renfrewshire, but they afterward removed to Lanarkshire, where the Mains of Kilbride had been their possession ever since the time of Robert the Second, and where their castle is still to be seen in ruins. They dwelt there in opulence and splendor till the beginning of the seventeenth century, when Alexander Lindsay of Dunrod, having 'some way or other,' says Crawford, become engaged in that dreadful and long-lasting feud between the Cunninghams and Montgomeries, killed by a shot out of the window of a farm-house of his own, at Hagton Hill, near Glasgow, Alexander Leckie, of that ilk, who was brother-in-law to Patrick Maxwell of Newark, a great hero, and a very bloody man on the side of the Cunninghams. The murder was never for a long while known, till Dunrod, in his declining days, told and discovered it himself. But as bloodshed always calls for vengeance from Heaven, so it fell heavily on this gentleman; for when he committed that act he had one of the best estates in the west of Scotland, yet from that day forward, it melted away visibly, from him, for in less than twenty years he sold all his estate, for the Laird of Leckie was slain in the year 1600, and he sold the barony of Dunrod in 1619 to Archibald Stewart of Blackhall."

According to "The Lives," Alexander Lindsay sank to the lowest penury, and really wanted bread, but what was offered to him from the charity of his friends. A sad conclusion to the career of one who had once been the haughtiest barons of the west country. He died, it is said, in a barn belonging to one of his former tenants.

Of his two grandsons, John Lindsay, the eldest, traveled to the Indies and was never heard of; and the younger, Robert, became a master-tailor in Edinburgh. I must also state this passage in the family history. During the reign of James the Fourth, the eldest son of David Lindsay of Dunrod (prior to the wicked Alexander), was set aside in the succession, and a younger son, John, preferred. "The disinherited heir acquired the estate of Blacksolm in Renfrewshire, and became the ancestor of a line of Lairds of Blacksolm, *who, on* the ruin of the *de facto* Lairds of Dunrod, assumed *the representation* of that House." Their crest was a withered branch of oak sprouting forth green leaves, with the motto "Mortua vivescunt." The last of them, continues "The Lives," William Lindsay of Blacksolm and Balquharrage, sold his estates about the beginning of the last century, and carried over a considerable stock to Jamaica, *where possibly the representative and chief of the House of Dunrod may still exist amongst his descendants*, if he left any.

It was this concluding sentence that aroused my suspicions as to the probable fact of the Lindsays of Port Royal, Virginia, being the descendants referred to by Lord Lindsay in his history; and on receiving the family pedigree from Miss Virginia Lomax of Warrenton, Virginia, whose mother was a member of the Lindsay family, I was, after perusal, more than certain of it, and hence assume it is so in this record. The eldest male member of this family (in the direct line of lineal descent), who I believe is Captain A. J. Lindsay of St. Louis, elder son of William Lindsay, who married a Miss Newton of Virginia, is, therefore, the representative of the Lindsays of Dunrod, and entitled to the honors and chiefships of this branch of the great Lindsay clan. William Lindsay, the founder of the family who settled in Jamaica, West Indies, married there. He had four sons, three of whom (according to tradition), were killed by the Maroons. The remaining one, William, disposing of the large Jamaica estates, came to Virginia and settled a home at Port Royal, in Caroline county. Previous to this, being of a wandering disposition, he had gone to the Bermudas, then wandered toward Virginia.

Port Royal, in his day, was famed for its society and wealth, and its seaport interest. It was on the Rappahannock. He possessed large tracts of land in this section, and also large flour-mills, called to this day "Lindsay's Mills," although long since passed out of the family. In 1749 or 1750, he married Miss Taliaferro of Virginia; by her he had four sons, no daughters; only *one* son survived him; the others, according to record, having died young and unmarried. The surviving one, William Lindsay, inherited his father's large property; he also possessed a fleet of merchant vessels, which service increased his means immensely; he was fond of travel, and made frequent voyages in his own ships; he lost thirteen in a storm at one time. At the breaking out of hostilities between the Mother country he put his vessels at the command of Virginia, and was appointed a cornet in Colonel Bland's regiment of Virginia State Line, on the 16th June, 1776, served till October 1, 1778, when he was severely wounded and compelled to retire from service for a while. He was afterward appointed major of cavalry in Alexander Spottswood's Legion, raised for the immediate defense of the State.

He married Miss Mattie Fox, a lady of Scotch descent, and lived for the most part with her in Norfolk, where he also had an estate; his health was now much impaired, and he had to travel a good deal on this account. In the summer of 1797, along with his wife, he took a voyage to Newport, Rhode Island, where, on the first of September of the same year, he died; he was buried there in Trinity Churchyard. He left his widow with six children, all young, and a vast estate; he left, as he supposed, a good will and executors, but they administered the estate so badly, and the heirs thought unfairly, that it finally dwindled away to a few negroes for the remaining child when she came of age. The children were:

I. Ann Lindsay, who married Francis Taylor of Virginia (see **). Her daughter, Ann Taylor, a maiden lady, died some years since in Fredericksburgh, Virginia.

II. William Lindsay, colonel of the Second United States Artillery, born in Norfolk, Virginia, died in Alabama in 1838. He married twice; his first wife being a Miss Newton of Norfolk, Virginia, and his second, Miss Motte of South Carolina. By his first wife he had three children, viz.: Virginia, who married a Mr. Wharton of Mississippi, and left a family; Martha, who married twice; first, Mr. Curphew of Alabama; secondly, William W. Lee; left no family; and Andrew Jackson Lindsay, who was educated at West Point, and served as captain in the United States Mounted Riflemen, and resigning at the beginning of the war joined the Southern army; Captain Lindsay also served in the Mexican war. He married Miss Julia Delany of Louisiana, in 1860, by whom he had the following children: Martha Newton, Mrs. Henry von P. Taylor of St. Louis; Mary Anne Lindsay, Catherine Graham Lindsay, John Delany Lindsay, Henry S. Lindsay and Andrew Jackson Lindsay, Jr.

Captain Lindsay and the family are residents of St. Louis, Missouri; by the second wife, Colonel William Lindsay had six children, viz.: Mary Ann, who married Mr. Bacon of Mississippi, and died, leaving twins (see †); Mattie died in

---

** Children of Mrs. Ann Taylor *nee* Lindsay, who married Francis Taylor of Virginia.

I. William Taylor.

II. Emily Taylor, who married Charles Handy of New York.

III. Ann Taylor of Fredericksburgh, Virginia.

IV. Sarah Taylor, who married Doctor Edward Carmichael of Fredericksburgh, Virginia.

III. Mattie Taylor, who married Captain Burk, United States Navy.

---

† Further issue of Colonel William Lindsay, Virginia Lindsay, daughter by his first wife, married first Hickman Lewis, by whom

childhood; Elizabeth, who died a few weeks after marriage; William, who died in childhood in 1834; Mellish Motte Lindsay, who is now a resident of Fulton, Tennessee, with a family; he married Frances Johnson in Noxubee county, Mississippi, in 1865; he was born at Round Botton, Limestone county, Alabama, in 1833; has a son Mellish Motte Lindsay, Jr., born March 13, 1873, in Fulton; and lost a young daughter, Martha, in 1879. Martha the second married her cousin, Dr. R. B. Stark, by whom she left issue, May Stark, who married Captain Rowen, United States Navy; Mattie Stark, who married Captain Poor, United States Navy; Emily Stark, who married Captain Ring, United States Navy; Powhatan Stark, who married Betty Organ; Ann Stark, who married Captain Cunningham; Mrs. Captain Rowen had no issue; Mrs. Captain Poor, a son, Rich Poor, who married Miss Warwick of Richmond, Virginia; Mrs. Captain Ring, a son, Robert Ring; they live on H street, near Seventeenth, Washington, D. C.; Mrs. Captain Cunningham had six children, viz.: Mattie Cunningham, wife of James Steel of Maryland; Sinclair Cunningham married Helen Stark, then

---

she had three children, viz.: Sam F. Lewis; died in Texas; Mary Lewis, married to Joseph Youngblood, Noxubee county, Mississippi; Clark Lewis, married to Hattie Spann in Noxubee county, Mississippi. Secondly, Doctor Spotswood Wharton of Noxubee county, Mississippi, by whom she had three children also, viz.: Elizabeth Wharton (dead); Mattie Wharton, and George Wharton, Professor of Greek, at Clinton College, Mississippi.

Mary Ann Lindsay, also daughter of Colonel William Lindsay, married Milton E. Bacon, May 6, 1856, in Columbus, Mississippi; she was born in New London, Connecticut, April 6, 1830; died September 29, 1859, at Aberdeen, Mississippi. Issue, Mettie Bacon, born in Tuscaloosa county, Alabama, February 24, 1858, married E. R. Oldham of Ripley, Tennessee. Issue, E. R. Oldham, Thomas Oldham, James Oldham.

Thomas J. Bacon, born in same county, February 24, 1858 (twins); married Minnie Landsum in Fulton, Tennessee, in 1883; issue, Milton E. Bacon and Myra Bacon.

a Miss Thompson. May Cunningham married Mr. Thompson. William Cunningham, Robert Cunningham and Lindsay Cunningham.

IV. George Lindsay, who died single.

V. Clement Lindsay, killed at fourteen, in the navy.

VI. Elizabeth Lindsay, who married Major Mann Page Lomax, United States Army, a distinguished gentleman, of one of Virginia's best old families, by whom she had the following children: Jane, Elizabeth, Thomas L., Ellen V., Ann C., Matty V., Julia and Mary; Lindsay Lunsford; William L., Mann P.

Ann C. married Thomas Greer of Virginia; no family. Lindsay L. Lomax, of the United States Army, until the late war, when he entered the Confederate service as major, and became a major-general. He was educated at West Point; married Miss Elizabeth Payne, daughter of Doctor Allen Payne of Virginia, now president of the State Medical College of Georgia. Major-General Lindsay L. Lomax has one child, a daughter, Elizabeth Lindsay Lomax. The Misses Matty Virginia,* Julia L. and May Lomax are single ladies and reside in Warrenton, Virginia, on a lovely little estate there. Four sisters and two of their brothers deceased.

Arms of the Lindsays of Blacksolm as recorded in the Lyon Register, Scotland. Gules a fesse-chequee, arg and az, in chief; a label of three points of the second, the label according to Crawford, " being to indicate that his ancestor was an eldest son of the family of Dunrod, though the succession was put by (past) him. Crest, a withered branch of oak, sprouting forth green leaves. Motto, " Mortua, Vivescunt." If any of the family possess the Arms of their ancestors, a

*I am principally indebted to the kindness of Miss M. Virginia Lomax of Warrenton, Virginia, for this American record of her mother's family; also to Mr. Mellish Motte Lindsay of Fulton, Tennessee.

comparison with the one here described, would, beyond doubt, prove my supposition that it is descended in the way I have set forth in this record, and which I discovered by careful comparisons of names, dates, etc., of the American Lindsays with the Scotch branch.

WILLIAMSBURG.

The descendants of a family who were, and still are, residents of this place, having lost the genealogy of their family, are only able to furnish me these few fragmentary points.

Jesse Lindsay and his wife Justina, who were once of Norfolk, Virginia, some time during the eighteenth century, had a son named Edward Lindsay, who lived in Williamsburg, and served in the war of 1812, and was killed therein when a young man; he left a young widow and three children in Williamsburg; his widow's maiden name was Anne Wilson; the children were—

I. Eliza, who married Mr. Thomas Basher, by whom she had children; a daughter of hers is still living, named Mrs. Hicks, probably in Williamsburg.

II. Edward Brook, who married three times; first, Harriet Bingley; secondly, Mrs. Sarah Bingley; thirdly, Sarah Ann Wave; and has two children living, viz.: Edward Brook, Jr., and Anne Elizabeth Lindsay.

III. Thomas, who married Miss Caroline V. Martin, by whom he had seven children.

1. Mary Anne E., who married Mr. J. Bunting, and had issue, Oscar, Caroline Lindsay, Minnie, Charles Laird, Mary J., Summerville and Lindsay.

2. Edward Joshua (deceased).

3. Jane Frances (deceased).

4. John Sommerville, a most popular and accomplished clergyman of the Episcopal Church, recently of Warrenton, Virginia, and of St. John's Church, West Washington, D. C.,

of St. John's Church, Bridgeport, Connecticut, but now of a church in New Orleans, Louisiana, a vacancy recently accepted by him. Doctor Lindsay has been nominated twice for bishop, and his ever-increasing popularity and winning character, not to mention abilities, will undoubtedly find him a prominent position in the church at no distant day. He married, about 1879, Miss Caroline Smith of Fauquier county, Virginia, by whom he has two children, named Mary Fitzhugh and —— ——.

5. Samuella, who married Charles Olphir of Hanover county, Virginia, by whom she has one child, Thomas Edzell.

6. George Bascome (deceased).

7. Edward Thomas (deceased).

Caroline and Albemarle Counties.

The following genealogy of this branch of Virginia Lindsays was derived from one of its aged members, whom, I was told, was better posted on such matters than others of the family—Mrs. Elizabeth Gordon *nee* Lindsay of Albemarle county (now deceased), a very old lady, I have heard, of remarkable memory and keen interest in life and things. While saying she knew little of her early ancestry, Mrs. Gordon, through her son, Mr. Mason Gordon of Charlottesville, kindly sent me this pedigree. Her grandfather, James Lindsay, lived and died in Caroline county, about twelve miles from Port Royal. Her impression was that two brothers came to Caroline county from near the Chesapeake bay; one was her great-grandfather, and the other was the grandfather of Major William Lindsay, who was a distinguished officer with Light Horse Harry Lee, and a great friend of her father, Colonel Reuben Lindsay; Major Lindsay belonged to the Port Royal, Caroline county, Lindsays, herein recorded, whose early ancestor came direct to Port Royal from Jamaica, West Indies, and was the only surviving son of his father (see preceding genealogy of these Port Royal Lindsays). This impression of the two brothers may doubtless apply to *her* branch, but not to theirs.

Her grandfather, James Lindsay, was born, she thinks, either in Scotland or Caroline county; he married, when very young, Sarah Daniel, by whom he had six sons and three daughters; his death occurred in 1782, in his eighty-second year. He was, says Mrs. Gordon, "a man remarkable for piety and uprightness of character; she remembered, when a girl, she once read to him Burns Cotter's Saturday Night," and on looking up from the book she found tears in his eyes, and he said that the poem recalled to his mind so forcibly what he had often witnessed at his father's, when a boy. She also recollected that a Scottish gentleman by the name of Adam Lindsay paid her father a visit when she was a girl, and gave him a copy of the History of Scotland, written by old Sir David Lindsay of "The Mount."

Sons and daughters of James Lindsay and Sarah Lindsay *nee* Daniel, his wife:

I. Caleb, of whom there is no record.

II. John, settled in Georgia and lost knowledge of.

III. William, of whom there is no record.

IV. Jacob, who is also supposed to have settled in Georgia.

V. Daniel, who married and left four sons, viz.: James, who had issue; Reuben, who left one son; Harry, who left one son; and George, who left no issue.

VI. Colonel Reuben of Albemarle county, who married twice; by his first wife, Mildred, daughter of Colonel John Walker of "Bellvough" in Albemarle, he had two daughters, Sarah and Mildred. The first married her cousin, Captain James Lindsay, elder son of Daniel Lindsay; the second married James Waddell, son of the famous blind preacher of Virginia. By his second wife, who was Hannah

Tedwell of Essex county, Virginia, he had three children, viz.: William, who died young, Elizabeth and Maria. Elizabeth married Mr. Gordon of the fine old family of this name in Albemarle, by whom she had two sons, Captain Charles H. Gordon of Fauquier county, and Mason Gordon, lawyer, Charlottesville, Albemarle county, Virginia. Both are married and have families. Maria married Meriweather Lewis Walker of Albemarle county, by whom she had three children, viz.: Isabella, Mrs. Doctor P. H. Gilmer, now a widow and a resident of the "Louise Home" in Washington, D. C.; Thomas L. Walker, M. D., of Lynchburgh, Virginia; and General Reuben Lindsay Walker, now Superintendent of Construction, State Capitol Board, Austin, Texas.

The three daughters of James and Sarah Lindsay *nee* Daniel were named Elizabeth, Sarah and Mary. The first two both married gentlemen named Coleman, and their descendants are very numerous. Mary married a Mr. O'Neal, and she has two great-great-grandsons, young men, who are Saunders O'Neal of Lynchburg, Virginia, and Albert L. O'Neal of Little Rock, Arkansas. (Data of 1880.)

Miss Sadie Patton of "Bentivoglio," in Albemarle, is a descendant of these Lindsays, her mother having been a granddaughter of James Lindsay, son of Daniel Lindsay, who married Sarah, elder daughter of Colonel Reuben Lindsay of Albemarle.

Rockbridge County.

The founder of this family was James Lindsay, who was the younger son of a wealthy county gentleman of Scotland; he was born, according to the family Bible now in possession of one of his descendants, in September, 1773, at the paternal estate or farm called "Dykehead," Evandale, in Lanarkshire, Scotland, near the great city of Glasgow. On the death of his father, and his elder brother coming into possession of the estate, he concluded to seek his fortunes in America, and emigrated here, and settled in Rockbridge county prior to 1795, where he married, June 30, 1797, Miss Nancy McCampbell, a member of a Scotch Presbyterian family that settled in the valley of Virginia about 1737, and by whom he had four sons and four daughters, whose names, births, deaths, etc., are here recorded from the old family Bible, which data I am indebted for to Mr. Charles Lindsay of "Alone," Rockbridge county; it is through his kindness and courtesy, and likewise through the courtesy of Judge William Lindsay of Frankfort, Kentucky, that I gained this record of the family.

Children of James Lindsay and Nancy Lindsay *nee* McCampbell, his wife:

I. Jane, born March 30, 1798, and married a Mr. Renwick of Virginia, and finally moved to Clinton, Hickman county, Kentucky, where she has descendants living, Robert Renwick of that place being one.

II. William, born January 9, 1801, died November 13, 1829; no record furnished of family, if he had any.

III. Sophia, born March 6, 1803, and married a Mr. Kirkpatrick of Virginia, and also moved to Kentucky.

IV. James Watson, born May 18, 1806, is still living at the good old age of seventy-six; no record furnished of his family, if he has any.

V. Andrew, born October 6, 1809, died July 4, 1883; married twice; first, in February, 1834, Sallie Davidson, of a Scotch-Irish family of the Presbyterian settlement already mentioned; secondly, Mary T. Gilmore, in 1847; by the first he had four children, viz.: William, James, Mary and Sally Lindsay. William Lindsay, the elder son, emigrated to Frankfort, Kentucky, in 1854, while quite a young man; he began the practice of the law there in 1858; served four years in the Army of the Confederation; from 1867–68 as

Senator in the Kentucky Legislature; was eight years Judge of the Kentucky Court of Appeals, the last two years of the term as Chief Justice; and is at present a prominent attorney at law of Frankfort. I have heard most flattering accounts of his abilities and intelligence, his friends' admiration for him, and his gentlemanly and handsome appearance. Judge Lindsay married twice; first, Miss Hetty Semple of Kentucky, by whom he has a daughter named Marion; secondly, Miss Eleanor Holmes, to whom he was married in 1883, in Frankfort, Kentucky. No record furnished me of James, Mary and Sallie Lindsay, his brother and sisters. By the second wife, Andrew Lindsay had four sons, viz.: Marion, Charles (already referred to), Warren and Bruce Lindsay, all residents of Rockbridge county, I believe.

VI. Agnes, born April 4, 1812, and married a Mr. Lackey; no further record furnished.

VII. Mary, born January 20, 1816, and married a Mr. Matur; died January 7, 1856.

VIII. Thomas M., born May 16, 1818, and died July 7, 1877; no record furnished of his family, if he had any.

Danville.

A family of Lindseys (spelled with the "e") living in this place are descended from one Archibald Clark Lindsey, born in Virginia, October 1, 1814; died in North Carolina, June 29, 1862, where he had principally resided in latter years, first in Guilford county, and latterly at Mebansville, where he was associate principal of Binghams School of that place. His father emigrated from Scotland, 'tis said, and settled in Virginia. The issue of Archibald Clark Lindsey were: Archibald Clark Lindsey, born October 4, 1847, and who died June 3, 1873, leaving a widow and two small children, who are still residents of Danville; the elder child, James Voss Lindsey, aged eighteen, is a student of the R. M. College at Ashland; the younger, Grace Lindsey, aged sixteen years, is attending a young ladies' seminary in Staunton. Mr. Lindsey was a prosperous tobacco merchant of Danville for many years, and served during the war (from a tender age) on the Confederate side, along with his brother, Captain Edwin Bingham Lindsey, coming home, as his widow says, with shattered health that was never restored. He served in Company K, Fifth North Carolina Cavalry, Barringer's Brigade, W. H. F. Lee's Division, Army Northern Virginia. His brother, the aforesaid captain, was killed by the last shot fired at Appomattox; he is said to have left a fine war record. His surviving brothers are Nathaniel Lee Lindsey, a farmer of Caswell county, North Carolina, and Walter Lindsey, a farmer in Guilford county, North Carolina. These gentlemen had an aunt named Margaret Lindsey.

Richmond.

Mr. J. L. Lindsay, manufacturer of mill supplies of this city, descends from an Anglo-Scottish or Scottish-Anglo branch. He says: "I was told my great-grandfather went from the North, I infer Scotland, to Lancashire, England, about 1700; he died when my grandfather was very young. I believe my grandfather was born in either Cumberland, England, or Scotland; my father was born near Glasgow, Scotland, where he married Alice Livingston, and shortly after their marriage, in 1833, they, with my grandmother, removed to Lancashire, England, but owing to meeting with some disappointments, they came to America in 1834, and settled a few miles from Bridgeport, Connecticut, where I was born in 1838, and where my parents died when I was very young."

From Mrs. Elizabeth S. Lindsay of this city, I have been kindly furnished with a fragment of her husband's family history, all she knows, she told me. Her late husband was James Garnett Lindsay, the only son of Major Reuben Lindsay of Orange county, Virginia, who was the only son of his father, Adam Lindsay, of Revolutionary fame. The family were, 'tis said, always proud of their ancient name, and claimed descent from one of the Lord Lindsays of Scotland or England, they were uncertain which. The only surviving member of the family is Julia V. Lindsay (Mrs. Stevens), Woodfolks, Orange county, Virginia, to whom I wrote for further history of her family, but did not receive any reply, to my regret.

I believe there are other families of the name in this city, but have failed to ascertain from them any knowledge of their families.

NORTH CAROLINA.

Greensborough.

(Guilford County.)

I am told by those who furnished this record or history of their family, that their first ancestor in America was John Lindsay, who settled in Guilford, then a part of Anson county, between 1725 to 1740, coming to America from the north of Ireland, and that he was of Scotch descent; one member of the family states that he was accompanied to America by one or two sisters. He took out patents for land in the above county, and established a fine farm or plantation here, upon which his sons and some of his grandchildren were born. He married and had two sons, viz.: John and Robert; the elder died single, and Robert perpetuates the family. He married twice; by his first wife he had two children, John and Elizabeth; of the latter, no record. *John* made a home in Davidson county, and married Elizabeth Wilson of Rockbridge, Virginia, by whom he had an immense family, viz.: fourteen children, who were, Samuel, Esther (who married twice, first Mr. Hargrave, then Mr. Clemons), Polly (who married a Mr. Campbell), Robert, Sallie (who married a Mr. Wright, and left issue), John W. (who married Miss E. G. Mock, and had five children, one of whom is W. A. Lindsay of Orinoco, North Carolina), Hugh, Thomas J., Eliza (who married Mr. Overman, and had eight children), Andrew (who married Sally Mock, and had five children), James M. (who married Catherine Clinnard, and had three children), Alexander H., and two others who died in infancy.

The second grandson of John, the early settler, was *Samuel*, by his father's second wife; he married and had issue, Doctor Madison Lindsay and William Lindsay.

His third grandson, *Robert*, settled a fine home at Martinsville, then the county seat of Guilford, and on the site of the battle field. He was a gentleman of handsome person, and great industry and energies, and all he touched or undertook seemed to prosper; he added year by year to his fortune, and would have soon been very wealthy had death not deprived his family of him in his early prime, at the age of thirty-five. He married Miss Harper of the distinguished Maryland family of that name, by whom he left five children, viz.: *Jeduthan* Harper Lindsay, who married a Miss Strange, by whom he had three sons, viz.: Doctor James Early Lindsay of Baltimore, who is married and has one child, Miss Margaret Lindsay; Ernest Lindsay, a resident of the West, and Doctor Edward Lindsay of Greensborough. *Jesse* H. Lindsay, who married a Miss Ellison, by whom he had two daughters, Annette, now Mrs. Colonel Wright, and Sarah, now Mrs. J. A. Gilmer. *Robert Goodoe* Lindsay. *Ann Eliza* Lindsay, who married Mr. John Motley Morehead of the old and noted family of this name in North Carolina, by whom she had eight children, viz.: Letitia M., Mrs. Walker of

Rockingham county, a lady of much ability, I have heard, and the representative of North Carolina, to the "Ladies Mount Vernon Association," she has several children — M. Corinna, Mrs. M. M. Avery, Ann Eliza, Mrs. P. G. Evans, Marie Louise, Mrs. R. L. Pattison; John Lindsay Morehead, married Miss Phiper; Emma Victoria, Mrs. J. A. Gray; J. Turner Morehead, married Miss Connally; Eugene Lindsay Morehead, married Miss Lathrope; Mary T., who married James Turner Morehead (brother to John Motley), by whom she had five children, viz.: Robert Lindsay Morehead, Henry Morehead, who married a Miss Lindsay; Ann Eliza, wife of the Reverend T. Whitfield; James Turner Morehead, and Joseph M. Morehead, who married a Miss Jones.

William, the fourth grandson of the early settler, married and had issue, Pinckney, Doctor Robert, Henry, Doctor Andrew, Lavinia, Amanda and Sarah Lindsay.

Andrew, the fifth grandson of the early settler, married and had issue, Andrew, Nancy, Eliza, Jane, Emily and Julia Lindsay.

David, the sixth grandson of the early settler, married and had issue, Doctor Dillon and Alpheus Lindsay.

Jenny, granddaughter to the early settler, is not recorded as having married.

Bettie and Nancy, the early settler's granddaughters, have no record, but Susan, his youngest granddaughter, married a Doctor Wood, and had issue, Doctor Sidney Wood and Doctor William Wood, late of New Orleans.

Currituck County.

Two brothers, Daniel and Jonathan Lindsay, were the founders of this branch. They came, as far as tradition goes, from somewhere near the Chesapeake bay or Williamsburg, Virginia, a short time after the Revolutionary war, and were, they say, of direct Scotch descent. Each made themselves a home in the above county, and in course of time became two of its most flourishing and well-known citizens; married and raised large families of handsome children, who received the advantages of education, which, on account of the troubled times of the country, their parents had been denied.

Daniel Lindsay was said to have been a remarkably handsome man, "tall, and of noble aspect and bearing," and gifted by nature with undoubted intelligence and brightness, as was also his brother Jonathan, *both* remarkable men of their county. Daniel Lindsay was immensely wealthy at his death, which occurred at an advanced age, in 1837. He left to his family large tracts of land and five hundred slaves in the above county; he was a representative of his county in the State Legislature for many years; his wife was Elizabeth Bray of North Carolina, to whom he was married in 1810. Some of the family spell the name with an "e" instead of in the old way, but this is an innovation, as the elder Lindsays, I am told, used the "a." The children of Daniel Lindsay were Susan, Elizabeth, Jane, Mary, Jonathan B., and Edmund C.

Susan became Mrs. John Barnard; left no children; Elizabeth married Mr. Reed of Durant's Neck, North Carolina, an Englishman, and descendant of the distinguished old family of Durant, and a gentleman of large means.

Jane became the wife of Wilson Corprew of Norfolk county, Virginia, a farmer and lumber merchant, and owner of considerable property.

Mary died unmarried.

Jonathan B. married Miss McDonald, by whom he had three children, Ambrose H., Daniel McD., and Virginia. The elder son, Ambrose H., resides in Portsmouth, Virginia, where he carries on large farming operations, and has seven children, viz.: William C., Jane McD., Jonathan B., Ambrose H., Jr., Addie C., Frank and Parke; all unmarried, except

Jane McD., who is the wife of Ensign Samuel W. Armistead of the United States Navy,

Daniel McD. Lindsay resides in North Carolina; has two sons and one daughter.

Virginia is the wife of W. W. Silvester of Washington, D. C.; has three sons and three daughters.

Edmund C. Lindsay, the younger son of Daniel Lindsay, who lost his father when too young to remember him, settled about thirty-five years ago in Norfolk, Virginia, where he is now in the real estate business. The war deprived him, as well as others of his family, of their large patrimony. He has served as Judge of the Probate Court of his State, and was, prior to the war, and during the war, a commander of cavalry; he married first, a Miss Silvester, daughter of a well-known physician of Norfolk; secondly, a Miss Owens, daughter of a Methodist clergyman of the same city, and has by her quite a family of fine-looking and intelligent young daughters and two growing sons. The elder daughter, Bettie Lu, who was cut off a year or so ago in the bloom of her young womanhood, was a most lovely character; she had one of the sweetest countenances I ever saw; it was, I might say, spirituelle in its beauty, a pure oval face delicately cut, dreamy brown eyes, a pale creamy complexion of remarkable purity, dark brown hair, and a tall, slender, and graceful figure. She had received an excellent education, and was so far advanced in her studies, that at sixteen she began teaching, and at her death she was an employee of the government at Washington, where she had been appointed to a position after a severe examination, from among five hundred applicants, and at the end of a year promoted to a higher grade.

SOUTH CAROLINA.

Waterloo.

Mr. W. L. Lindsay of this place is of Scotch descent; his father, he says, was born in Dundee, Scotland, in 1788, and came to this locality when a boy; he had an uncle in Scotland called David Lindsay. I believe his family are connections of the Fox Lake and Milwaukee, Wisconsin, Lindsays.

GEORGIA.

Matilda S. Lindsay of Georgia, second wife of Mr. Andrew B. Stephens (who was the father of the noted Georgia statesman, Hon. Alexander H. Stephens), was a daughter of Colonel John Lindsay, a Georgia planter of Wilkes county, of Scotch-Irish descent, and a distinguished commander of a Georgia regiment during the Revolution. She had five children by Mr. Stephens, three reached maturity, one of whom is Mr. John Lindsay Stephens, an attorney at law of western Georgia.

ALABAMA.

Tuscumbia.

A family of Scottish-American Lindsays reside here whose late head was Robert B. Lindsay, Esq., at one time Governor of his State, and who filled the honorable position with dignity and credit. He was, I am told, a very handsome man, and of considerable abilities. He was elected the Democratic Governor of Alabama in 1870; after the expiration of his term he retired entirely from political life and settled down in his attractive home in Tuscumbia, where he resided, surrounded by his family, until his death, which, I have heard, was not very long since. In 1854 he married Miss Winston of Alabama, the daughter of a wealthy planter, originally from Virginia, and the sister of the late Governor John A. Winston of Alabama. The issue of the marriage were: Mary K., now Mrs. Robert H. Watkins of Birmingham, Alabama, and whom I once had a charming correspondence with; Minnie Burns, Mattie Isabella and Maude McKnight Lindsay.

Ex-Governor Robert B. Lindsay has a brother, also of Tuscumbia, or not far from here, Doctor David R. Lindsay, a physician, who has a married daughter, Mrs. McGregor, that resides on her plantation home named "Glengerry," at Town Creek, Lawrence county, Alabama; has a husband, and daughters named Florence and Alma.

I have long hoped, from his promise to me, to receive from Doctor D. R. Lindsay a full history of this family, which has taken root like many others in America.

MISSISSIPPI.

Walnut Grove.

There are some Lindsays (they use the "e" in the name) residing in this place, who, I believe, trace their ancestry to Virginia and North Carolina. One of them, a Mr. William F. Lindsey, believes his grandfather moved from Virginia to North Carolina; his father, Thomas C. Lindsey, was born in Nash county, North Carolina, and died in Jackson, Mississippi, during the war, while his son William F. was quite young. Other residents of Walnut Grove, distantly related to this latter Lindsay, are Mrs. Virginia Castul *nee* Lindsey, Mr. J. L. Lindsey and Miss Mattie Lindsey. I addressed letters in reference to their ancestry to some of them, but to my regret failed to get replies.

KENTUCKY.

Boonesborough, Clark and Bourbon Counties.

About 1809 there emigrated from Culpepper county in Virginia, to Boonesborough, Kentucky, a widow and her family of sons and daughters, who doubtless were nearly all adults; this widow was Mrs. Margaret Lindsay *nee* Thomas of Maryland; her husband's name was Thomas Lindsay of Culpepper county, a gentleman of Scotch-Irish descent, whose early ancestor, 'tis said, came to America from the north of Ireland. The family have no record of themselves beyond Thomas Lindsay. By degrees Mrs. Lindsay's sons started out on their own pathway in life, and founded homes of their own in Kentucky, leaving the good and enterprising mother on the early homestead, which she maintained with wonderful cleverness and ability until within a few years of her death at a good old age. She had seven children, Jacob, Reuben, Thomas, Eliza, Nimrod Long, Charles and Elizabeth.

Jacob served in the war of 1812, and died unmarried.

Reuben married in Virginia and left a child; history unknown.

Thomas, who also served in the war of 1812, married Elizabeth Elkins, and settled a home in Clark county of this State; his issue was William and Sallie Lindsay, who both married, histories unknown; William was last heard of in Texas.

Eliza died single.

Nimrod Long appears to have been the bright, particular star of his family, being a gentleman of marked abilities, intelligence and nobility of character. He settled a home in the famous Bourbon county, famous alike for its women, horses and whisky, and soon, through his forethought and enterprise, became the leading stock raiser in this locality; he imported the best breeders from Europe, and spared no expense to improve and beautify his farm and stock; at his death he left one of the finest and best ordered stock farms in the State, I am told. He was a fine specimen of manhood, in person as well as character; a deep and devout believer in religion, and a pillar of his church, and left sincere mourners at his death. His wife was an intelligent and pleasing lady, a native of Kentucky, by the name of Grimes, who brought her husband somewhat of a fortune. The issue of the union was Richard, Volney, Nimrod, Henry Clay, Margaret A., Mary and Henrietta Lindsay; the four sons all married and passed away from earth in their prime; no knowledge has been furnished me of their issue, if they had any.

Margaret A., the elder daughter, married a Mr. Scott, and became a resident of Louisville, Kentucky; she has two accomplished and handsome daughters, Mrs. Rathbone and Mrs. Faulds, both of Kentucky, the former of whom I once had the pleasure of meeting and talking with in Washington, D. C.

Mary, the second daughter, married Mr. Warren Rogers, a gentleman of English descent, and has three children: James (a captain in the Confederate army), single; Lundie, who married Joseph W. Jones, and died young; Alice, who married Colonel Robert Stoner of the Confederate army. Mrs. Mary Lindsay Rogers resides at her beautiful home called "Glenwood" in Bourbon county. The third and youngest daughter of Nimrod Long Lindsay, Henrietta, married, first, Archibald William Hamilton of Montgomery county, Kentucky, who was educated at Oxford and Harvard in England, and who died five years after their union. Their issue: James Carroll, who died in childhood; Archibald William, a colonel in the Southern army; and Ida Penelope Stuart Hamilton, these latter of whom own a beautiful home in Montgomery county, called "Longwood," and a winter villa called "Naples," in Florida. Mrs. Henrietta Lindsay Hamilton next married John S. Williams, respectively a colonel in the Mexican war, general in the Confederate army, and a United States Senator from his

State, Kentucky. These ladies have been described to me as all handsome, accomplished and clever, and a decided ornament to the great Clan of Lindsay.

Charles Lindsay, the sixth child and youngest son of Thomas and Margaret (Thomas) Lindsay, was born in Virginia November 27, 1795, and married Malinda Elkins (sister of Elizabeth, his brother Thomas' wife) August 26, 1826; these ladies were granddaughters of Zacharia Elkins, one of the first pioneer "old ironside Baptist preachers" of Kentucky. The children of Charles and Malinda Elkins Lindsay: William, Thomas, Elizabeth, Mary. William Lindsay, the elder, married Rebecca Scott, and had issue: Thomas, Daniel, Nannie, Willie and Charles Grant. William and his family reside on their fine farm near Lexington, Kentucky. Thomas Lindsay, the second son, died en route to California in 1850, single. Elizabeth, the elder daughter, married D. J. Pendleton, and had issue: John T. J., Charles and Franklin Pierce Pendleton. Mary, the youngest daughter, married William Scott August 27; 1851, and has issue: Lutie and Charles Scott. Both ladies reside in Kentucky.

Elizabeth, last child of Thomas and Margaret (Thomas) Lindsay, married a Mr. Skinner of Kentucky; no issue.

I am of the opinion that this Kentucky branch of the Clan Lindsay descend from some of the numerous brothers Lindsay who came out before or during the war of the Revolution from Ireland, and settling in different parts of Pennsylvania, left children who went from here to many of the Southern and Western States, and settled homes and families.

Heydens Station.

(Near Frankfort and Scott Counties.)

Having been furnished with two or three records of this family, in justice to those who kindly sent each to me, I insert them all.

The first was that the early ancestor of the family, a wealthy Scotch sea-captain, who was lost at sea, had several sons who settled in America long before the Revolution; one in Maryland, twelve miles from Baltimore; some in Virginia, and some in South Carolina. The one who settled in Maryland being the parent tree of this branch, and whose name was Anthony, and who married a daughter of one Lloyd Dorsey of Maryland, he first moved to Pennsylvania, and then to Kentucky, with part of his family, about the year 1784.

The second was that three brothers Lindsay landed in Charleston, South Carolina, *from* Scotland, and that one of the three went to Virginia, whose son emigrated to Kentucky at an early day, and was the founder of this family, his name also being Anthony.

The third was that three brothers came over from Scotland long before the Revolution, one, Anthony Lindsay, settling near Baltimore, the other two going into Virginia; that said Anthony Lindsay was in America long enough before 1775 for his eldest son, John C., to be born and attain sufficient age to serve in the American army. At the close of the Revolution, the family removed from Maryland to Scott county, Kentucky, having bought a farm with the Continental money received for the one in Maryland. He took with him a wife, five sons and three daughters.

In the fourth, the record states that Anthony Lindsay and wife *nee* Dorsey emigrated from Maryland county, Maryland, to Heydens Station on the Kentucky river, just above where Frankfort now stands, in 1784. They had twelve children, viz.:

I. Kate Lindsay, who married her full cousin, John Lindsay of Baltimore county, Maryland, and there resided.

II. John C. Lindsay, who married Sukie Dowden and lived in Henry county, Kentucky, and had children: Kate, Betsey, James Anthony, Eliza, John, Orlando, Joshua, Nat, Hazel and Cyrus.

III. Sallie Lindsay, who married Sam Bartlett, and lived in Virginia, in the Allegheny mountains; issue: Bob and Tom Bartlett.

IV. Nicholas Lindsay, who married Miss Cresenberry; issue: two daughters, and sons Vincent and Ross; the former resided in Kentucky, then in Illinois; the latter died in an Indian block-house in 1812.

V. Anthony Lindsay, who married Alice Cole in Woodford county, Kentucky, in December, 1788, and finally settled a home which was called Lindsay's Station, in Scott county, Kentucky. He was one of the prosperous farmers of his day. His eldest son was General Jesse Lindsay, who served in the war of 1812–13, and who lived in Ghent county, Kentucky, where his family were raised, some of whom are: J. H. Lindsay of Carrollton, Kentucky; Colonel John A. Lindsay of Lindsay, Arkansas; two daughters in Kentucky, one in Illinois and two in Missouri, and the family of his son, R. T. Lindsay, in Pettis county, Missouri. Further children of Anthony: William Lindsay, Lucy, Richard C. Greenberry, Ann (Mrs. Sandram), Sally (Mrs. Cole), Elizabeth (Mrs. Calvert), John C. (father of Benjamin I. Lindsay, lawyer, of Gallatin, Kentucky), Mrs. Ann Grigner of Augusta, Ill., James M., Polly, who married her cousin Charles Lindsay.

VI. Vachel Lindsay, who married Annie Cresenberry in Kentucky, and moved to Dearborne county, Indiana, and died in Gallatin county, Kentucky; issue, Thomas, Sallie, George, Vachel, Nicholas, Elijah, Charles, Polly, John, William. (Vachel is the grandfather of Mrs. Eudora Lindsay South* of Jett, Kentucky.)

---

* Mrs. South has written and published a very pretty and interesting book of her travels in Europe a few years ago, including some lovely poems. She has two brothers, who are physicians in Springfield, Illinois, Vachel C. and Johnson C. Lindsay.

VII. Elizabeth Lindsay, who married Mr. Whitaker, and lived in Shelbyville, Shelby county, Kentucky; issue, six children, names not given.

VIII. Lydia Lindsay, married first, Mr. Whitaker, brother to the above; secondly, Mr. McCrockland; resided in Ohio county, Kentucky; issue by each.

IX. Rachel Lindsay, who married Daniel Applegate in Franklin county, Kentucky, and lived in Henry county, Kentucky, and after husband's death moved to Chariton, Missouri; one son, Lisbon Applegate.

X. Charles Lindsay, who left no family.

XI. Elisha Lindsay, who married Sallie Holmes; lived in Shelby county, Kentucky, and died in Florida; issue, Mahala, Anthony, James, Peggie, Lucinda.

XII. Lucy Lindsay, who married a Mr. Meeks, and moved to Indiana.

COLD SPRING.

(Fifty-four miles south of Newport.)

The early ancestor in America of this family was Thomas Lindsey (they use the "e" in the name), who was born in Ireland, but was of Scotch descent, like all those of the race in Ireland, and who, after residing in Cork for a time, emigrated with his wife Rebecca *nee* Hanie, to America, landing in Philadelphia, October, 1789. From here, he and his wife went to Pittsburgh, where they remained until the spring (possibly they had relatives here, which may have been an inducement to visit this place); they built themselves a boat at Pittsburgh, and came on it to Limestone, now Maysville, Kentucky; stayed here two years, then crossed Licking river, and stayed for a short time near Lexington, and from here removed to Leithe station, on the Licking river, twelve miles back of Newport, Kentucky.

Thomas Lindsay died in 1817, on his farm in Cold Spring, Kentucky, fifty-four miles south of Newport; his wife survived him a long number of years, and then died in 1838, and was buried beside him on the old homestead. They had eleven children; the following is a record of them:

I. Thomas, who married a Miss Colin, and lived at Point Pleasant, Ohio, where he died; issue, seven children: 1. Thomas, who married twice, both wives named Meals; no record of their families, if they left any. 2. George, who married and lived at Point Pleasant, Ohio; issue, Mollie, who married, first, a Mr. Lindsey, then a Mr. Richards, resides at Springfield, Missouri. 3. Benjamin. 4. Rebecca. 5. Janet. 6. Marian. 7. Mary, who married James Noble, who served many years ago as United States Senator from Brookville, Indiana; he died in Washington in 1826; issue, James Sedgewick, Southgate, Kitty and Rebecca Noble.

II. John Brown, born April 21, 1775, came to Newport in 1805, married Maria Noble, January 4, 1806; he built the first brick dwelling in Newport in 1798, ere he came to reside here; the house is yet standing on Frank street. He was Mayor of Newport; died October 21, 1849, aged seventy-four years; his wife died August 9, 1850. They had twelve children: 1. Thomas Noble, born December 22, 1807; married Isabella Weisegar, then Louisa Applegate; he died November 22, 1877; issue, seven children, viz.: General *Daniel W.* Lindsey, who served in our late war, and is now a prominent attorney at law in Frankfort, Kentucky; his wife was Miss Kate Fitch; children, Antoinette, Noble, Henry, Weisegar, and Kate Lindsey. *John B.*, also a lawyer of Frankfort; wife was a Miss Helen Talbot; children, Helen, Maria, Willie, Isabella, Cordelia, Dudley, John, Lilian and Genevieve Lindsey. *Maria*, husband, John Thomas of Lebanon, Kentucky; issue, Owen, Emily, Lucy, John and Daniel Thomas. *Lucy*, husband the Reverend Mr. Blainy, a Presbyterian minister; has issue, two children. *Thomas*, wife was Stella Ralston; lived in Louisville, Kentucky, and has issue. *Bella*, husband Henry Fitch ; lives in Louisville ; has issue, six children. *Joseph*, wife was a Miss Maria Watson ; has issue, five children. 2. Marcus, born November, 1809, died 1810. 3. Rebecca, born 1812 ; married Reverend Joseph Marree, and had eight children. 4. John, born October, 1813 ; died in childhood. 5. Maria, born February, 1814 ; died 1838 ; married Jacob Scoggin ; had one son. 6. Louisa, born November, 1815 ; died in 1840. 7. Emily Christian, born May 28, 1817 ; married Doctor H. L. Ross, by whom she had three childen. 8. James Noble, born December 11, 1818 ; married twice, Mary Price, then Sallie Prettyman ; issue, Sallie, George, Mary Louisa, Augusta, James and Helen Lindsey. 9. Lazanis Noble, born July 15, 1822; married twice, first, Miss Swigert, then Mary J. Fisher ; issue, Mary, Thomas, Emily and Pegrim Lindsey. Mr. Lazanis N. Lindsey and family are residents of Vicksburgh, Mississippi. 10. William Holman, born March 7, 1824 ; died in Nevada in 1860. 11. Henry K., born March 13, 1825 ; married Augusta M. Sewie (now deceased) ; issue, Aurelia (who lives in Ashville, North Carolina), Lizzie M., Henry A. (who lives in Ashville, North Carolina), and Augusta Lindsey. Mr. Henry K. Lindsey is general agent of "The Lancashire Insurance Company" of Cincinnati, Ohio ; he resides across the river at Covington, Kentucky. I am indebted both to him and his daughter Aurelia, for this history of the family, the latter having taken much interest in, and pains to collect as true a genealogy of it as possible. 12. Martha, born June 18, 1828 ; died in 1834.

III. Mary, elder daughter of Thomas and Rebecca Hanie Lindsey, born in Ireland in 1783 ; died in Columbus, Indiana, September 29, 1836 ; married James T. Noble, and had issue, Betscy Noble, who married a Doctor Milton in 1826 ; she died May 4, 1878 ; she left issue, John Lindsey Milton, and nine other children.

IV. Sallie, the second daughter, married Joseph McPike, and left issue, Charlotte McPike, who married first, Doctor Fronnie, then Mr. Caldwell, and she left issue, two children.

V. Rebecca, the third daughter, married Archibald Smith, and left two children.

VI. Marcus, was a great Methodist minister of Marion county, Kentucky; he died in Shelbyville, Kentucky, in 1834; he married a widow named Hardin, by whom he left issue, Kitty, Sarah, Maria and Rebecca Lindsey.

VII. Richard, of Greenville, Indiana, married Nancy McPike (sister of Joseph McPike), and left issue, Thomas, Harriet, Frances, Richard, Nannie, William, Joseph, John, Amelia, and Eliza Lindsey.

VIII. Emily, the fourth daughter, born November, 1782, married Owen Thomas, and had issue, three children, Marion, Lewis, and John Thomas.

IX. Liza, the fifth daughter, died single.

X. James, of near Alexandria, Kentucky, married Mary Beall, and has issue, Janet, Mary, James, Thomas, Ellen, Rebecca, Amaliza, and one other daughter.

XI. Kitty, the sixth daughter, married Captain Ward of the regular army; she died in Columbus, Georgia, in 1872, leaving three children, James, Marcus, and Laura Ward.

TENNESSEE.

Jackson.

A Lindsay, resident of this place—Mr. Edward A. Lindsay, agent for the Western Department of the Hartford Fire Insurance Company—was unable to furnish me with *his* family record, owing, he said, to its having been destroyed by fire many years ago, and its renewal being neglected; having, as he says, relatives in Kentucky and North Carolina, he may possibly see some connecting links of his family with some families herein recorded.

OHIO.

Belmont County, now of Illinois and Missouri.

(Formerly of Pennsylvania.)

James Lindsey (spelled with the "e"), who came over to America as a British soldier in 1776, being of Scotch origin, was the early ancestor of this family. He was taken prisoner by General Washington at Fredericksburgh, Virginia, and at the close of the war settled in some part of Pennsylvania, where he made himself a home and married Miss Elizabeth Moody, of Irish descent, by whom he had five sons and five daughters, who were—

I. John, who married and had a large family; four of his sons are said to be ministers of the Gospel, and are scattered in the West, names and cities not furnished me.

II. Letitia, who married Samuel Clark, and had issue, John, George, Samuel and Eliza (twins), Mary Ann, then Nancy and Lavinia (twins), and Polly, who died young.

III. James, of whom no record.

IV. Mary, who married George Clark and had issue, Mary Ann, George Waterman, and Elizabeth.

V. Rebecca, who married Robert Clark, and had issue, Stansbery, Julius, Joseph, John, Elizabeth, Waterman, Samuel and Caroline.

VI. Robert, who married Miss Rebecca E. Simmons of Morefield, Hardy county, Virginia, where they resided for a while, then emigrated to Belmont county, Ohio, where he died in 1870, leaving her a widow with four sons and one daughter. (See further notice.)

VII. Elizabeth, who probably died single.

VIII. George, who married Miss Alice Hatton, by whom he had issue, Abner, Sarah Jane (deceased), Elizabeth, Mrs. Stout, Rebecca (deceased), Mary Ann, Mrs. Poulson, James (deceased), Maria (deceased), George (deceased), Hulda (deceased), Louise, Mrs. Stewart, Adeline, Mrs. Timberlake, John (deceased). Mrs. Poulson and Mrs. Timberlake reside in Belmont county, Ohio.

IX. Samuel, who married Miss Margaret Hart, and had issue by her, Samuel, Josephus, and Elizabeth.

X. Jane, who married William Bright, and had issue by him, Elizabeth and William.

The children of Robert Lindsey and Rebecca E. Lindsey *nee* Simmons, of Belmont county, Ohio:

I. Mary Elizabeth, who married twice, first, Mr. Kemp, by whom she had issue, Joseph Kemp (deceased), and William L. Kemp, who resides in Brookfield, Missouri; secondly, a Mr. Reeder, by whom she had issue, Mary E., Mrs. Conant (deceased), Rachel M., who resides in Brookfield, Missouri, Rebecca Ann, Mrs. Pancoast of Hyde Park, Missouri, John A. of Brookfield, Missouri, and Lewis L. Reeder (deceased).

II. Thomas L. of Millersburg, Iowa; married and has issue, Mary, Mrs. Hatcher of Leigh, Nebraska; Catherine, Mrs. Watters; Susanna, Mrs. Barrett; Lavinia, Mrs. Chase; George (deceased), Robert (deceased), Rebecca (deceased), Alice, Anna, Joseph V., and Maydella.

III. Robert W. of Armstrong Mills, Ohio, married and has issue, William P., John Alexander, David of Mahomet, Illinois; Mary H., Mrs. Armstrong; James M. Elsworth, Laura and Elonzo.

IV. Valentine S. of Farmer City, Illinois; married and has issue, Mary Virginia, Mrs. French; and William Phelps Lindsay.

V. William M. of Farmer City, Illinois; married and has issue, Joseph L., William, Charles, Flora, Samuel and Robert.

Zanesville.

The founder of this family was James Lindsay of Scotch descent, who emigrated from some part of Pennsylvania to

Winchester, Virginia, when in 1805 he removed to and settled in Zanesville; he served in the war of 1812; was under General Harrison; was in Hull's surrender; was paroled; then came back. He was recruiting officer for a time, then went to Virginia, where he re-enlisted. He came back to reside in Zanesville in 1825; married a Miss Sarah Shrack, by whom he had seven children; those deceased are, James, Francis, and Eliza Lindsay; those living are Thomas, who married and has a son Henry C., who is an architect of Zanesville; Jane, single; Margaret E., Mrs. G. M. Fell of 57 Elm street, Zanesville; and Mary, Mrs. Pine, said to reside in Winchester, Virginia.

Mr. James Lindsay died in Zanesville about fifty years ago. His children are all in the prime of life.

Am indebted to Mr. Thomas Lindsay for this record of his family, which he regretted was not a better one, owing to the loss of old books and papers relative to it, during his father's life-time.

Canton.

A Lindsay, residing here, Mr. George C. Lindsay, is a native of Lawrence county, Pennsylvania, where his father, Boyde Lindsay, resided, also his grandfather, George Lindsay. For lack of knowledge, he was unable, he said, to give me further data of his branch. Possibly he belongs to some of the numerous Pennsylvania families of Lindsays.

Knox County.

(Formerly of Lancaster county, Pennsylvania.)

The early ancestor of this family was born in England in 1719, lived there and married a Scotch lady, and shortly afterward emigrated to America, and settled in Lancaster, Pennsylvania. He entered the Revolutionary army, and died in the service; after his death his wife returned to Scotland, taking her daughter Pastell, with her; their two sons remained in Lancaster county, whose names were James and William; the elder died after his mother's return to her native land; William Lindsay, the remaining son, who was but ten years old at his father's death, and who was born in 1768, in the county in which his parents settled, was adopted by Richard Clees of Maytown, Lancaster county, and lived with him till his twenty-first year; after leaving Mr. Clees, he went to Montgomery county, Pennsylvania, and remained there till 1792, in which year he was married, and returned to Lancaster county, remaining there some time.

In 1801 he emigrated to Ohio, settling first in Stark county; after living there about eight years, he removed to Knox county, of the same State, where he died in 1836. His wife was a Miss Reed, and one member of the family says, a native of Virginia, daughter of General Reed of Virginia, a noted officer of the Revolutionary army, and that the match was a runaway one; she survived him about eight years. They had eleven children, three boys and eight girls; nine were living at their father's death, one son and eight daughters. The son William, being the third of the name from the early settler, was born in Knox county, in July, 1812; at eighteen years of age he went to Pittsburgh, Pennsylvania, and stayed here three years learning the carpenter's trade, and one year longer after finishing his apprenticeship; from here he removed to New Castle, Pennsylvania, for one year, then to Youngstown, Ohio, where he located as a contractor and builder; a number of buildings are still standing which owe their origin to him. He was married twice; one of his wives was Mary McDougal of Youngstown; he died here in February, 1876. Nine children survive him, viz.: William I., who is in the lumber business in Cleveland, Ohio, firm name, W. I. Lindsay & Co., office No. 1 Central Way; Albert, a locomotive engineer of Youngstown; Gilbert, a carpenter of

Youngstown; Charles, a machinist of Cleveland, Ohio; Grant, in a carpet firm of Detroit, Michigan.

Am indebted principally to Mr. W. I. Lindsay of Cleveland, Ohio, for this record of his family.

ILLINOIS.

WAUKEGAN.

(But first of New York City.)

The founder of this family in America was David Lindsay, who came to the United States in August, 1848, from Old Castle, County Meath, Ireland, accompanied by his wife and children, one of whom was married. He landed in New York, where he resided for several years, and finally joined his elder son, Charles Lindsay, in Waukegan, Illinois, who had settled here, and where he died in 1867, aged seventy-seven years. His other sons were James and Thomas Lindsay. Charles was born in Ireland, and was accompanied by his wife and a little son, on his arrival in New York, with his parents and brothers. James was born in Ireland in 1825. Died in America in 1871. Thomas, who was also born in Ireland in 1823, died in America in 1882.

Issue of Charles Lindsay, who settled in Waukegan:

I. Charles M. Lindsay, who was the son to accompany his parents and grandparents from Ireland, where he was born June 9, 1842.

II. Lewis F., born August 27, 1843; married Mary A. Hall, by whom he has issue — Cora H., born May 23, 1870; Hattie B., born March 23, 1873. Is a merchant tailor in St. Louis, Missouri.

III. David J., born June 14, 1845; married Victoria Nidull, by whom he has issue — Sarah F., David M., and Robert; residence, St. Louis, Missouri.

IV. Thomas H., born March 22, 1847; married Mary Kellogg, by whom he has issue — William and Charles; residence, Waukegan, Illinois.

V. Sarah F., born May 22, 1849. Died 1873.

VI. Samuel W., born September 11, 1851; married Lucy Curtis, by whom he has issue — Lewis S., born December, 1886; residence, Omaha, Nebraska.

VII. Mary C., born July 26, 1853.

VIII. James F., born 1855.

IX. Franklin, born 1858.

CHICAGO, ELGIN AND HYDE PARK.

(First of New York City.)

William Lindsay, the early ancestor of this branch, emigrated to America from Perth, Scotland, in 1832, accompanied by his wife (who was a Miss Moncrief of Scotland), and one child. He landed and lived in New York city until his death in 1850, leaving two children: I. Catherine, born in Perth, Scotland, in 1828, and married a Mr. Kilpatrick, and moved to, and still resides in Elgin, Illinois. II. James, born in New York in 1835, and married, and had issue, four children: 1. Parmale Estha, born in 1856, married a Mr. F. McCairn, and resides in Hyde Park, Illinois. 2. Catherine Rosetti, born in 1859, married a Mr. H. Hattenban, resides at 876 Thirty-fifth street, Chicago. 3. Jannette Francis, born 1864. 4. Edward James, born 1866, also residents of the same home and city as Mrs. Hattenban.

AUSTIN.

(First of St. Johns, New Brunswick.)

The founder of this family was John Lindsay, who came from Londonderry, Ireland, to America, and settled in St. Johns, New Brunswick, in 1840. His father had emigrated from Scotland to Ireland. John's wife accompanied him to America, by whom he had the following issue:

I. Martha, who married David Tennant, and died in 1880.

II. Mary, who married James Keltie.

III. Ellen, who married Thomas Bell.

IV. Matthew, who died single in 1887.

V. Margaret, who married William Finley.

VI. Eliza J., who died single in 1841.

VII. Andrew, who married Jane Armstrong of Peabody, Massachusetts (see issue below).

VIII. Isabella, who married Samuel Tufto.

IX. Rebecca, who married Uriah McDowell.

The issue of Andrew and Jane Lindsay *nee* Armstrong: Alfred, born in Boston, 1865; William G., born in Boston, 1866; Charles Edward, born in Austin, Illinois, 1874.

Andrew Lindsay emigrated from New Brunswick to Boston in 1849, married his wife here in 1863; after the birth of his second child, moved to Chicago, thence to Austin, Illinois, where they now reside.

Sangamon County.

The ancestor of this branch was John Lindsey, born in Fort Pitt, Pennsylvania, in 1773, and married in Kentucky (where he had removed) in 1800. From Kentucky he latterly moved to Sangamon county, Illinois. His issue—Rebecca, who married Andrew Orr, and died in Sangamon county. Polly, born in Kentucky, married, and had one child, Amanda. David H., born in Kentucky in 1807, married, and had children. Marquis D. lives in Laonie, Illinois. George G., born 1808; died in Sangamon county, leaving one son, James. John P., born in Kentucky, 1814; lived in Lincoln, Illinois, at last accounts; had issue—James N., of Centreville, Iowa, and John W., Russell county, Kansas. Abraham, born in Illinois, 1819; lived in Ottawa, Kansas, in 1876; issue—William H., George B., Eva B., Harriet O.; who all live *near* Elkhart, Illinois.

Chicago.

A Lindsay emigrated from County Cavan, Ireland, about 1838–9, to America, and settled in one of our States; married, and left a widow and several children. The only male member of the family now living in America, according to information furnished me, is Thomas S. Lindsay, treasurer of "The Wilson Sewing Machine Company of Chicago." His widowed mother is a resident of Cleveland, Ohio. This family are of Scotch-Irish descent.

WISCONSIN.

Fox Lake and Milwaukee.

The early American forefather of this family was one David Lindsay, a native of Dundee, Scotland, born there in 1778, and only son of James Lindsay of Dundee; he emigrated to America, and settled in Fox Lake, as above, where he died September, 1849, leaving the following children:

I. Jessie, Mrs. George L. Scott of Paris, Ontario.
II. Matilda, Mrs. A. F. North of Pewaukee, Wisconsin.
III. James of Fox Lake.
IV. David of Dundee, Scotland.
V. Edmund, in partnership-business for the sale of agricultural implements, etc., 236 East Water street, Milwaukee.
VI. William, partner with Edmund.
VII. Thomas of Rochester, Minnesota.
VIII. Anne, died 1861.
IX. George of Detroit, Michigan.
X. Henry of Milwaukee.

Of the above children of David Lindsay of Fox Lake, all were born in Scotland, except the few youngest.

Am indebted to the courtesy of Mr. E. Lindsay of Milwaukee, for this record of his family.

KANSAS.

McPherson.

Mr. D. P. Lindsay, attorney at law of this town, has kindly furnished me the following few points about his branch of the American clan: David Lindsay, his grandfather, came (along with his father, and brothers and sisters, apparently) to the United States from County Antrim, Ireland, about 1806, landing on one of the shores of the Carolinas; his great-grandfather then went North, and some of the family remained in the South; his grandfather, David Lindsay, died at Garnett, Kansas, in 1880, aged eighty, and his grandmother, Mrs. Martha Lindsay, at the same place, in 1886, aged eighty-five. They had ten children, five sons and five daughters, who reached adult years.

The oldest of the sons, Dr. Thomas Lindsay, is a resident and physician of Garnett, was a surgeon during the late war, and served three years in the Kansas troops, and is the father of Mr. D. P. Lindsay of McPherson; the remaining son living, is Captain J. G. Lindsay, who also served as a captain of the Kansas troops in our late war, and is now an attorney at law in South Pasadena, California; Robert Lindsay died in Iowa in 1866, leaving a family; Houston Lindsay, unmarried, was killed in Iowa, by an accident, before the war; Samuel Lindsay, the youngest of the sons, was killed near Vicksburg during the war, unmarried. He was serving as first lieutenant of his company, in the Iowa troops.

Of the daughters, Lydia A. Lindsay is the wife of David Collier of South Pasadena, California, by whom she has one son and three daughters. Mattie Lindsay is married to L. K. Kirk, an attorney at Garnett, Kansas, besides a member of the State Senate. Lizzie Lindsay is the wife of A. G. Huey of Dwight, Illinois. Mary Lindsay (Mrs. D. W. French) died at South Pasadena, California, last February.

NEBRASKA.

Peirce.

Mr. Benjamin Lindsay, attorney at law of this place, traces his ancestry to his great-grandfather, who was a Scotchman who emigrated from Scotland to King's county, Ireland, where the family has since resided, except some members, who pushed out and settled in other lands; one of whom was his father, who came to America in 1846, and to Iowa in 1849, where his family still reside, with the exception of himself.

Am sorry not to have been furnished with further data of this branch.

Places in the United States called Lindsay.

Those marked thus * are Postal Stations.

Lindsay*	Lawrence county	Arkansas.
Lindsay*	Polk county	Minnesota.
Lindsay*	Platt county	Nebraska.
Lindsey*	Washington county	Georgia.
Lindsey*	Sandusky county	Ohio.
Lindsey	Jefferson county	Pennsylvania.
Lindsay's	Albemarle county	Virginia.
Lindsay's Mills	Caroline county	Virginia.
Lindsey	Ottawa county	Kansas.
Lindsey's Mill	Trigg county	Kentucky.
Lindseyville	Worcester county	Maryland.
Lindsey Creek	Ottawa county	Kansas.

CHART

TO ILLUSTRATE THE DESCENDANTS AND REPRESENTATIVES OF CHRISTIANA DE LINDSAY, LADY OF LAMBERTON, AND DAME DE COURCY, 1335 TO 1885.

Christiana de Lindsay, Lady of Lamberton = Ingelram de Guignes, Sire de Courcy.

- William, Sire de Courcy = Isabelle de Chatillon, daughter of Count St. Pol, by Mary of Brittany.
  - Ingelram VI, Sire de Courcy. = Catherine, daughter of Leopold the First, Duke of Austria.
    - Ingelram VII, le Grand, Sire de Courcy, Count of Soissons and Earl of Bedford, prisoner to Bajazet in 1397. = Isabelle, daughter of Edward the Third, by Phillipa of Hainault.
      - Marie, Dame de Courcy, Countess of Soissons. = Henry, elder son of Duc de Bar, by Mary of France.
        - Robert de Bar, Count of Marle and Soissons. = ...
          - Jeanne de Bar, Countess of Marle and Soissons. = Louis de Luxembourg, Count St. Pol.
            - Jean died without issue.
            - Pierre de Luxembourg, Count of St. Pol, Marle and Soissons. = Margaret, daughter of Louis, Duke of Savoy.
              - Marie, Countess St. Pol. = François de Bourbon, Count of Vendome.
                - Charles, Duke of Vendome = Françoise, daughter of Rene, Duke of Alençon.
                  - Antoine, King of Navarre = Jeanne d'Albret, Queen of Navarre.
                    - Henry IV of France, father of
                    - Louis XIII of France, father of
                    - Louis XIV of France, father of
                    - Louis the Dauphin, father of
                    - Louis, Duke of Burgundy, father of
                    - Louis XV, father of
                    - Louis the Dauphin, father of
                    - Louis XVI, father of
                    - Marie-Therese-Charlotte, Duchesse d'Angouleme.
                    - Henry IV, King of France.
                    - Heir at line et supra.
                    - Henri V, Duc de Bordeaux, who died 1885.
- Ingelram, Viscount de Maux. =
  - Jeanne de Courcy = Jean de Bethune.
    - A Quo, all the branches of that House.

Postmasters of the Name of Lindsay throughout the United States in 1855.

From Postal Directory of that year.

H. H. Lindsay.....Jefferson, Green county......Pennsylvania.
Benjamin Lindsay..Unionville, Frederick county..Maryland.
John T. Lindsay...Berry's Ferry, Clark county...Virginia.
Thomas N. Lindsay.Churchville, Augusta county..Virginia.
H. P. Lindsay......Bridgewater, Burk county.....N. Carolina.
M. P. Lindsay......Linville River, Burk county...N. Carolina.
Thomas C. Lindsay.Carthage, Leak county.......Mississippi.
J. W. Lindsay......Van Buren, Itawamba county.Mississippi.
J. A. Lindsay......Powhatan, Lawrence county ..Arkansas.
T. R. Lindsay.....Dry Creek, Kenton county....Kentucky.
R. T. Lindsay.....Foster, Bracken county.......Kentucky.
S. S. Lindsay......Lindsay's Mills, Trigg county..Kentucky.
Samuel Lindsay....E. Springfield, Jefferson county.Ohio.
Samuel Lindsay.....Enoch, Monroe county.......Ohio.
C. Lindsay.........Campbellton, St. Clair county.Michigan.
F. A. W. Lindsay ..Deerfield, Randolph county...Indiana.
A. Lindsay........Naples, Scott county.........Illinois.
Joseph Lindsay....Rochester, Cedar county.....Iowa.
J. N. Lindsay .....Parks Bar, Yuba county......California.

List of Lindsay Grantees in Virginia from 1657 to 1766, from the Land Office, Richmond, Virginia, September 8, 1888.

David Lindsay granted 236 acres on Perrie's Creek, in Northampton county. Patented March, 1567.

It is not improbable that the said David Lindsay was the Reverend David Lindsay of Northumberland county, the former county being but a short distance across the Chesapeake from the latter, and it was not unusual to own land in separate portions of the Colony. This land might have been bequeathed to his son during his life. The loss of the ancient records in this, as in many other counties, precludes all possibility of posterity ascertaining any information upon the subject.

John Lindsay, granted 700 acres in Middlesex county, 1674.
James Lindsay, granted 390 acres in Gloster county, 1674.
Jeremiah Lindsay, granted 174 acres in New Kent county.
William Lindsay, granted 174 acres in Brunswick county, 1745.
William Lindsay, granted 400 acres in Brunswick county, 1746.
William Lindsay, granted 490 acres in Brunswick county, 1755.
William Lindsay, granted 294 acres in Caroline county, 1759.
Jeremiah Lindsay, granted 231 acres in Hanover county, 1760.
Cahill Lindsay, granted 404 acres in Brunswick county, 1761.
Samuel Lindsay, granted 170 acres in Augusta county, 1766.

CHARTERS AND CONSTITUTIONS OF THE UNITED STATES, PART II PAGE 1893.

In the second charter of Virginia of date May 23, 1609, the name of Captain Richard Lindesay is given as one of the grantees.

A Robert Lindsay lived at James Island, over the river (I suppose from Jamestown), Virginia, in 1623. He *may* have been related to the Lindsays of Northumberland county.

NINETY DIFFERENT WAYS IN ORTHOGRAPHY OF THE SURNAME LINDSAY, FROM CHARTERS AND OTHER ANCIENT DOCUMENTS.

Limesay.
Lyndeseya.
Lyndeseia.
Lindeseia.
Lindessaya.
Lindesseye.
Lindisseia.
Lindesaia.
Lindisin.
Lyndesins.
Lindesins.
Lindesans.
Lindensay.
Lynddessay.
Lynddessaye.
Lynddesai.
Lyndessay.
Lindessaye.
Lyndyesaye.
Lyndisseye.
Lyndessaye.
Lindesaye.
Lindesaie.
Lyndeseye.
Lyndeseie.
Lindeseie.
Lyndesheie.
Lyndeshey.
Lyndessey.
Lyndyssey.
Lindessey.
Lindessi.
Lyndessai.
Lindessay.
Lyndissay.
Lyndissai.
Lindissay.
Lyndyssay.
Lindyssay.
Lyndissai.
Lindissa.
Lyndysay.
Lyndisay.
Lindisay.
Lindiesay.
Lyndezay.
Lindeszey.
Lyndyssey.
Lyndessay.
Lindyssey.
Lindessey.
Lyndessy.
Lyndesy.
Lindesy.
Lindesye.
Lyndesie.
Lindesie.
Lindesi.
Lindeci.
Lyndesey.
Lindesey.
Lindesei.
Lindesee.
Lindese.
Lindesay.
Lyndesai.
Lyndesay.
Lindesa.
Lindsai.
Lyndsai.
Lyndsay.
Lyndsa.
Lindsai.
Lyndsaie.
Lyndsay.
Lyndsa.
Lyndsey.
Lyndsy.
Lyndseye.
Lindseie.
Lindsey.
Lindsai.
Lindsay.
Lindsa.
Lindsaye.
Linsaie.
Linsai.
Lynsay.
Linsay.
Lynsey.
Linsey.
Lynse.
Lyncay.
Linzee.

Family Record and Additions.

Family Record and Additions.

Family Record and Additions.

Family Record and Additions.

Family Record and Additions.

www.ingramcontent.com/pod-product-compliance
Lightning Source LLC
Chambersburg PA
CBHW061716270326
41928CB00011B/2007